The Man Who Wouldn't Die

Adventures of a Hobo and
Central American Soldier of Fortune
in the Early 1900's

The Man Who Wouldn't Die

Adventures of a Hobo and Central American Soldier of Fortune in the Early 1900's

Frank Kavanaugh

Edited by Ken Cooper

TotalComm Press
St. Louis

The Man Who Wouldn't Die
Adventures of a Hobo and Soldier of Fortune in the Early 1900's

By Frank Kavanaugh (Ken Cooper, ed.)

This publication is designed to provide accurate and authoritative information in regard to the subject matter covered. It is sold with the understanding that the publisher is not engaged in rendering legal, accounting, or other professional service. If legal advice or other expert assistance is required, the services of a competent professional person should be sought.

ISBN: 978-0-9850949-7-3

All names, companies, brands, products, and services mentioned in this book are the trade names or registered trademarks of their respective owners.

Book design: Peggy Nehmen. This book is set in Latino URW Regular and Gotham Bold.

Printed in the United States of America.

To Mary Frances and Brother ...

and all the Kavanaugh offspring.

CONTENTS

Editor's Note

TO OUR FAMILY, FRANCIS JOSEPH (FRANK) KAVANAUGH was Grandpa. To many south of the border, he was the *norteamericano* known as *El Señor Diablo* (Mr. Devil.)

I was too small to remember him, but everyone describes him as a quiet man who lived a regular life and liked to write. His vocal cords had been damaged by disease during his war service, so there was always a hesitation to his speech.

For decades he worked the night shift for two Kansas City newspapers, keeping the Linotype machines up and running. He could fix just about anything. He lived the ultimate regular existence, marrying later in life and raising two children—Charlie and my mom, Mary Frances. At the end, he died peacefully in his sleep in his seventies.

It's hard to reconcile this with the person who wrote these memoirs. But indeed, this middle-class family man is the same person who was an expert on railroads and machine guns, who managed an opera singer, who was a colonel in the Guatemalan army and a bodyguard for the president, who served warrants as a deputy US Marshall, who ran con games, who smuggled contraband, who stood trial for mutiny, and was an itchy-footed hobo traveling throughout North and Central America in his "thousand-mile shirt"... all as described in this book.

My dad, Frank's son-in-law and a fact-driven engineer, did whatever he could to confirm as much of the book as possible. It was his opinion that it's all true. For example, Dad heard about the frantic telegram from the president of Guatemala begging Frank to come back and save him from a revolution, that the palace was surrounded. Dad ran across stories about Frank's smuggling in New Orleans. He heard first-hand from Frank about most of the adventures retold here in this book.

When you see the detail in the descriptions, names, and conversations, when you see the linear nature of the book as a connected series of events, it's easy to agree with my dad. This isn't a bunch of short stories, although that's how it's organized. This is clearly a man's life, from his discharge after the Spanish American War, near death, to hoboing throughout the world.

This book covers the period of Frank's life from 1898 to 1906. As the book states, some of these stories were written up and submitted to magazines of the day. But the manuscript in this form was written around 1942.

As you read this, you'll get a real understanding of what life was like in the early 1900's. It was a different world of manners and sensibilities. There was no such thing as political correctness, and everyone had labels. It was also the forerunner of the Great Depression that was to come. It's probably as near as you can possibly get to what the old Wild West was like, only with early 1900's technology.

They don't make men like this anymore. In some ways that's good. Not all of this book shows Frank in the best light. He was a complex man—kind in some ways and ruthless in others, scrupulously honest in some ways and totally crooked in others. His was a life unlike any other you've ever encountered.

This book is the original text scanned in from Frank's typed manuscript and hand-written corrections. I merely fixed the scanning errors and did some minor formatting for readability.

So enjoy. It was a different world back then, and it sure was exciting!

Ken Cooper
May, 2020

About the Author

THE AVAILABLE PAPERWORK SAYS that Francis Joseph (Frank) Kavanaugh was born in Galveston, Texas, on May 25, 1876. This may or may not be accurate. On a birth certificate, his father, Albin Kavanaugh of Dublin, Ireland, listed his profession as "railroader." His mother, Mary (nee Stanley), from Near Hearne, Texas, listed hers as "housewife."

Frank left home at 15. He lied about his age and enlisted in the US Army in Nocogdoches, Texas. At induction, the Army described Frank as 24 years old, 5 foot 6 inches in height, light complexion, blue eyes, light hair, occupation of machinist, and single.

Frank served in Companies K and B of the 2nd Regiment Texas Infantry Volunteers and saw action in the Philippines in the Spanish American War, which later earned him a war pension of $60 per month. He was honorably discharged on November 9, 1898 after suffering a bout of malaria which left him near death. This is where the book begins.

Frank's parents had died. He lost what was left of his family in the great Galveston hurricane of 1900, leaving him essentially an orphan. He had only distant relatives in Ireland.

After his Army service, he became a hobo and soldier of fortune traveling throughout the US and Central America. South of the border, he was known as *El Diablo*—the devil.

After the events described here plus more, Frank married, settled down in Kansas City, got a regular job, and raised a family. It was the exact opposite of his previous life of travel and adventure.

Frank continued to write about his experiences for adventure and railroad magazines of the day. He also published and mailed *The Kavanaugh Kronikle*, a weekly humor and family news sheet, from 1940 to 1946 that was sent free to hundreds of service members. He was frequently quoted in national publications such as *Colliers, Readers Digest,* and many others. Major magazines of the day called him the "Kansas Philosopher."

Frank died on April 23, 1946 in Kansas City, Kansas.

Why This Is

THIS BOOK IS DEDICATED to the many good people and the few bad people I have met in my wanderings, and to the United States Army, which taught me self-confidence.

You may learn from reading this book a few things you may not have known before, such as:

You can laugh your way around the world, but if you're hunting trouble you'll find it.

No nationality, color, tribe or breed can claim a monopoly on good citizens.

There is nothing that will fit a young man for what comes after than a "hitch" in the United States Army.

If a physician tells you that you are going to die, keep a stiff upper lip. Maybe you'll fool him by forty or fifty years.

———————————

Several of these adventures have been published in *Munsey's Railroad Magazine, Everybody's, Youth's Companion, Adventures,* and other magazines which were in existence forty years ago. Some of them are still being published. I have fooled a lot of editors into sending me real good checks.

Yours truly,

Frank Kavanaugh

1942

Cities Frank Kavanaugh references.

1

The Man Who Wouldn't Die

THE TRANSPORT SHERIDAN, CROWDED with soldiers returning from the Philippines, docked at Honolulu. The soldiers, anticipation in their eyes, looked forward to several days shore leave. To make things still more pleasurable, the paymaster had given notice that the soldiers would receive a month's pay before they left the transport. With fifteen dollars and sixty cents, a soldier could have a helluva time in Honolulu. Everyone was happy.

Everyone was happy with the exception of four men down in the sick bay. One of these men was conscious—the others knew nothing of what was going on. The conscious man was in such pain and so weak that he didn't care whether he was in Honolulu or Hell.

A shore doctor came aboard as soon as the vessel docked. The army surgeons aboard had given the men the best of care. The conscious man in one of the berths could hear the conversation of the doctor.

"They're about gone, eh?" the shore doctor asked.

"Almost gone," one of the ship's doctors agreed. "We'll want to take them ashore if you have a place for them."

"We've got a good hospital here now," the shore doctor went on. "Call your orderlies and get them topside. There'll be ambulances to take them away."

"Good," a ship's doctor exclaimed. "The skipper, a civilian, doesn't want to take them any farther. Declares he doesn't like burials at sea. After we get them out of here, come over to the officers' club and we'll have lunch and a few drinks. We've got a dandy little club here now."

"I'll be with you in a few minutes."

Orderlies carried the men, one by one, to the waiting ambulances. Having sent their patients on their way, the orderlies joined the line of men waiting for their month's pay. The four sick men got no pay, as they were too sick to

1

stand in line and too weak to care whether they ever got paid or not. A man about to die is not interested in a month's wages or anything else.

The hospital was nice, clean, comfortable. At one time or other the four sick men came to, looked around with lackluster eyes and saw they were in a new place, a place that didn't sway and heave. Slowly it came to their cankered brains that they were ashore somewhere. Just where they were was no concern of theirs. They didn't care. Men as sick as they were didn't worry about what portion of the globe furnished them clean beds.

As the days passed they slowly began to put two and two together and it made four. It came back as in a dream that the ship had coaled at Nagasaki. They remembered that because the coal was loaded by Japanese women who carried it aboard in baskets balanced on their heads. They remembered how the coal dust had sifted into the sick bay and caused them to cough and spit black.

They remembered there had been a fight on deck just above the sick bay while the transport lay at the Japanese port. One of the sick men wondered at the time whether he would ever be able to again take part in a knock-down-and-drag-out fight.

Then came the remembrance of a rolling ship. At one time the vessel rolled so sharply the orderlies were compelled to strap the men in their bunks to keep them from rolling out. There seemed to have been days and days of this rolling and tossing, but now they were ashore again and the ship had gone on towards God's country. The civilian skipper of the Sheridan didn't like burials at sea.

They lay there and thought. One man whimpered for his mother. Another thought of a girl back home who had sewed his first corporal's stripes on his sleeves when he had been promoted. That was when his outfit was a part of a state militia.

The third man thought of a little hill farm back in Tennessee, of his bearded father and work-worn mother. His sisters and brothers were older now, of course, and worked as hard as he had worked to draw a scant living from the rocky hillside farm. He resolved, if he recovered, never to go back to that rocky farm except for a visit.

He'd get a job in some city where he could see the bright lights and go to a show once in a while. In his entire life on that farm he had never been to a show. His first had been while his outfit was camped at the Presidio, near San Francisco. He chuckled foolishly when he thought how dumb he used to be. He had pictured the Philippine Islands as only a day's sail from San Francisco. It had been a voyage of thirty-two days—thirty-two days on beans and hardtack.

Number Four was a soldier of the regular army. The other three were from regiments recruited later, after the islands had been pacified—with the aid of Krag-Jorgensen rifles. Number Four had been in the islands for two years and eight months. A soldier who served in the islands that long becomes hard-boiled.

Number Four thought of many things, but nothing sentimental. He had grown too hard to be sentimental. He cursed the men next to him—the man who whimpered for his mother. He turned away from the orderly who wanted to wash his face. He refused the offer of the surgeon to have a barber come and shave off two months' growth of red beard. He demanded and didn't get a slug of American whiskey.

Sentiment had been squeezed from him by that term in the islands. Sentiment and fear, both. When a doctor examined him one morning and shook his head, Number Four asked, "What's the score, captain?"

"I might as well be frank with you," the surgeon said. "You've got about one chance in a million."

"Less chance than I'd have in a crap game, you mean, captain?"

"A great deal less."

"Then bring me a bottle of good American whiskey and let me go out happy."

"That's out, definitely," the doctor declared.

"Then to hell with you. I'll get that millionth chance. Someday I'll meet you and remind you that you guessed wrong."

The doctor did not reply.

Number Four lapsed into unconsciousness. In his dreams he was back in the islands, seated on the tripod of a machine gun which spit little pellets of death at a group of little brown men. That dream faded into one where he was back in the states, where there were streetcars filled with men and women in clean, stylish clothes. He started to board one of the streetcars but it faded away. He woke to find himself still in the hospital.

He looked around. The man in the bed next to his, the boy who whimpered for his mother, wasn't there anymore. The bed had been remade and was awaiting another occupant. An orderly passed along the row of beds, checking the record hung on the foot of each bed. When he reached the cot of Number Four, that individual inquired, "What became of that punk that was there—the cry baby?"

The orderly made a motion with his hands, indicating the man was gone—gone west.

"Cry baby," Number Four remarked as he fell asleep again.

Then followed memories of visits from the doctor, of someone washing his face, of being fed some sort of dope that was watery and tasteless, of seeing forms moving back and forth in the passage way between the beds. He woke at last to a new sound.

It was late at night, for the lights were dimmed and there was no one about. But that sound disturbed him.

2

Smuggled Death

IT WAS A QUEER SOUND, something like a giant hiccough, then a silence, then another giant hiccough. After listening for a few minutes, Number Four located the source of the sound. It came from the throat of the man on his right, the boy from the hillbilly farm down in Tennessee.

It took a lot of effort, but Number Four reached up to the head of the bed and found the cord that a patient pulled when he needed an orderly. Number Four pulled the cord with all his strength. He could hear a bell tinkle in another room. Presently an orderly came in, rubbing sleep from his eyes.

"Here," Number Four said. He indicated the man on his right. "Get this bird outa here. I can't sleep while he hiccoughs. He's going over the big divide anyhow. That's a dying man's hiccough. Get him outta here."

The orderly came closer and looked at the man from Tennessee. As he did so the hiccoughs ceased and the man, after a violent contraction of his face, lay still.

"That's better," Number Four said as the noise ceased. "Now I can go to sleep. That bird was a helluva long time dying."

Number Four went into a coma again.

When he again was able to notice things, the boy who remembered the girl who sewed on his first corporal's stripes wasn't there. Number Four knew there was no need asking where he was. Number Four knew.

Days and nights passed, blending into each other like paints blend on a palette. There was a calendar on the wall across the room and Number Four knew time was passing when pages of it were torn off. November was showing when he first noticed it. It seemed but a few hours until he looked up and December snowed. A few hours more and a new calendar was there and it was January and the year was 1901. He wondered if the orderly tore

5

off a month every day to make time pass quicker. Finally, after rolling it over in his foggy mind for a while, he decided he didn't give a damn what they did with the calendar.

One morning an officer came to his bedside. This wasn't a medical officer. He wore the insignia of a second lieutenant on his shoulders. His face wasn't burned by a tropical sun and Number Four knew he had probably just reached the islands from West Point. He was glad to see him. He had served under West Pointers and he liked them. You obeyed their orders pronto or else, but they took care of their men and they had guts. Number Four was glad to talk to a man with guts who was not a medical officer.

"Through an error," the lieutenant began, "We haven't your record here. It went on to the states with your outfit. I'd like to get it for our records. Age?"

"Twenty-one, sir."

"Native of…"

"Texas, sir."

"Who would you wish notified in case of your death?"

"Hell, lieutenant, I'm not going to die."

"I'd like the information."

"No one, sir."

"Haven't you any relatives?"

"No, sir. None that would care whether I was dead or living."

The lieutenant was little older than Number Four. He had not served in the Philippines long enough to become hard-boiled. In fact he had never been there. Number Four thought he detected a look of sympathy in the officer's eyes.

"Anything I can do for you?" he inquired.

"You might give me a few slugs of American whiskey," Number Four suggested.

"I'm afraid that's out," the lieutenant explained. "The chief surgeon outranks every other officer here in the hospital and I wouldn't dare give you anything except on his order. We received a letter from Lieutenant Kirkland, in command of your company, inquiring about you and requesting us to see that you got the best we had, but I couldn't bring whiskey in here except with the surgeon's permission."

"I'm going to get up tomorrow and sit on the porch," Number Four declared. "If someone—some private that doesn't give a damn was to be passing and slipped me a bottle no one would care."

"You may not get up," the lieutenant warned.

"I think I will, sir," Number Four said. "Thank you."

The lieutenant was leaving when Number Four called to him. "Haven't I got some pay coming, lieutenant?" he asked.

"I think so."

"How soon do I get it?"

"When you are able to come down to the paymaster's office."

"I'll be down there in a day or two."

The lieutenant smiled as he walked away. At the entrance he met the surgeon on duty. "That man over on bed thirteen," he began. "How about him?"

"He's had a slight turn for the better," the surgeon replied, "but he's apt to go any time. He may linger for months or he may go within an hour."

"He wants some whiskey."

"If he took a drink of whiskey now, he'd pass on before he could set the glass down,"

"I see," the lieutenant remarked as he left the building.

Number Four waited impatiently for the next day to come. Something in the lieutenant's manner gave him a slight hope that if he sat on the porch long enough something might happen.

After an argument with an orderly, he was furnished a wheelchair and wheeled to the long porch just off the sidewalk. He sat there and waited.

Natives, Japanese, Chinese, United States soldiers and the usual conglomeration of peoples of the Hawaiian Islands passed. Some of them, passing, glanced up at the invalids sitting on the porch of the hospital but no one stopped. Number Four was about to give it up as a bad hope.

At length a lanky soldier walked down the street. As he approached the hospital he paused and looked up. There were half a dozen men in wheel chairs on the porch but only one sported a month's growth of reddish beard. The soldier looked closely at Number Four's red beard. Number Four's eyes lighted in anticipation. The eyes of the soldier on the sidewalk and the man in the wheelchair met.

"Hello, you damned sucker." the soldier on the sidewalk exclaimed. "Thought they'd have blown taps over you before this."

"But they didn't," Number Four told him. "Come on up and chin a while."

The soldier climbed the steps to the porch and drew a vacant chair close to the wheel chair. "Can you stash a bottle in your nightie?" the soldier whispered after he had taken a seat.

"Till I can stash it in my belly," Number Four said.

The bottle was slipped under the robe of the man in the wheel chair. The other soldier had served in the Philippines and they talked awhile. Finally the soldier left.

Number Four wheeled himself into the ward and slipped into bed. When the orderly's back was turned he put the bottle to his mouth and drank. He waited a few minutes until the orderly left the room and took another drink. A few minutes more and he took the third drink which finished the bottle.

Having finished the bottle, Number Four waited. The effects of the whiskey made things change a little. His whole body warmed up. The sun shining through the windows seemed brighter. Perhaps, Number Four thought, that was how the sunlight appeared to a man about to go over the great divide. The wind coming through the windows seemed softer, but that might be how the wind felt to a man who was about to croak.

Number Four remembered a joke he had heard at a vaudeville show years before and laughed at it again. If this was death, he concluded, it wasn't so bad.

Then he remembered one thing he had to do before he went out. It wouldn't do to give away the lieutenant and that soldier who had smuggled the booze to him. When the orderly left the room for a moment, Number Four got the empty bottle, laid it carefully on the floor, and sent it sliding across until it stopped under the fourth cot from him. Then he lay down and remembered another vaudeville joke he had heard in the days before he enlisted. He was laughing at it when he fell asleep.

He didn't expect to wake again and he didn't care much because he felt so good. But he got fooled and woke with a slight hangover. He was surprised to find himself still in the hospital in Honolulu instead of in Heaven or Hell. He felt almost as good as ever, except that he was weak. Having nothing else to do he lay in bed and made plans. He would go places and do things.

Instead of killing him the whiskey had helped him. Two or three days later he swore at the orderly who brought him his meal of belly wash, and demanded steak and onions, which he didn't get. A week or so later he demanded a new uniform.

"That'll come out your clothing allowance," the orderly warned.

"What'n hell will a clothing allowance be worth to a dead man?" Number Four countered.

He got the uniform. The first day he wore it he tried to walk and did go the length of a block. He rested a while and then walked the block back.

The next day he walked three blocks, rested and walked back. By walking a little farther each day he finally made it to the paymaster's office. There he was paid $46.80. In those days soldiers received $13.00 a month, with 20 percent extra for foreign service. Number Four found he had three months' pay coming and got it. But the long walk had tired him and he didn't spend a cent of his pay that day.

A few days later he made it downtown and fell in with a corporal of a regular outfit who had served down at Iloilo and Zamboango. They had a few drinks together and talked of the time Jimmy Pendexter had been found cut into quarters because he had tried to make love to a Mohammedan girl; of the Gugu art of throwing a bolo through a man; of the time the bird from the Twenty-first had thrown a glass through the mirror back of the bar in McCarty's saloon, and lots of things dear to the man who had served over there.

The corporal had one ambition, it appeared. A Chicago policeman, Number 315, to be exact, had once sapped him with a billy club. Now the corporal was going to get out of the army and go back to Chicago, hunt up Number 315 policeman and punch his head off. After that his plans were uncertain. But that sapping he had taken from Number 315 had stuck in his craw all the time he was in the army.

So they drank a little more and talked about how the natives never had more than three centavos when a busted soldier held one up to get the price of a drink, and various other things.

The corporal got Number Four interested, and the drinks made life in the states seem like Heaven. He wasn't sore at any policemen back there, but he'd like to get back anyhow. He was too weak to punch a policeman right then. That evening he told the hospital surgeon he'd like to join his outfit again.

"Do you think you can stand the trip?" the surgeon asked.

"I do, sir."

"Your enlistment's almost expired?"

"Yes, sir."

Number Four was standing at attention and he found it hard to do. He wavered a little. The captain noticed it. "At ease. Sit down," he ordered.

When Number Four was seated the captain continued, "You've recovered from a condition I thought would kill you. But even though you are now feeling better, you haven't long to live. If you wish, you may stay here indefinitely. It isn't the policy of the army to turn sick men out, willy-nilly. So if you wish to stay here, where climatic conditions are ideal, you may."

"I'd like to go back to the states, sir."

"We'll send you. But buck up until the vessel is out at sea. Civilian skippers do not like burials at sea and are permitted to refuse to take on men likely to die aboard. And you are likely to. So buck up until the vessel is a day or two out of here."

"Thank you, sir."

Number Four left Honolulu for San Francisco and wasn't buried at sea.

The story following is the story of the man who wouldn't die.

3

On His Own

FORT BLISS, TEXAS. PARADE GROUND. Companies lined up in formation. Sergeants calling the roll of company members, then turning to the officer in command with the usual announcement, "All present or accounted for, sir."

April 30, 1901. A pleasant sunny afternoon. The soft notes of a bugle sounding retreat. My company stood at ease as Lieutenant Kirkland strode down the company front and stopped before my position in the ranks.

"Forward two paces, Private Kavanaugh," First Sergeant Gene Fowler ordered. I did so and the lieutenant handed me a long envelope.

"I am sorry to see another man of the company mustered out," the lieutenant began. "Of the eighty-two men who sailed with us about three years ago, eleven remain. I am sorry it is so, for we have been through good times and bad together, and not one has ever flinched from danger or neglected a duty. Dismiss the company, sergeant."

The formation broke and, as I turned to go to my quarters, Lieutenant Kirkland touched me on the shoulder. I turned quickly and saluted.

"Get into civvies as soon as you can, Frank," he said. "I have transportation to El Paso and I want you to come and have dinner with me."

(As long as I wore a private soldier's uniform, I couldn't eat with the lieutenant. But when I dressed in civilian clothes, I could. I had purchased the civvies several days before in anticipation of my release from the army.)

We walked into the dining room of one of the finest hotels in El Paso and were seated at a table. The lieutenant ordered drinks while the waiter was getting our dinner order. We drained our glasses and then he asked, "How much money have you, Frank?"

"I got four hundred and thirty-two dollars on my final settlement."

"And what are you going to do now?"

"As you know, lieutenant, the doctors say I am going to die. But I'm going to fool them."

"You may," the lieutenant agreed.

"I will," I asserted.

"You should get interested in something," the lieutenant went on. "Try some sort of work that would keep you interested. If you find you are healthy a year from now, say, marry. Have children. Be what you term a home guard. A good citizen."

"And kick myself in the pants, synthetically, when I have a yen to point a machine gun at someone and hear it rattle until my nose bleeds from the vibration, and can't because I'm tied up with a bunch of kids and a wife? No."

"But consider, Frank, you have a good grounding in mechanical engineering. You are an expert telegrapher. You told me you learned the printing trade while you were attending school. You should settle down and go to work."

"Perhaps I couldn't find a job."

"I have a cousin who is an executive in a big manufacturing plant in Brooklyn. He'll find you a place on my recommendation. Want to try it?"

He handed me a letter addressed to a man in care of the Mergenthaler Linotype Company, Brooklyn, New York. I put it in my pocket, intending to tear it up as soon as I had parted from the lieutenant.

"Sometimes I think of resigning my commission, now that the excitement is all over," Kirkland mused. "From now on promotion will be slow and uncertain."

"Unless you marry a senator's daughter," I suggested.

Kirkland smiled. "I wouldn't put it that way exactly," he said, "but I may be a lieutenant for several years to come."

We shook hands and parted about 10 o'clock, Kirkland to drive back to Fort Bliss, me to...

When the doctors tell you that you may live for two years and then again you may go west in a month or two, and the army tells you it is through with you because your three-year enlistment has expired, and you can't enlist because you're going to kick in before long, it gives a fellow a certain feeling of freedom and relief.

It's a cinch you're not going to be afraid of anything, because you're due to go anyway. It's another cinch that you're going to try to get the most out of what time you have left.

But after you've served a hitch in the army you lose touch with what has been going on in civil life. After you've sat on the tripod seat of a machine gun and pumped hot lead at a shadowy group of little brown men, after you've slogged through rice paddies and climbed over hills, after you've beaten the Gugus out of a town and then searched the place for what loot you could find, it's hard to get interested in the little things civilians are interested in and for which you have contempt.

It's hard for a soldier to settle down to an active civil life after he has lived for several years in an atmosphere of dirt and blood and guts. Some of them do, some of them never do. This is the chronicle of a man who never did.

I registered at the hotel wherein we had enjoyed dinner, and went to my room. For the first time in a little more than three years I was free to come and go as I liked. But I didn't know what to do with my new freedom. A train for the East was due to leave El Paso about midnight. I could take that.

I left my room and wandered down to the lobby. The money I had was burning a hole in my pocket. It was more money than I'd ever had before. Perhaps I could get into a good craps game. In the army I was something of a champion crap shooter.

But caution came to me. If I went broke, I wanted to go broke farther from the Fort. Finally, I deposited four hundred dollars with the hotel clerk and walked out into the street.

Half an hour later, I had crossed the international bridge and was in Juarez, Mexico. I had been partly educated in the City of Mexico when my Father was superintendent of the Interoceanic Railroad and I could speak Spanish—or Mexican, rather, for there is a difference—better than many natives.

I was taking a drink in a Mexican saloon—I had avoided those kept by Americans—when I noticed a short, heavy-set man next to me at the bar. Full of freedom and tequila, I asked him to have a drink with me.

"I've just got out of the army," I explained, "and I'm enjoying my first freedom in three years."

"I'm Shorty Hurd," the short man introduced himself. "I'll take a drink. I'm a printer when I'm not a vaudeville actor. Someday, when I get enough filthy lucre to get my things out of hock I'll show you some swell press notices."

"Why the busted situation and all that?" I asked.

"A natural development of an inherent tendency," he explained. "When I'm in the money I'm afraid of getting robbed. When I'm broke I'm happy."

"And just now?" I inquired.

"I'm happy," he replied.

"I think I'll go east," I mentioned as we drank.

"So will I," Hurd said. "You might as well travel with me. Good eats, a free life, and nothing to worry about."

"You're busted and you're promising me that?" I exclaimed.

"It'll cost us a few dollars to start on," Hurd explained. "I'm banking on you furnishing the capital. After that it'll be all beer and skittles, if you know what skittles are. I don't."

"I still don't get you."

"I'll explain tomorrow. By the way, that's a pretty Mexican girl over there. That tall one. Are you good for the loan of a dime, so that I can dance with her?"

"She's a foot taller than you are," I said.

"I like tall girls," he returned.

"That rosy-cheeked little fairy next to her looks good to me," I mentioned.

"She's a foot shorter than you are," Hurd observed.

"I like short girls," I explained.

We danced and danced, always with the same girls. After each dance we would belly up to the bar and drink. The girls took checks instead of drinks. Each succeeding dance was done with more abandon, as the added tequila took effect. Finally I was carrying my girl along, swinging her feet clear off the floor. I stumbled and sprawled on the floor. The orchestra ceased playing until I got up and lifted my little partner to her feet. Once we were upright the orchestra resumed its music.

I was swinging my partner around and around, her feet sticking out, when someone slapped me on the shoulder. The slapper was a Mexican. The music ceased.

"Theese is not allowed," he began. "Hugging the girl while in the dance. And theese girl, she not a dancing girl at all. She a waiter."

"She's been dancing with me," I countered.

"She think you dance like all gringos dance."

The girl had disappeared, and so had most of the others. They did not know what drunken Americans might do. They might start shooting. Shorty's girl stood by him, however, towering above him a foot.

I walked over to the bar and ordered drinks. The Mexican shoulder-slapper followed. Numerous drinks had addled my eyesight. When I looked at the man, I could see two of him. The bartender was twins. I looked around at Shorty Hurd and he was twins, too, as was his tall girl. So it came about that when I had swallowed my drink and turned suddenly and took a poke at the Mexican I saw two of him and poked at the wrong one—the one that wasn't there. My fist fanned the vacant air.

Shorty pulled at my sleeve. "We'll be murdered if we stay here." he exclaimed. "Let's move."

"I'm due to die anytime, anyhow," I returned, trying to get my eyes in focus. "Might as well make it right here."

Just then I remembered that I could speak Mexican with a vocabulary greater than most Mexicans. I turned, with my elbow on the bar, and told the Mexican shoulder-slapper what I thought of him, in his own language. I dissected his ancestors to the fifth generation or thereabout, and they were all scrawny pigs. His mother, I mentioned, was a nanny goat and smelled like one.

It is astonishing how insulting one can be with the beautiful Mexican language if one knows how.

I hadn't really finished when something hit me on the head. Perhaps it was the bartender, using the beer-keg mallet. Whatever it was, it sent me into a complete blackout. I didn't even see stars.

4

Fooling the Yokels

I RECOVERED CONSCIOUSNESS AT the Mexican end of the international bridge. Shorty told me about the fight, in which I had taken no part other than being on the receiving end. The bartender and several of the house men had hit me at once with anything that came handy. He and his girl had dragged me out of the place but not until I was badly battered up. He had gone through my pockets and given the girl a half-dollar for her help in rescuing me.

We held a council of war. I was for going back and wrecking the place, as I was going to die soon anyhow, but Shorty vetoed the plan. He wanted to live a while longer. They would certainly kill us, he argued, and throw our bodies into the Rio Grande river. Shorty asserted he didn't need a bath bad enough to be thrown into the river.

"Have you any other plans?" I inquired.

"Creep along till we get almost to the center of the bridge," he suggested, "and then we'll run for it. After midnight the collectors are at the center of the bridge. We'll be several blocks into the good old United States before they know what's happening."

"Why not pay them the two dimes and walk across?" I queried.

"Because we haven't got any dimes," Shorty explained. "I gave that girl your last half-dollar. And I don't think those birds back at that saloon would lend us twenty cents if they saw us dying."

It was about 2 o'clock. The international bridge was deserted. Everything in Juarez, with the exception of the saloons, was closed. Across the river the lights of El Paso twinkled. I had four hundred dollars over there and not a dime with which to pay bridge tolls.

"What are we waiting for?" I asked.

We ran for it. We passed the collector's hut in the center of the bridge before anyone saw us. As we ran we heard shouts behind us, but we kept on running and were soon within the confines of the good old USA.

Just as we came off the bridge on the United States side we ran into the arms of two El Paso police officers. They listened to our story and looked at my head, which was bleeding. They took us along with them.

As soon as we reached the police station and the surgeon there had patched up a few cuts on my head, we fell asleep. They didn't lock us up in a cell. I showed my soldier papers and Shorty had a printer's union card and a lot of vaudeville identification papers. The booking sergeant had served time in the Philippines, so he let us sleep on a bench in the booking room.

The police judge hadn't served in the army, and hadn't any mercy. He didn't like the idea of two nondescripts running the bridge, so he said it was ten dollars apiece or ten days, take it or leave it.

After an officer had accompanied us to the hotel to get my money and we were free again, Shorty unfolded his plan to work his way eastward. But first he insisted that I buy a money order on New York with my money, less ten dollars, to be used as working capital. Five of that went to get a mandolin belonging to Shorty out of pawn.

What we were about to do to work our way east may not have been exactly ethical, but it worked. Moralists may call us perverted, but our plan was no more dishonest than many things then being used by what was known as big business. We merely followed, in a small way, the plan of selling phony stuff to men who were suckers enough to bite.

At that time, and for years later, phony mining stock was sold openly. Banks and insurance companies were organized, collected a lot of money, and then folded up. Railroads and express companies had no arbitrary rates for service, and an agent was complimented if he could bilk a shipper or a passenger out of more than the regular rate—if he turned the overcharge money into the company.

Shorty and me were just little fellows in a big puddle, so to speak.

Shorty bought several bars of white laundry soap and a bar of tar soap. A bottle of gasoline cost us twenty cents, as there were no filling station in El Paso or anywhere else at that time. A roll of red wrapping paper cost us twenty cents at a printing office. We were now ready for work.

We hired a horse and buggy at a livery stable and drove out a mile or two, where we took off a rear wheel. Using the gasoline, we cleaned the hub and axle thoroughly. While it was drying, we cut the big five-cent bar of white laundry soap into small cubes and wrapped each cube in red paper. Before we replaced the buggy wheel we smeared it liberally with the tar soap. By the time we drove back to town the tar soap resembled axle grease so much that no one not in on the secret could tell the difference.

Back in town, Shorty attracted a crowd with his mandolin and a few jokes. Then came the hokum.

We used one stock joke. It smelled as much as the goat it referred to. Shorty would tell me about seeing a goat without a nose. I would ask how it smelled. "Rotten." he would explain. This joke and several others just as ancient and rotten, got us laughs and the crowd remained in good humor while we bilked it.

I would take off the wheel we had doctored with the tar soap. Shorty would borrow a nice white handkerchief from some man in the crowd. He would wipe the handkerchief on the greasy hub until it appeared to be ruined beyond repair and could never be cleaned. Then he would hold it up between thumb and forefinger and show it to the crowd.

"If I wasn't so sure what our magic soap would do I would be buying the gentleman a new handkerchief," Shorty would say as he began to wash it.

He would dip the handkerchief into a bucket of water we kept handy, rub it with some of our magic soap, the cheap laundry soap we had cut into cubes and wrapped in red paper, rinse it out and lo, it was as white as it was before he borrowed it from its owner. The tar soap on the hub and the water would have cleaned the handkerchief without using the magic soap, but the audience did not know that.

We sold out on our first pitch right there in El Paso, clearing about six dollars, and were ready to hit the road.

As I had my army discharge papers showing that I had participated in three battles, twenty-seven skirmishes, and was wounded twice, no license was required for selling in many towns, State laws protected veterans who wished to sell on the streets if they got permission from city officials. Usually this permission was received from the Chief of Police or, in smaller towns, from the city Marshal.

Late that night we caught a train toward the East. We rode in the ice compartment of a fruit refrigerator car. At some point out of El Paso a brakeman came over and Shorty showed his union card which squared us for the ride. The brakeman asked us if we could find a loose board in the wall between the ice compartment so that we could get out some oranges, but the wall was solid. The brakeman told us that occasionally he found a loose board in the wall and the crew secured all the oranges they wanted by reaching through and breaking open a crate.

Toyah, Big Springs, Palo Pinto, Mineral Wells, Fort Worth...We made them all. Shorty had conscientious scruples against paying railroad fare, so we rode freights. Shorty's union card and my discharge papers got us in good with the train crews, usually good fellows.

We took about six dollars profit out of each town. Sundays we went out to the hobo "jungles" at the edge of the town we happened to be in, near water, and washed our underwear and threw away our week-old shirts. We wore what was known then as "thousand-mile" shirts, made of black sateen, which cost us from 35 to 50 cents each. The thousand-mile shirts were so called because a man could travel in one, via freight trains, a thousand miles or more and arrive at his destination fairly presentable. We bought a new shirt every Saturday afternoon and on Sunday we threw the old one away or gave it to some hobo who needed it worse than we did. We carried no luggage.

Fort Worth, Dallas, in that portion of Texas, little towns were thick. We played three or four a day around Dallas and made that city our headquarters. In this way we used the same horse and buggy all day, which saved tar soap, which cost us five cents a bar. Then we went north on the Houston & Texas Central Railroad, along which, were many nice little towns, and, incidentally, many yokels we could bilk.

We rested one Sunday near Sherman, where there was a nice clean creek about two miles south of the city. We rested and washed our underwear as usual.

Monday morning, when we reached the town, we met with an adventure which netted us several dollars extra and we didn't have to sell soap to get it.

They had built a nice new jail in Sherman. That Monday morning the jail was surrounded by a mob bent on lynching some inmate of that new jail. I never learned who it was the mob wanted or what they wanted him for. We mingled with the crowd.

Four officers armed with shotguns stood at the entrance of the jail and watched the crowd. The crowd howled for blood and did nothing but howl. They feared those shotguns. The officers did nothing but watch the crowd and kept their guns poised under their right arms so they could shoot from that position quickly.

Shorty took in the situation and said, "We might as well cash in on this. If I know anything about mob psychology, we can make more here in two minutes than we can in three or four pitches of the soap game."

"How?" I queried.

"Take that side of the crowd, and do as I do," he instructed.

He started on one side of the crowd. I began on the other.

"Dynamite," he shouted. "Let's get some dynamite and blow the jail open."

He took off his hat and began passing it. As he did so he shouted, "Who'll throw in for dynamite? Who'll throw in for dynamite?"

I followed suit on my edge of the crowd.

Nickels, dimes, and even quarters were dropped into our hats. We circled the crowd and met at the outer edge, the side toward town.

"We'll have it here in a jiffy," Shorty shouted as we sprinted toward the business section of the city. No one had thought to ask who we were or where we would get the dynamite. That's mob psychology. All the mob cared about was getting that prisoner.

We walked through the business section of the town and walked on. Out near the union station we counted the money we had collected. The stunt had netted us a little less than twenty dollars—very little less.

Unethical? Of course. Unlawful? Yes, but no more unlawful than the act of a mob storming a prison. I never learned whether the mob got its man or not. Probably not. Those officers with the shotguns looked determined.

We paid fare to Denison, nine miles north, and in the same county. We were still too close to Sherman to make it healthy for us, so we ate dinner and walked north across Red River. We were in the Indian Territory.

It was the same all the way up. We sold cheap white laundry soap to the yokels for about a dollar a bar, using the tar soap and buggy racket. Only once did we get into near-trouble and that was due to the inquisitiveness of a girl. Perhaps that is why I was girl-shy. Every time I had anything to do with a girl, I got into trouble or lost or gave away every cent I happened to have at the time.

That trouble came in Logansport, Indiana. My army papers had squared it with the Chief of Police and we were going through the usual hokum.

I had the buggy wheel off and the handkerchief had been daubed with the tar soap that resembled grease after the buggy had been driven a mile or two. A girl came up, looked at the hub a moment and put her finger on it. Then she held her daubed finger to her nose and smelled it.

"That stuff's nothing but tar soap," she said. "You're fakes.'"

"I've just been discharged from the army, sister," I told her in a low voice, "and I've got to make a living somehow."

I let go the buggy wheel and pulled out my discharge papers. She glanced at them.

"I won't report you, soldier," she said with a smile. "But you'd better leave Logansport."

Shorty had sensed something was wrong when I pulled out my discharge papers. I caught his eye and gave him a signal we had agreed on. He was just washing the handkerchief, as usual, before making a selling talk.

"Now folks," he began, "I have just shown you what you might think was a miracle. But I could have washed this handkerchief clean without the use of this white soap. The black stuff that resembles axle grease is just tar soap.

We are here in the interests of the Anti-Fraud League of America and I have just demonstrated to you one of the ways in which frauds are perpetrated on innocent, unsuspecting persons. I will now return your handkerchief, damp but clean, and I trust every one of you will remember this lesson and not bite at every faker that comes along."

The crowd dispersed and the girl, looking somewhat mystified, walked away.

We took eight dollars out of Peru, Indiana, the next day, no inquisitive girls being present.

All the time we traveled, when we had accumulated ten dollars or more, Shorty would insist that we buy money orders, payable to ourselves in New York. I would buy one, Shorty the next and so on. These money orders were sewed in the seats of our underwear. Each Sunday, when we washed our underwear and threw away our thousand-mile shirts, we would cut out the seams and lay the money orders away until the underwear dried. We never kept more than three or four dollars with us, aside from the money orders, cashable in New York.

We had accumulated quite a number of these money orders. So at Youngstown, Ohio, we decided to quit the soap graft and go on to New York. Shorty said he had once worked the country between Youngstown and New York before with the soap game, and was afraid to try it again.

Shorty wanted to go to Boston, where he had a sweetheart, but I didn't care to accompany him. I had never been in New York before and wanted to explore it. Beyond that, I had no plans.

5

Meet Amy Zubar

I LOAFED AROUND NEW YORK several days before I met a girl. She was seated opposite me at a restaurant table. She had ordered just as I did and had finished her meal while I was drinking my coffee. Then she reached for her pocketbook. She uttered an exclamation that attracted my attention. When I looked up tears were streaming from her eyes.

"I've lost my pocketbook!" she exclaimed again. "What'll I do? I haven't a cent with which to pay for my meal."

I glanced over at her check—55 cents. Many a gentleman would have thrown over a dollar or even a five-spot if he wanted to be liberal. I didn't. But of course I wasn't a gentleman.

Instead, I said, "I'll pay the check. Just sit here and talk a few minutes. How much do you make at this graft?"

"Graft?" she repeated. "I'll have you know, sir, that I am an honest girl!"

"I'm glad to hear that," I told her. "For I've got a graft far better than yours. We can clear fifty dollars a day at it. And I need an honest girl, with a good front, to help me."

"If it's something like going to a room with a man and blackmail, you know, nothing doing."

"Nothing like that, sister," I assured her. "Just a little film-flam on the outside."

She became interested. "What is it?" she asked.

I reached over and got her dinner check.

I worked with that girl for more than two months and we both made money. There was nothing sordid or unduly intimate about our partnership. We met once a day at a restaurant, planned the scene of our campaign for the day, and then parted after we had worked out a definite schedule. After that we parted and I would not meet her again until late that night, when we divided our take and ate a light lunch while we counted the money.

Until the day we parted I did not know where she lived. And she was not curious about my personal affairs. She was a good dresser and a good looker and that's what counted. Her name was Amy Zubar, or at least that's the name she gave me.

Our only social meeting was one Sunday. We had planned a campaign in a certain part of the city, but it rained hard about noon, so we chucked the idea of working that afternoon and went out to Coney Island. We played every concession there. An Italian named Delgado living in San Antonio, Texas, had just lately put on the market a new dish, chili con carne, which is "peppers with meat" when translated into English. We ate some and I drank a bottle of beer. That was as far as our intimacy went.

Our graft was a cinch, and depended for its success on the stupidity, cupidity, and gullibility of our fellow citizens.

Amy would be walking along a residence street where, in the warm summer evenings, men would be sitting in their yards or on their porches. When she was sure a man was watching her, Amy would clutch one hand with the other and utter an exclamation of surprise, horror, et cetera, which she could do to a queen's taste. Then she would begin hunting something on the sidewalk or in the gutter. Nine times out of ten the man or men who had been watching her would come out to find out what was wrong.

By that time Amy was weeping, shedding big crocodile tears. She could cry on the spur of the moment or without any spur at all. She occasionally gave me demonstrations of this crying ability while we were seated at a restaurant table. If some dish she had ordered didn't please her she would call the waiter and with tears in her eyes ask him to substitute another dish, which he usually did, as restaurants do not want weeping women in their dining rooms.

When Amy had attracted a man or men to help her search she would tell them about losing a valuable ring, or a necklace, almost priceless, as it was a family heirloom, she asserted.

"And mother told me never to wear it," she would wail. "Now I have lost it. What'll I do?"

A hunt would ensue. The missing piece would not be found, of course, because it wasn't in the neighborhood just then. Finally Amy would give up the search, but she invariably left a card with the address of a swanky hotel or apartment house engraved thereon.

"If you should find this ring" (or bracelet or whatever our schedule called for her to lose at that point), she would say, "Please bring it to this address and mother or I will give you a hundred dollars reward. If you will ask for me personally and give it to me when mother is not present, I will make the reward larger as I do not want her to know I wore the bauble."

Then my part in the graft came. Well-dressed, prosperous-looking, or sometimes, dressed as a Westerner, I would saunter along, not long after Amy had lost the jewelry. Suddenly, when I saw anyone noticing me, I would look down, stoop and pick up something. I would examine it closely. Usually I asked if anyone had lost a piece of jewelry. As they could not describe it they couldn't claim it, but when I showed it and let them see the initials stamped inside the ring or on the necklace or whatever it was, they would begin to dicker for its purchase. I would refuse to sell.

"It's just the thing I've wanted for my girl back home," I would assert. "She'll go wild over it when I give it to her."

It may appear strange, but among all those honest householders not one ever gave me the card Amy had given him and let me collect the reward myself.

There would be more or less bargaining. The bargaining resulted in all cases in my taking anywhere from $20 to $50 and releasing the find. Invariably, I refused to take checks. One man walked me six or eight blocks to a store where he was known well enough that the cashier would cash his check for $50.

Of course, when the purchaser took the ring or bracelet to the address on the card Amy had given him, he would either find no one of that name residing there or find the one whose name was on the card had never had a daughter.

Once we found a card bearing the name of a well-known Wall Street man. We made $50 on that deal. I learned later the man was a bachelor. I wondered what he said when the purchaser of the ring told him his daughter had lost it.

Usually we had the cards printed in small lots with fictitious names on them.

Fear of ridicule kept the bilked men from reporting their losses to the authorities. A Spaniard down on Vesey Street sold us the ritzy jewelry for about fifty cents apiece, and stamped initials on them to match the cards we were going to use next.

Our best night was over in Brooklyn. Amy lost six rings and I collected $105. Our worst night was away out in the hundred numbered streets. A thug came along while I was dickering with a man to whom Amy had given a card. He held both of us up and got the last ring and also most of what I had collected on two plants before that one.

But all good things must come to an end. One night Amy showed me a little story in a newspaper—about ten lines of six-point type—which told of police being on the trail of a couple who had worked that graft on several citizens. That would be us, of course. Once one man squawked all would squawk and we would be arrested.

Amy announced she was going home—home being somewhere in Ohio, I believe. We were both prosperous, and had money and fine clothes. We celebrated that last night after we had bilked two men over on Long Island out of $35 and $25, respectively. Evidently they had not read the papers closely.

Amy did not drink or smoke, but I did, and we went to a midnight show, ate dinner later and then went over to Coney Island for an early morning swim.

We were lying on the sand, watching the sun come up out of the ocean. I got sentimental.

"I could almost marry you, Amy," I began, "if I wasn't due to die soon. But you'd make a nice looking widow when I kick in."

"Almost is right," she returned. "Almost, but not quite. I've tried married life, and I'm all washed up with it. I lived with a man for more than a year after I married him. He wanted me to stay at home and vegetate while he ran around. You're a good fellow, all right, and I might as well admit I was getting pretty desperate when I met you. But I wouldn't marry you if you were the best man in the world."

"But I'm not," I said.

"You're not what?"

"The best man in the world."

"Forget it, then. I'm leaving for home at noon. Want to come and help me pack?"

"Why not? By, the way, how much did you ever make by the lost pocketbook racket?"

"Not a cent. But I got acquainted with a nice young man."

"Who?"

"You. You were the first man I ever tried that gag on."

As we parted at the steps of the train that was to take her home I kissed her.

Ships that pass in the night? Perhaps. Amy was a good girl, and wherever she is today I wish her well. I still remember her as a girl who could wear clothes well, think quickly in an emergency, and shed tears when she wanted to shed tears.

For a week or two I looked around for another girl partner, intending to go up to Boston for a month or so. I interviewed several I met in unconventional ways, without telling them my plans, but every one of them wanted a closer relationship, a closer intimacy, after a short acquaintance. I was girl-shy anyhow and did not gang up with any of them. Amy was gone and the graft was shot as far as I was concerned.

I didn't know what to do. Inaction palled. As long as I kept busy I felt well. A few days of loafing brought back the old illness. I either had to keep busy all the time or that doctor would be right. It was either work or get sick and kick in. I decided to go to work.

I remembered the letter of introduction given me by Lieutenant Kirkland. I went over to Brooklyn and found the Mergenthaler Linotype factory on Ryerson Street.

I little thought at the time that my visit to the factory was one of the steps that would lead to my becoming a colonel in the Guatemalan army. Guatemala was and is a republic down in Central America. No one could have predicted any connection between a factory in Brooklyn and a colonelship in the Guatemalan army. But there was to be.

As far as I knew when I went over to Brooklyn, I was going to get a humdrum job to occupy my time for a while. I didn't intend to stick. If I was doomed to die soon I wanted to go places and see things. I knew I would be a long time dead. Just for the time being I wanted to keep myself busy. So I crossed the big bridge, not caring whether I got the job or not.

6

You Sail Saturday

"YOU WISH TO WORK HERE, I take it," the cousin said, after he had read Lieutenant Kirkland's letter.

"Yes, sir."

"Ben says you have had some mechanical engineering training and worked in a printing office while you were in grade school," he went on, referring to the letter. Although it had been unsealed, I hadn't taken the trouble to read it. He laid it aside and asked, "Broke?"

For answer I showed him my savings account book showing deposits of almost a thousand dollars. In addition to that, I pulled a wad of bills from my pocket and threw them on his desk.

"I thought perhaps you were just asking for a job to get a chance to panhandle. However, your work here will be in overalls. We need no white collar men."

"Just so you keep me busy," I said. "Anything will be all right with me."

"The man you'll work under will see that you keep busy," he said with a smile. "Show up tomorrow morning at seven o'clock. I take it you're Irish and the man you work for is Irish. He'll be boss, and he'll let you know it. He's a good man with his fists."

"I'll get along with him."

"Glad you take that attitude. Don't be late, for the doors close at exactly seven."

"Thank you, sir," I said as I walked out to find a boarding house near the factory.

I worked in the assembly department. At that time Ford hadn't started his well-known assembly line, on which each man either puts on a piece or tightens a certain bolt as the machines moves along on a belt. We set up the machines in a big room. instead of having to fight my boss we became great friends. One day at luncheon I was beefing about my boarding house when my boss said, "We've got an extra room. I'll ask the wife if she can put you up. She's a good cook and cooks plenty of everything."

So I fell into a good home.

A linotype is an intricate machine, but I had my engineering knowledge to back me up so that in a month or so I could make the adjustments, from the first seven adjustments, which had to be made in the proper sequence, on up to those on top—the distributor. And that knowledge was to make me a colonel in the Guatemalan army. But I didn't know it then.

Just before Christmas time, a notice was posted on the bulletin board asking for a man familiar with the linotype who could read, write. and speak the Spanish language. He had to be free to travel as well. The notice was on the board several days before I got the sense of it. When I did, I realized that here was a way to go somewhere, to get out of the factory. If they wanted a man to go somewhere, I was the man. I didn't care where I was sent. Any old place in the world was agreeable with me. So I told my boss I was the man.

Next day he sent me over to New York City to fix a linotype that was giving trouble. There were few linotype machinists in the country then. I fixed the machine to the satisfaction of the man who owned the shop. Next day the boss sent another man over to check on my work. He found it satisfactory. As soon as he got back with his report the boss called me.

"Tomorrow you will not come to work in the factory. Tonight as you go out ask the timekeeper for a letter to the Guatemalan consul in New York, which he will have. Go over and satisfy the consul you know Spanish. If you do, and want the job, you'll sail for a place called Porto Barrios on Saturday."

"I'll go anywhere to get out of this factory," I exclaimed.

"You bloody spalpeen." he cried. "Haven't we treated you fine?"

"You have, Mac," I returned. "But have you ever heard of a bird in a gilded cage?"

"So you call yourself a bird, eh?" Mack grouched. "Judging from your appetite, maybe it's an Irish ostrich you are?"

"No, Mac," I explained. "You don't get what I mean. After being in the army three years and fighting and sweating and drinking, it's hard as hell to settle down and live decently, like you fellows do."

"Mebbe it is, me boy," he admitted. "Mebbe it is."

I went over next morning to see the Guatemalan consul. He proved to be a nice fellow. We talked Spanish. We talked English. Finally we made a trade and went out and took several drinks on the strength of it. After several drinks we mixed the languages so that the bartender looked at us in amazement and then gave us one on the house.

I was to get $100 a month, this to be paid in United States money. As the United States money at that time was worth twenty to one in Guatemalan money, my pay after I got down there would amount to $2,000 a month of that money.

"After you land at Porto Barrios," the consul instructed, "you will be responsible for the machines landing in Guatemala City. The railroad runs only to El Rancho. From there on to Guatemala City it is by cart and mule back. Can you do it?"

"I can do anything," I boasted.

"Alright. Come to my office Friday afternoon for your transportation and expense money. Your company will see that the machines are loaded on the steamer. It sails at eight o'clock Saturday morning. I will give you a letter to the commander of the army post at El Rancho. He will furnish you men and mules for the journey over the mountains."

Then I went out and got drunk to celebrate my release from the factory. I recollect having a fight in a barroom. I recollect a policeman putting me out of some place, while I was trying to tell him a funny story.

Somewhere along the route to drunken unconsciousness I bought a shoulder strap holster and a revolver to go in it. It was a curiosity to me, as I had never seen anything like it before. I woke up in a bed in a second-class hotel. There was another man in bed with me. Whether he put me to bed or I put him to bed I will never know. I had most of my money, so no one had robbed me.

I was sober as a judge and on the steamer before seven o'clock on Saturday morning. I was on the second lap of the journey to becoming a colonel in the army of a beautiful little Central American republic.

7

Porto Barrios and the Mountains

PORTO BARRIOS. SUN AND MOSQUITO-BITTEN little hole. Dirty, feverish, stinking. Dirty women, men and children grabbing and scrambling for the too-ripe bananas discarded as the bunches were carried aboard the steamer. United Fruit Company men carrying wicked-looking blue revolvers at their hips. Faded white women watching the steamer and wishing they had fare to go north in her. One of them saw me light an American cigarette and asked me for one. I gave her a full package.

"Are you broke down here?"

"Most of the time, since this damned climate faded what beauty I had."

"Why did you come down here?" I asked again.

"Came down here with a musical comedy show. It went broke. Then I had to do the best I can, as every other white girl has to do around these coffee-colored men."

I gave her a five dollar bill, United States currency.

"What do you want me to do for this?" she asked. "Murder somebody?"

"If I might make a suggestion, I think you'd better get something to eat."

"I'll eat a long time on this—a hundred dollars of this monkey money. Thanks, kid."

A dinky locomotive was switching cars. I saw my machines unloaded from the steamer and loaded into a box car. Fourteen boxes. I counted each box carefully as they were transferred from the steamer to a box car. I was responsible for them. Then, after I had locked the car doors with locks I had brought along for that purpose I went over to an estanca and had a few drinks. You couldn't get breakfast in Barrios until about eleven o'clock. My train was due to leave at eight.

The train crew, that is, the engineer and conductor, were Americans. As my trunk was placed aboard the one passenger coach, the conductor noticed it and asked, "Got an extra shirt in there, old man?"

I noticed he had on a ragged shirt. I had caught the "old man" stuff, too.

"I can let you have one." Then I asked, "What outfit were you in?"

"First Texas. We got to Cuba and went to sleep for six months. Then they sent us home. The tropics got me. I had lost my seniority on the Texas and Pacific. So I came down here."

Regardless of ages, it was the custom of Spanish-American war soldiers to address each other as "old man." It was a sort of friendly greeting. If you were sore at a man you used a more forcible method of greeting.

The railroad from Porto Barrios to El Rancho, the Guatemala Northern, was operated on the hit-and-miss plan. It had been built by New York capitalists, and when they went in the hole a few million dollars they quit and left it to the government. The government operated it by hiring American hoboes who happened along, and these were mostly discharged soldiers. After the close of the war, many of them went south. They had lost their jobs and seniority while serving Uncle Sam, and there was nothing for them to do but hit the road.

There wasn't anything like a payday on the Guatemalan Northern, so the men paid themselves by collecting what money they could and keeping it. No one cared. There were no auditors or accountants employed by the railroad. No supplies were ever purchased. The rolling stock was run down. If a locomotive or cars happened to leave the track and topple over, they were left there. Section men were scarce and the vegetation grew right up to the tracks, breaking windows of the passenger coaches as they went along.

The locomotives were fired with wood, and it was amusing to see an engine pull up to a wood pile and the whole crew go out to dicker with the native who had cut the wood. Sometimes the bargaining took an hour, sometimes only a few minutes, according to how much money the crew happened to have.

At one time, I was told, shortly before I got there, some railroader leaving New Orleans had bought a bundle of facsimile Confederate bills, used for advertising purposes. This money circulated for awhile as United States currency, the natives knowing no better than to accept it and pass it on.

Railroad trains had no schedule and didn't try to get anywhere on time. But in Guatemala no one hurried, Why hurry, when there were always new days coming that hadn't been used yet?

The train on which I shipped my machines and rode myself was due in Gualán about five hours out of Barrios. We left the port about nine o'clock in the morning. We reached Gualán just at sunset and could go no farther that night, as none of the locomotives had headlights that worked.

At Gualán, an ex-convict operated the eating house patronized by the railroad men. He detailed to me the highlights of his escape from the Joliet, Illinois penitentiary. He asked my name and hastened to add, "Of course you don't have to give your right name down here. Any old name will do."

I had him change a five dollar United States hill and he got interested. While he counted out the soiled Guatemalan currency he said, "What you want down here in this country is a native wife to wait on you. I've got a servant here who has two fine girls. I can sell you either one for five dollars and she'll make you a good wife while you stay in Guatemala."

I told him I was down there on business and it was no girls for me.

"But you need one."

He went to a door leading into an inner room and called something to someone inside. Two young girls came in.

"Either one is yours for five dollars. And they're good healthy girls, too."

They were clad in a sort of dress that came to their knees. They didn't look very clean.

"How do you like 'em?" he asked.

"I'm not falling for natives," I told him.

"Oh, all right," he said, waving the girls away. "Come on and have another drink."

The railroad men in Gualán treated those who hadn't made a run that day and therefore had no money. I had money—some of my own and some that had been given me by the consul in New York—and I treated several times and paid for the suppers of all of them. Late that night, one of the trainmen invited me outside.

"You've got money," he warned me after we had stepped outside. "Better sleep with us tonight. If you sleep in that convict's hotel you'll have no money in the morning and you may be dead."

So I slept with the railroad men that night. They occupied a coach which had windows. It was hot in there, but there were no openings by which little insects could enter. I slept and sweated all night, but I had my money and my life when the sun rose.

Living in Gualán was cheap. One could get a drink of aguardiente for one cent. If you wanted water for a chaser it cost another cent.

The train left early next morning, but we got only as far as Zacapa. The flues in the locomotive were leaking badly. So the cars were switched to a siding, an unnecessary proceeding, for there were no other trains on the division. The locomotive was coasted down to Gualán to get another to pull the train into El Rancho.

Zacapa was a nice little town. As the engineer and conductor had gone back to Gualán with the engine, I was the only foreigner in town.

I ate at a little estanca where I got lots of food and attention, for I had money. The old woman who kept the estanca sat at the table, and talked while I ate. Three or four girls stood in the background. I asked them all to have dinner with me but they only giggled and did not come near the table except to bring food. After dinner I sat there a long time and ordered a drink once in a while.

Once or twice a native came in and had a drink with me. About nine o'clock that night, the engine having failed to come up, I went over to a big shed near the station and slept. I was not afraid of being robbed. There were no foreigners there.

At sunup next morning the old woman sent one of the girls over to wake me for coffee. Zacapa was above the mosquito line and I had slept well. The girl appeared as if she had bathed recently and she smelled of strong soap, but she was not bad looking. Her dress had been freshly washed but not ironed.

I started up the street and the girl fell in behind me, a native custom. I reached out and drew her to my side.

"In my country," I explained, "the girls walk by the side of the man."

"But this is on the street," the girl objected.

"And it is not allowed?" I inquired.

"It is not done," she said as she fell in behind me.

"What is your name?" I asked over my shoulder.

"Carnación," she replied.

"Are you married?"

She giggled. "No, señor."

"Are you going to marry soon?"

"I cannot marry until a man comes for me."

"Would you like to marry a man from my country?" I inquired.

"No, señor."

"Why?"

"Because they do not stay here long."

"And you do not want to go to a far-off country?"

"No, señor. I would be lonesome away from my own people."

Along about the middle of the morning a locomotive came up from Gualán, coupled onto the train and we went on up. It was after dark when we reached El Rancho.

From El Rancho to Guatemala City I knew it was mules and men. I found the colonel in charge of the post there and presented my credentials. He merely glanced at them and asked me to have a drink or two before dinner, which I must surely have with him. As a government agent, he explained, I was to stop at the comandancia while in El Rancho.

I didn't want to stay in El Rancho longer than necessary. The comandancia was both hot and dirty. The woman who served us drinks stopped just inside the door to reach down and scratch her legs. I suspected fleas, as that town was too high for mosquitoes and too hot for cooties.

Over the drinks I inquired: "How soon can I get men and burros?"

"Poco tiempo," the colonel said. "Tomorrow I will confer with my officers and see what can be done."

We sat and talked and drank until late. I was given a room in the comandancia and found that sure enough the insects that had caused the woman to scratch her leg in our presence were really fleas. I climbed out onto the flat roof and slept very well.

The sun woke me next morning, and I had a helluva hangover. It was late and I expected to see my men and mules ready to go. But no one was about.

I found the colonel and woke him. He had a hangover just like mine. As we drank coffee with aguardiente in it, I repeated my request for mules and men.

"I remember you spoke about it last night," he said. "You have certain machinery you wish transported to the capital. Tomorrow, of a surety, I will confer with my officers about the matter. Usually I let my junior officers attend to details. Have another cup of coffee with this delightful aguardiente in it, and we will speak further about the machinery which is now here and will soon be taken to the capital.

"I have discovered," he went on, "that when I am worried about anything, a few drinks of aguardiente in coffee makes me forget just what I am worried about."

"I'd like to get the stuff up there," I said.

"We will help you get it up there," the colonel assured me. "In the morning I will consult with my officers and see what can be done."

"Can't you do that today?" I asked, but without a great deal of anxiety. The colonel's remedy for worrying had gone to my head a little, yet I had the stuff in me, aside from coffee and aguardiente, to declare, "I've got to get those machines up there."

"That is true," the colonel soothed. "But if you deliver them in a hurry they will become old and worn out much sooner. New machinery looks nice. Old machinery is dusty and greasy. So wait until tomorrow (mañana) and I'll consult my officers. One of them will have a plan to help you, never fear. They will attend to all the details. I believe several of them have left the garrison for some journey or other, but they will return sooner or later. In the meantime, while you remain here, my young friend, you will make the comandancia your home."

That afternoon I tried to telegraph to the capital, but the government line wasn't working well. In fact, it wasn't working at all. There was just enough juice in the line to work the relay spasmodically, and the batteries which were supposed to work the sounder off the relay had been allowed to deteriorate until they had no power, so it was impossible to receive a message. I asked the operator why he did not renew the batteries and he said he had no blue vitriol.

"How long has the line been working this way?" I asked. "Or not working?"

"Maybe three months, maybe four," the operator replied. "I am not certain."

"And you don't care?"

"Why should I, señor?" he asked. "I do not have anything to do as it is. If the wires were working I would have to sit here all day."

El Rancho was noted for its fleas. I became accustomed to pulling up a trousers leg and dislodging a flea regardless of what company I happened to be in, without exhibiting the slightest embarrassment. Everyone did the same thing. There was no real society there, all the garrison officers being bachelors. A railroad man told me that the sand around El Rancho was so full of fleas that if you scooped up a handful of sand and held it a moment, after all the fleas had jumped out of your hand there would be no sand left. I never tried it.

I lived with the colonel. As all the officers had to pay their own way, I stood my half of the food. Every head mozo was given one dollar of that money with which to purchase food for the day. After the first day I gave the dollar on alternate mornings.

I learned to drink coffee with aguardiente and like it. We bought the aguardiente by the garafone, which is a sort of jug. One might hold a gallon and the next might hold five. But a garafone of aguardiente always cost a dollar.

Every day I tried to get the colonel to get mules and men, and every day he shifted the responsibility onto the shoulders of some subordinate officer who didn't appear particularly interested. As a last resort I hunted burros myself until I had about twenty available. The colonel promised to detail as many soldiers as I wished if he had that many. He was uncertain just how many he had as they were coming and going all the time. Each soldier drew twenty cents per day ration money and had to buy rations himself. I think that was the only pay they received, for I never heard of a payday there.

I was in El Rancho twenty-one days before I started over the mountains toward Guatemala City with my linotype machines. I could imagine what my old boss back in Brooklyn would have said if he had been along. He'd have gotten so angry he might have bitten himself. Loafing was a cardinal sin in his department. And while he seldom fired a man, he would have given a loafer a tongue-lashing.

My old boss would have told the colonel plenty. I didn't say much. That old colonel was a good coot. The only thing that got monotonous was the hangover I woke with every morning. But the colonel's aguardiente with coffee soon killed that.

If I tried to hurry either him or one of his officers, they had one stock reply: "Why hurry today? Think of all the fine days coming that haven't been used yet."

It was a good philosophy and could well be practiced today. We might not be so well advanced as we are if we adopted such a life, but we would live better—and perhaps longer.

Despite the fact that El Rancho was full of fleas and heat I never felt better in my life. I knew now I would fool the doctor who said I hadn't long to live. In fact, I forgot all about dying.

It was about ten o'clock one morning when I got my outfit started from El Rancho. We had made about three miles by siesta time. It took us until about five o'clock to get started again, as the burros had wandered back to El Rancho and we had to send men after them. By dark we had made about seven miles.

For three days we hauled those fourteen boxes in carts. From that point on carts could not be used, as the trails were too narrow. At one point, instead of swinging the heavy boxes between burros we had to swing them between four burros traveling single file, two in front and two behind. I had to make a long harness to do this. The boxes containing the lighter parts were packed on the backs of burros.

Many an evening, when we camped for the night, I could look back across a valley or a barranca and see the place from which we had started that morning.

But my gang of native soldiers was of the happy-go-lucky type. We had fun. They had a miramba, homemade, and they would sing and play after we had camped for the night. Occasionally, when we camped in a village, there would be a dance.

When we reached a village or a rancho, I would give each man a coin with which to purchase food. I got liberal one evening and gave each of them three coins. Within an hour I had a bunch of amiable drunks on my hands. I would whistle "Give My Regards to Broadway" and the musicians would try to play it on the miramba. I couldn't get them started next morning until nearly noon. After that, one coin.

At length, after a hard journey, during which I became brown and felt as tough as when I enlisted in the United States Army, we rounded the side of a big mountain and saw before us a broad, winding road, paved, well-bridged and drained. President Don Manuel Cabrera had caused the road to be built, using both convict and paid labor.

This road followed the route of a road that had been built in prehistoric times. Landslides, floods and time had obliterated it in places. But for miles, disconnected from the other good places, little work was required to make it a modern highway.

What sort of people built this road or for what purpose it was built will never be known, but they were engineers, surely, for the curves were banked and the tangents were level and well drained. The road was paved with some sort of stone that had gradually hardened and became as smooth as a road paved with cement in modern times.

I reached the village near the end of the road and my troubles were over—almost.

I needed carts. There were none in the village that answered my purpose. I noticed a wire running into the intendencia, or city hall, and knew it was a telegraph line.

It worked like the one at El Rancho. But I cut the wires and grounded out the El Rancho end so as to cut out as much resistance as possible, and found I could work with Guatemala City by listening carefully to the gentle ticks of the relay. The sounder batteries weren't there. The intendente told me someone had borrowed the glass jars to brew aguardiente in.

I waited five days while the carts were coming from Guatemala City. They were drawn by burros. It took us a day to load and seven days to get to the city. But we had every box intact.

I landed in Guatemala City March 14, 1902, three months out from New York.

8

Guatemala City

GUATEMALA CITY. RUINED TIME AFTER TIME by earthquakes, it still stands, a city of one-story buildings scattered over a wide area. The San Marcos building, owned by the railroads, and the government buildings were the only ones rising above two stories when I reached there.

Street cars, electric lights, nice saloons and restaurants. Pretty women, ugly women. Native men in evening dress and native men in rags. Native women in Paris creations and native women with only a short chemise to hide their brown bodies.

Street cars bearing the signs, "No fumar aqui," which meant you shouldn't smoke on the cars, but no one ever paid the least bit of attention to the signs.

A friendly city. No one hurried. No one worried. No one worked when they could get by without working. If one attempted to hurry he was reminded that hurrying was useless, as there were new days coming that hadn't been used yet.

By skirting around and eating meat at one stand, vegetables at another, and coffee somewhere else in the city market, one could get a real good meal for about 10 cents, but not all of it at any one stall in the market. One had to get around and pay one centavo for a dish of beans here, another centavo for a cup of coffee and so on until one had a meal.

While eating a man could pass compliments to the young or old woman who operated the stand he happened to be patronizing at the time. Like women the world over the Guatemalan women liked compliments, and if a man complimented the owner of the stand he would get the pick of her edibles or perhaps a larger helping for one cent.

Meals at the principal hotel of the city cost about $5 of that money and were poor imitations of French meals. Restaurants patronized by Americans or Europeans charged about the same. The native restaurants were better and charged about a fourth of the price. But in the native restaurants you had to risk swallowing a fly occasionally.

I was a week putting up the machines. Then I set about teaching the native printers how to operate them.

I was furnished a house, as per contract, with mozos, or servants. My mozos were an old man and woman, husband and wife, slow-going, indolent, living for today and caring little for tomorrow. Each day I gave the old woman a dollar with which to purchase food at the market. One never laid in a supply of food ahead in Guatemala City. There was always a new day coming when one could buy more food.

I fell into a routine that was pleasant at first but soon became as monotonous as the factory work in Brooklyn. I would spend the morning at the printing office, instructing. About noon I would walk home for my noonday meal.

In the afternoon, after a siesta, I would either loaf with Americans or Europeans at a bar uptown or go down to the Central Railroad station where I would drink and talk with the railroad men at a little estanca just across from the station. Drinks could be bought there for a cent, the same drinks that cost ten to twenty-six cents uptown. American railroad men came and went. The turnover in trainmen on the Central Railroad was about twenty-five percent a month.

The old woman who operated the estanca near the station had a large book, once the ledger of some business house, in which her guests wrote their names and the date of their visits to Guatemala City. The woman could not read, but she treasured that book. I looked it over and found it dated from about 1672, when Guatemala was little known in the United States.

In that book were names written in old-fashioned script that was taught before the present business writing. Those men had come over the mountains for some reason or other. It would be a treasure to a man who wanted to delve back into the years when Central America had no railroads and burro trails were the only highways. The old woman scorned my offer to purchase the book.

I had been in Guatemala City about three months when something happened that changed my life altogether. I had tired of my routine. I might as well have been back in the Brooklyn factory for all the excitement I was having.

The men I was teaching were becoming good mechanics. They could go on from there without my assistance. It got so I would loaf around the office a few hours each day and do absolutely nothing. My feet became itchy. I wanted to put on a thousand-mile shirt and go over the next hill and around the next curve and see what was there.

But I did not know the Guatemalan officials.

Occasionally in the office I praised the men for learning the linotype so quickly, and declared my intention of going on somewhere. Someone probably reported my desire to the authorities.

One morning, as I walked to the office, I noticed a little soldier following me. While I was in the office he sat in the doorway, dozing. Later in the day he was relieved by another. Wherever I went after that a little soldier followed me. He never bothered me or spoke to me, but he was there all the time. At night he slept with the mozos just outside my bedroom door.

The second or third day I questioned the one who happened to be following me at the time. He knew nothing, he declared, except that he had orders to keep me in sight at all times, and if I attempted to leave the city he was to prevent my doing so. Failing in that, he was to telephone his superior officer.

Life with a little soldier at my heels and sleeping on my doorway at night became distasteful, to say the least. I became jittery.

I wandered around in the most disreputable portions of the city at night, hoping someone would try to hold me up so that I might fight both the holdup man and the little soldier. The nearest I came to having a fight was in a low-class saloon or estanca when a group of tough-looking customers insisted I drink with them. I did, so we didn't fight.

I sat in the lowest class saloons and drank, treating the little soldier, and tried to get him drunk, but the officers must have known my capacity and sent a well-seasoned soldier at night, for by the time I was woozy the little fellow would be taking drink after drink with me and not appearing to feel them.

I attended shows, thinking they wouldn't admit my guard, but a word to the ticket-taker passed him in without question.

Finally, one day, after I had been followed for about 10 days, I went to see the man above the soldier. He didn't know what it was all about, but advised me to see the commanding general. I located that individual away out in the suburbs. He was watching while some soldiers were trying out machine guns.

They were having poor success with the guns. They would fire until the guns jammed and then it would take as much as thirty minutes to dig out the jammed bullets, sometimes longer. I butted in and looked one over while the soldiers were digging out a jammed bullet. They were of the Benet-Mercie type, evidently rebuilt, for they had parts I believed belonged to another make of gun. In the Philippines I had become something of an expert with machine guns. The experience had been wished on me, so to speak, but I had liked it.

I told my troubles to the commander, a nice old gentleman. I asked why a soldier had been detailed to watch me all the time, just as if I were a convict.

"It was learned you were about to break your contract," he explained. "Your contract calls for a year's duty here. So you will not be permitted to leave until the year is served. Have you been treated fairly?"

"I have been treated nicely," I replied, "but I just wanted to go."

"If you will give me your word that you will not break your contract, the guard will be recalled," the general offered.

"I'll give my word," I said, and the general turned and gave an order to a junior officer.

When he had finished I remarked, "Those men are not very well trained in the use of machine guns, general."

"Are you familiar with those guns?" he asked.

"I learned something about them in the Philippines, where I served in the United States Army," I explained.

"Would it be a trespass on your good nature if I asked you to assist us in teaching those men the use of machine guns?" he asked.

"You mean for me to train machine gun crews?"

"Yes, señor."

"Nothing would suit me better," I exclaimed, and went on to explain, "That is why I wanted to leave here. I have nothing to do. The men I came here to teach the operation of typesetting machine are intelligent and I can teach them little more. I was becoming ennuied and wanted to go somewhere where there was something doing. I'll train you a fine company of gunners."

The following morning I was commissioned a captain in the Guatemalan army. The little soldier guard was gone. The boys down at the Central shops heard of my promotion and insisted on calling me General. I gave my two mozos five dollars each in United States money when I dismissed them. They could live a year on that.

I spent ninety dollars of that money setting a tailor to fit me in a suit of uniform. With it on I was a captain and was entitled to a salute from any private soldier I happened to meet. But most of them thought perhaps I was a passenger conductor on the Central Railroad who had purchased a new uniform and passed me by without a glance.

I happened in a barroom uptown where foreigners congregated in the evening, and one of them asked me if I had gotten a job on the railroad. When I explained my promotion they all addressed me as General.

With the appointment came a change in my routine. As a commissioned officer of the army I no longer lived alone. I joined a sort of officers' club where a number of young officers had a sort of co-operative arrangement for paying board and room. As I could speak the language and knew something of their etiquette I got along famously.

My salary as per my contract continued, but because of that I received no captain's pay. That was nothing to me, anyhow, as the monthly pay of a captain, reduced to United States money was about as much as Shorty Hurd and myself had taken in one day when we were selling phony soap to the yaps between El Paso and Youngstown.

In my leisure time I still went down to the Central Railroad shops and drank and talked with the boys there. They took great pleasure in introducing me to a newcomer, and there were many newcomers, as General.

It was a pleasant life, but the fireworks were yet to come.

9

President Cabrera and Señorita Sugusta

I TRAINED THOSE MACHINE GUNNERS by a method all my own. Those Benet-Mercies were good only for a number of shots before they jammed. I had twenty guns, mounted on tripods. I taught my men to count as they fired and each of the other squads would count in unison: "One, two, three, four, five."

This counting was done in Spanish, of course.

When the count of five had been reached, the gun which had been firing would cease, and the next would begin. Then the next, and so on. By the time the first one was ready to fire in its turn the barrel would be cool and there was no danger of jamming.

After I had taught my men in this manner, I tried it out in batteries of five guns and found that the intervals between blasts were sufficiently long to allow the barrels to cool so they would not jam.

To teach the men to count in unison I had to station a tall man at one side and slightly in front of the firing line to lead the counting. At every count he would raise and lower his arm, outstretched. Soon every man jack of the idle guns would raise and lower his right arm in time with the tall man. It looked comical to see each man swinging his arm up and down, but it did what I wanted. We could shoot half a day and never jam a gun.

One afternoon, when I had been training the men for a couple of weeks, President Cabrera visited the field and I gave an exhibition for his benefit.

We had planted a row of posts, dressed like scarecrows I have seen in fields in the United States, and used them for targets. After my crews had each fired two intervals of blasts at these not one of the posts was left standing.

Then I gave my men a rest command, at which they sat flat on the ground and began rolling cigarettes, and an officer escorted me to where the President stood. Thus I was introduced to a man who remained my friend as long as he lived.

Much has been written about President Cabrera being a dictator and always surrounded by guards. All chief executives are guarded, even the President of the United States. Cabrera had to be a sort of dictator in those days or he wouldn't have served six months. He tried to pattern his actions after those of presidents of the United States and succeeded in part. He built highways and railroads. I knew him intimately and found him to be a square shooter.

But he did not believe in giving the resources of his country to American or other foreign exploiters. His people lived simply and happily. They were poor financially and did not care.

When I was presented to the President he shook my hand and congratulated me on the showing my men had made.

"There will be a meeting of officers and diplomats at the residency this evening," he said. "I would be pleased to have you come, as I wish to talk to you. I am well pleased with your exhibition of machine gunnery."

I saluted, turned away and went to dress for dinner with the presidents.

I decided I should have some decorations to wear on my uniform and looked in two hockshops and found nothing suitable. A young locomotive engineer I met told me he had several and I went to his room with him and looked at them. One was from a fishing club out in California and was for telling the biggest fish story. Another was for collecting the most box tops of a popular cigarette. So I went without decorations.

Leslie Coombs, a Kentucky politician, was United States minister to Guatemala at the time and was the only Yankee present except myself. We were introduced and he asked why I hadn't called on him. He appeared so patronizing that I told him I had no business with his office as I could take care of myself anywhere under any circumstances. That was the last time I ever spoke to him. It was a case of mutual dislike.

But the others at the dinner presented a conglomeration never to be forgotten. Plain Indian army officers looking bored and frightened, dresses from Paris, native dresses, lights and sparkling champagne. Lovely ladies side-by-side with ladies whose faces would stop a clock. One man alone stood by himself, eyeing all present, watching every movement. That was Volters, the president's German body guard. Aside from myself, he was the only man in the gathering who wore a weapon. Had he known I was armed he probably would have shot me.

Two courteous gentleman at the entrance expertly frisked each man as he entered. The frisking was not done openly, but with efficiency. I happened to be carrying a fountain pen. Why I carried it I don't know, as the thing wouldn't write, but perhaps it was in the nature of a decoration. While one of the men passed his hands over my uniform the other borrowed the pen, tried to write with it, gave it up as a bad job and returned it to me with a word of excuse. He had investigated and found it not to be a lethal weapon.

It was something of a joke to me, this casual search for weapons. I wore my shoulder strap holster with a revolver in it, but it was a new thing then and no one thought to look under a man's arm for a gun.

I did not like the first drink of champagne I ever tasted, which was right there, so I confined myself to native wine or tequila, which choice appeared to please some of my comrades-in-arms.

"The captain likes our native drinks," one of them remarked.

"I do," I said, "and I do not like the foreign champagne."

"Some day you may become a Guatemalan, perhaps," another suggested.

"I would never regret becoming a citizen of your beautiful country," I returned. "I have never found a better people."

"Perhaps the actions of the Captain and his deportment while here makes us a good people in his estimation. There are foreigners who have come here and left with a poor opinion of the Guatemalans. But their actions were not of the best, however. A good man finds good people everywhere."

As I was nothing but a captain I did not sit at the President's table, that being reserved for diplomats and the higher officers.

When giving a formal dinner, President Cabrera aped the customs of United States and British officials and paired off ladies and gentlemen to go into the dining room together. Usually this is not the custom in Latin-American countries.

I stood uncertain when they began pairing off to go into dinner, and looked inquiringly at the officer who seemed to have that part of the program in charge. He glanced at a paper in his hand, looked around, located my partner and motioned me over to where she stood. A moment later I was being introduced to Señorita Sagusta, then about seventeen years old, spirited, independent, chic, modern. She did as she pleased around Guatemala City, I learned later. Her parents were dead and she was in the care of a distant relative who was a leading politician at that time.

The señorita was to have me banned from Guatemala City, but it really was not her fault and it happened months later.

After the introduction I offered her my arm and took her into dinner. I learned later that she had demanded I be paired off with her, as I was a new foreigner and somewhat of a novelty—a man who had been jerked, so to speak, from the position of a mechanic instructor to a captaincy in the army.

She was trying to learn English and could speak a few words with no sense of grammar, She tried to converse with me in English all through dinner.

As we seated ourselves at the table, she said: "I am trying to learn your language and will converse with you as much as I can in it. If I make an error in construction, señor Captain, will you do me the favor to correct me? I will not resent it, as I wish to learn to speak the language as it is spoken in New York."

"As much as it will pain me to criticize such a lovely young lady, señorita," I told her, "I promise to correct your English."

Occasionally I glanced around the room. Four long tables, three of them presided over by senior officers, the fourth by the President himself. Cut glassware flashed back the gleams of the diamonds worn by some of the women. Conversation flourished. I looked over the place and my thoughts went back a few months to the days when Shorty Hurd and I camped on a creek near a town and washed our underwear and threw away our thousand-mile shirts, to the times when we sold little cubes of laundry soap to the hicks in the towns between El Paso and Youngstown, and to the days when Amy Zubar and I had worked the lost-ring game on the big town hicks in New York and Brooklyn.

I said to myself, audibly: "You've come a long way, old timer. I wonder how soon you will be down to wearing a thousand-mile shirt again."

I imagined I was thinking, but I must have been talking to myself, for Señorita Sagusta asked, "What said the mister?"

"What did you say, sir?" I corrected.

"What did you say, sir?" she parroted.

"Nothing at all," I replied. "I was just talking to myself."

"And you no to me talk?"

'And you do not talk to me?" I corrected.

She repeated the correct question and I could see her lips move as she repeated it over and over.

"When I talk to you, señorita," I said in Spanish, "I have to be very careful and use words suited to the ears of a very pretty and accomplished young lady. When I talk to myself I do not have to be so choice."

"The Captain is not so different from other gentlemen in Guatemala City," she observed. "Every woman is a lovely lady. I understand in New York men are far more rough with women. Is it true?"

"In some classes," I replied. "But when I say you are lovely I speak the truth."

She smiled.

After the dinner was over and the ladies had left the room, the President motioned me to a seat beside him and asked, "You are a good shot with a revolver, are you not, Captain?"

"A little above the average, sir," I confessed.

The president went on, "I have a reason for asking that question. A man in my position has enemies, just as every executive has. I have a bodyguard, as you know. There is a German, Volters. He is a good and devoted man as long as I pay him. The others are army officers I have detailed from time to time. Would it be amiss if I asked you to serve in that capacity occasionally? I like men of your nationality, and I noticed tonight you liked our drinks even better than the foreign beverages we import."

"I would like nothing better than to serve you, sir," I told him. "But I would like, also, to have a chance to go out into the field. You realize, sir, that after having served three years in the United States Army one does not fall readily into a monotonous routine."

The president smiled.

"I will see that you are sent out with the very next expedition. Not all my people are satisfied. We have uprisings. You will have your chance for field service, with your machine guns."

"I am at your service, sir," I said.

"Do you carry arms?" he asked.

"Yes, sir. But I might as well carry none. I haven't fired a revolver since I came to Guatemala."

"And the gentlemen at the door? Did they take your revolver?"

"No, sir. One of the gentlemen looked at my fountain pen a moment, but returned it."

"And you are now armed?"

"Yes, sir."

"I see no weapon."

I threw back my coat and showed him the shoulder strap I had purchased while on a drunk in New York.

"You see, sir," I elaborated proudly, "I am prepared right now to kill anyone who would attempt to molest you."

"It is astonishing," he exclaimed.

"No one told me it was against the rules to wear my weapon."

"We'll let it go," the president said. "Men of your class are seldom traitors. I was told you are a mechanical man. There is something about a mechanical man which makes him trustworthy. I don't know what it is. A short time ago an American locomotive engineer went to his death in a railroad accident when he could have jumped and saved his life. But he chose to give his life to save his passengers."

"They do that often," I said. "It is the same code of ethics that makes a ship captain go to his death rather than desert his ship."

"Have you had occasion to use your weapon since you have been in Guatemala?" the president asked.

"No, sir," I replied. "I have been treated royally since I have been in Guatemala City. I have taught five young men to operate the machines I brought in, and they are now proficient. I am glad to be able to teach your soldiers how to operate the new machine guns."

The president indicated that we were to join the ladies in the drawing room. Once there I singled out Señorita Sagusta.

"I was going to leave Guatemala, señorita," I said. "But I'm afraid you'll be the magnet that will make me stay in this country forever."

"Do you say that to every young woman you meet?" she asked.

"You are the only whom I have met that was attractive enough to make me say it."

"And you will teach me English as they speak it in New York?" she asked.

"I will teach you English as they speak it in Kankakee, as long as I can be near you."

"I do not understand that, that Kankakee."

"I'll teach you all that, señorita."

10

Promoted, Via a Dead Man

I LED A BUSY LIFE, one that I liked. Every afternoon I drilled my gunners until they could shoot surely. It was comical to see each disengaged man at a waiting gun counting aloud and bringing an arm up and down each time he counted. Two or three times a week I would go down to the printing office to see how things were getting along. The men were becoming good operators on the linotypes. They took great care in keeping the machines cleaned and in tiptop condition. I was proud of them and told them so.

I drank with foreigners at a bar catering to the wealthier class and occasionally went up to the San Marcos building where railroad headquarters were located. The Guatemala Central Railroad had headquarters there as well as the Ferro Carril de Ocós, or Ocós Railroad.

The Ocós Railroad was to play a great part in my life later. I got chummy with the railroad's president and general manager, Herr Welmyer. He was a German who could speak English as it is spoken in Brooklyn and his sole duty, it appeared, was to send American hoboes down there to operate the railroad. They would go down, stay a while, come back to Guatemala City and try to kill old Welmyer. I was to discover the reason for this afterward.

President Cabrera decided to follow the custom of the United States presidents and hold a hand-shaking match one Sunday, with a long line of citizens of all classes passing in single file and shaking the hand of their president. It was a well-advertised event, as no other Central American president had ever had the nerve to try it before, and long before the time set there was a mob of citizens of all classes, high and low, waiting to get into line.

It was a fine Sunday morning and a long line of men and women were passing the place where President Cabrera stood, giving his hand a shake and then passing on. His German bodyguard stood at his left side, the side from which the line approached, while I stood directly behind him. We watched as each person drew up, to see that no one carried weapons. There were any number of men in that country who would cheerfully have killed the president.

The line had been passing for about half an hour, and I was ready to call it a day, for my feet was hurting in a new pair of shoes, when my attention was attracted by a man in the advancing line. One of his hands was covered with a handkerchief, as if it had been injured. This man was about ten or twelve from the man in front of the president when I noticed him.

That hand covered with a handkerchief caused something to click in my brain, but it didn't click clearly. I couldn't remember what it was. He was second or third from the president when my brain clicked efficiently. Then I recalled that a man with his hand covered with a handkerchief had murdered President McKinley.

I did not have time to warn the German, on whose side the man was approaching. The man with the handkerchief was just in front of the German when I stepped between him and the president, drew my revolver from its shoulder strap holster, put it against his side and pulled the trigger three times.

What I really meant to do was to order him out of line, but I didn't have time. Within a second or two he would have been directly in front of the president.

The sound of the shots was not loud. My revolver was a .32 caliber with a long cartridge. The man stood still a moment, and I was about to give him the remaining two bullets that were in the gun when he toppled over. A stubby revolver fell from the hand that had been covered with a handkerchief clattered across the floor. The man following him turned as if to run. As he did so, the German, Volters, saw a gun in his hand and fired. I placed myself in front of the president.

"Sorry to interrupt you, sir," I said, "but those men were going to shoot you. Please stand still."

The German called a few soldiers and had the bodies dragged to a corner of the room. A minute or two more and the line was passing as it was before. The president made no sign that he had noticed the incident. I instructed a couple of my own soldiers to go down the line and see that all hands were uncovered, and if anyone looked suspicious to take them into another room where we would examine them. Half an hour later the audience was over.

Twenty or more officers just behind us had drawn their revolvers to use in case of a stampede, but it was a useless precaution. The native Guatemalan sees death too often to get excited when it approaches.

As soon as the end of the line had passed and the president had retired to his chambers, I went to a bathroom and vomited. My new shoes began to hurt my feet again, too. I was so weak I had to sit down a few minutes. I thought for a few minutes that perhaps the Honolulu doctor was right, that I was going to croak then and there. I hadn't been a bit excited while the excitement was going on, but now that the excitement was over the reaction was too much for me.

Finally I recovered so that I could walk, but I was still shaky when I went in to see the president. He was talking to some officers when I went in. He grasped my hand.

"You saved my life," he exclaimed.

"My brain had a blind spot in it for a few moments, sir," I explained, "or I would have taken those men out of line long before they approached your person."

"What do you mean?" he asked.

I told him the incident of the handkerchief and reminded him of the recent murder of President McKinley. When I had finished he turned to the German, Volters, "Had you heard of the manner in which the assassin approached President McKinley of the United States when he was murdered?"

"I know nothing of it," the German replied.

The president turned to me, "Then I have you to thank for saving my life, Colonel. You alone," he said.

"I beg your pardon, sir," I inquired, "but did I understand you to address me as..."

"You did, my friend," the president interrupted. "I will have your commission made out as soon as possible and your promotion will be published tomorrow."

Thus it came about that in less than a year after I had been washing my underwear in the hobo jungles and throwing away my thousand-mile shirts, I was commissioned colonel in the Guatemalan army. Things were coming along nicely for me, but there is always a chance for a fall or a bump. The bump came afterward.

The life I led as colonel differed little from that I led as captain. I still ate, slept, drank, and played with my brother officers at the co-operative club. I still visited the printing office, and if anything happened that needed my services I took tools and fixed it. I still drilled my machine gunners. I still visited the Americans down at the Central Railroad roundhouse and drank one-cent aguardiente with them at the estanca across from the station.

But I was a colonel and was respected as such. It was a far cry from selling phony soap to the hicks up in the States. My monthly salary was not much more than Amy Zubar and I had taken in a good day with the lost ring graft.

It was late in the autumn when news reached the capital of a revolt brewing down on the Guatemala-Honduras-Salvador border. The three republics were at odds over frontier lines and helped along revolutionists against the other when they could.

So one day I received orders to prepare my gunners for an immediate departure for Esquipulas. I had the guns dismounted, oiled, and covered with canvas. The tripods were packed so they could be carried, with the guns, on the backs of burros. This done, I was ready to start for Esquipulas or any other place.

11

The Battle of Esquipulas

THE REBELS HAD GOTTEN AS FAR as Esquipulas and were recruiting there. Any man who could pay soldiers and furnish them food could recruit an army down on the border. It was common knowledge that this revolutionary movement was financed by foreign interests who wanted President Cabrera overthrown, as he was very cautious about giving foreigners concessions to exploit the resources of the republic.

Anyhow, the revolutionists were at Esquipulas and we marched toward that city on foot because we couldn't get there any other way.

There was another American in the outfit. A colonel named Jarvis, who had been stationed somewhere down in the Peten for several years, went along with the expedition.

I had fourteen machine guns and commanded them, having the same rank as Jarvis. But Jarvis outranked me by several years' service and therefore, technically, I was under him.

The general was a good old coot who drank too much when he was away from his wife and the capital. His adjutant was a younger officer, trained partly in the United States, an educated man who could speak perfect English, but who seldom uttered a word in any language. He would go for a whole day without saying a word, except when it was necessary for him to speak. I had met his wife, a beautiful woman, who talked all the time. But they were a devoted couple.

Esquipulas was almost directly south of Guatemala City, but we marched east to get there. This was because of the mountains and canyons, or barrancas, and also because we did not all travel the same route.

We divided forces so that the rebels would think the government was sending only a small force against them. Two of my machine guns were with each detachment, while my group had four and a company of infantry. This was done so that if the scouts of the enemy spotted us, which they could easily do, the reports they brought in would serve only to confuse them. The rebel commanding officers would think each separate report was about the same force and therefore would not prepare to engage a large expedition.

I had been furnished with a detail map, but threw it away after we had run against the edge of a thousand-foot cliff where the map said there was a good road with no obstructions. I could see a large volcano down about where the boundaries of the three republics met, and I guided my course by that. None of my men had ever been in that part of the country. We were seven days making the march.

All the detachments met on a tableland near the top of a mountain and rested one day. The Guatemalan is prone to rest as much as possible.

There was a spring of pure water there. The water gushed out of the side of a mountain and threw a spray down into a canyon for a distance of a thousand feet or more. All we had to do to get pure, ice-cold water was to lay a trough made of hollowed trees about a hundred feet. This brought the water right into camp.

At daylight the second morning we started for Esquipulas. A native who claimed to know the way volunteered to lead us and he did, but not to Esquipulas. He should have made the town in a couple of hours, but at nine o'clock, after having traveled since about five, we were still trying to locate it.

Finally we met an old woman carrying a load of faggots. We asked her how to find the town and she pointed obliquely back the way we had come. We had missed the town by several miles. It was high noon by the time we reached the place.

For the last mile or two out of Esquipulas snipers worried us. I lost three men and a burro by snipers' bullets. A bullet also hit one of my guns square on the bandolier-carrying mechanism and put it out of business. So I had 13 guns with which to go into battle.

We finally got into town. I was for breaking my battery into little one-gun detachments and circling through the town, getting what cover they could while they did so. By doing this we could come in behind the comandancia walls, as the side of the square toward the town was open. The comandancia wall protected three sides of the building only.

But Colonel Jarvis placed me in a position just before the blank wall of the comandancia. This was a twelve-foot wall extending for a block in front of the building. All my men had to shoot at were a lot of little square holes in that wall. And the rebels were peppering us through the same little square holes.

I retreated a little and got my men and guns into a depression where there was a lot of broken crockery. At one time the hole must have been the site of a pottery, but now it was only a hole in the ground, about four feet deep, twenty feet wide and three times that in length.

"Fire when you see anything to fire at," I ordered. "But fire by count as I taught you."

Then I crawled back and circled around to locate Jarvis, after investigating several houses in our rear and finding them deserted.

I found Jarvis behind a large house studying a map. I wondered if it was as accurate as the map given me in Guatemala City, which ran me squarely against a cliff where it said there was a road.

"Have I your permission to divide my force into one-gun detachments and circle through the town?" I asked.

"No, you haven't," Jarvis growled. "Stay where you are until you get orders to move."

"But they'll pick us off one by one out there," I protested.

"Better obey my instructions," Jarvis said, without even turning to look in my direction. "I've been fighting these little battles for years. Get back to your command."

I made it back to my gunners, swearing a blue streak. "If that man Jarvis would let us go around," I told a lieutenant, "we'd have the town within an hour."

"And the Colonel Jarvis will not allow you to do so?" the lieutenant asked. (By the way, I didn't have a captain with me. I was a colonel and my junior officers were four lieutenants.)

"He will not," I exclaimed. "He says to stay here where it will do no good and they'll pick us off one by one."

Spanish was not expressive enough for my feelings, so I turned to pure Americanese, as it is spoken in Kansas, Hoboken and other places, "In this position we won't last as long as a snowball in hell."

The lieutenant didn't understand the Americanese, of course, but he knew it was something expressive. Saluting, he crawled across the broken crockery and talked a few minutes with several privates, who were Indians. Three or four of the Indians crawled out of the depression, skirted the houses in the rear and then ran. The lieutenant crawled back to where I sat.

"Where did you send those men, lieutenant?" I asked.

"They have gone to busque a little water to drink, señor Colonel," he replied.

We lay there for a long time, shooting once in a while. Bullets whined over us. One of my men stood up to look around and fell with three bullets in his head. Those rebels could shoot.

The sun beat down unmercifully. The temperature must have been 150 degrees in that hole. I thought of all the nice cool drinks in Guatemala City. Here I was in a hole in heat that would have fried eggs in thirty seconds.

I don't know how long it was, but finally the men sent by the lieutenant returned without water. I was ready to go over and upbraid them for not bringing any, as my throat was dry and my tongue ached. I couldn't raise moisture enough to spit. The lieutenant spoke to the men a moment and came over to where I sat.

"I regret to inform my colonel that Colonel Jarvis has met with a fatal accident," he reported.

"How?" I asked in surprise.

"Someone was carrying a large knife while running and he fell and the knife went through the body of Colonel Jarvis," he explained.

I began to smell a mouse.

"Send one of those men over here," I ordered. "I want to know more about this."

One of the men came to where I sat. He was pure Indian and his duty on machine fourteen was to keep the bandoliers full of cartridges. Now that No. 14 was out of commission he was at liberty, so to speak.

"How did the accident to Colonel Jarvis happen?" I asked.

The Indian studied a moment or two before replying. Then he detailed, "A man was running, holding a large knife (machete) in his hand. Near Colonel Jarvis this man stumbled and fell and the knife went through the body of Colonel Jarvis."

"Do you know the man whose knife went through the body of Colonel Jarvis?" I queried.

"How could I, my coronel? I know many men in Quexaltenango. I know many men in Casa Blanca. I know many men in Guatemala City. But I know no man in Esquipulas."

"Are you sure it was none of our men?" I asked.

"I do not know very well all of our men here," the Indian replied. "I know many men in Quezaltenango. I know many men in Casa Blanoa. I know..."

"That's enough," I interrupted. "Get back to your bandoliers."

The lieutenant smiled. "Shall we now divide and perform the maneuver suggested by our Colonel to Colonel Jarvis?"

"Yes."

Nothing more was said about the queer accident that happened to Colonel Jarvis. It was one way of getting rid of an officer who would not let us do as we pleased. Death meant nothing to those Guatemalan Indians. A man had to die sometime, anyhow, so if he happened to be in the way, it was no great crime to hasten his death by a matter of a few years.

We left two guns in the hole. The others we took along and crawled back to the houses in the rear. We left one there to protect the rear of the men in the hole if they should have to retreat, or if some of the enemy encircled them. Then we made a detour of several blocks and finally came around in sight of the open front of the plaza, across which was the comandancia.

Our infantry had got around so they could shoot across the wall into the plaza, but they were doing little damage. They had to shoot too high to get over the wall.

The front of the comandancia and the plaza were full of rebels, and they weren't taking our attack too seriously. Some of them were cooking a meal in big kettles right on the plaza!

We hadn't attained our positions without casualties. At every corner we met the rebels and had a little shooting, but those were mere sentry outposts. We left them dead, but in doing so I lost three men and got a wound in the thigh myself.

My plan was to begin by sending a rake of bullets from number one gun, the farthest around. Then number two gun would start and so on until it came number one's time again. While a gun was idle it was to move up as much as possible.

Just as we had gotten in range of the plaza, as we were turning a corner, several shots raked us from a little building across the street. Without waiting for orders four of my men ran across the street to the house. Two circled to the rear, two went in front.

We could hear sounds of conflict inside and a moment or two later a man ran from the house, followed by one of my men.

Seeing the rest of us there, the man started to turn and as he did so the gunner following him brought his machete down on the man's shoulder. The machete split the man's body to below his breastbone, but the victim kept running for a few yards, veered around in a sort of circular course and dropped right at my feet.

As he dropped the other three gunners came from the house. One of them was wiping the blade of his machete with a woman's inner garment.

"Get the names of those four men, lieutenant," I said to the officer nearest me, "and I will see that they are properly rewarded."

When we reached the point from which our guns could rake the plaza, the rebels were the most surprised men ever. Our first rake from a gun sent cooking pots into the air and men fell. The blast from number two gun took another quota and the third and fourth got them from a different angle.

I had to smile while my men were firing, for, true to their training, each disengaged man raised and lowered his arm and counted in the proper cadence.

Then, while the soldiers on the plaza ran amuck from the surprise attack, we advanced until the whole nine guns were in range of the plaza. Number one would spit its quota of bullets, number two would start where the first left off, and so on. After each series of blasts we would advance until those poor devils in the plaza were right in the mouths of those death-spitting guns, you might say.

At one time an officer tried to reform some of the milling rebel soldiers. He got at their head, gave a command, and they started running toward the left side of the plaza. They were within fifty feet of my number six gun when it started peppering them. Before it had sent out its count there wasn't a man of that company left. All were on the ground, some dead, some squirming. They hadn't known I had so many guns, almost entirely surrounding the plaza.

Infantry observers must have noticed the shambles on the plaza, for by the time we had reached its edge that portion of our force had moved around the wall and the battle was over.

Mopping up those soldiers in the comandancia was easy. Other than the guns in the crockery hole, my outfit did not participate. But those guns in the hole helped. When the rebels tried to crawl out of those little square holes in the wall my gunners let them have it. Those who got past the two guns in the hole were nailed by the gun in the house in the rear.

As the excitement abated I became aware of the wound in my thigh. It began to hurt like sixty. I sent two men to tell the rest of the gunners to come to the plaza. Then I went to a house back in town several blocks and asked an old woman for some hot water and rags. The blood had run down into my boots. One of my lieutenants, seeing I was wounded, accompanied me to the house.

"I'm all right, lieutenant," I said. "Please go and report to the general that I am at his orders, and beg his pardon for me that I had no chance to consult him before trying our flanking move."

"Yes, colonel," the lieutenant agreed. "But I will leave a man with you."

I looked at the man. He was the same man who had explained away the accident to Colonel Jarvis, the man who knew so many men in Quezaltenango, so many in Casa Blanca, etc.

I wore a dark shirt, with the insignia of my rank on the shoulders. It had not been damaged much except a small portion of the tail which was soaked with blood. I cut that part off with my knife. The Indian helped me pull off my boots and trousers.

"Do you know how to dress a wound?" I asked the Indian.

"Yes, Coronel. Once, between Mazaltanango and San Felipe I cut off the leg of a companion who had been bitten by a ratita and his blood poisoned so that he would swell up and die. I did a very fine job."

"And he lived?"

"No, Coronel, he died. But he was stubborn and might have wanted to die anyhow. I had to hit him with a club before he would let me cut the leg off. Perhaps I was too slow and all his blood ran out because my machete wasn't very sharp. But I did a nice job—with only my machete. And I surely saved him from the poison of the ratita, for when we passed going back three days later the jackals and ants had picked his bones clean. They will not eat the body of a person who has ratita poison in his blood."

12

The Widow of Esquipulas

BETWEEN THE INDIAN AND THE OLD WOMAN we got the wound washed. Several pieces of loose flesh were torn and hanging.

"We must cut these off," the Indian observed, "or they will gather disease that poisons the blood through the air."

The old woman brought out a pair of scissors and the Indian proceeded to cut off the pieces of flesh close to the hide. That operation hurt like hell, but I dared not show it. To have cringed or cried out would have blasted my reputation forever with my men. Someday, if they branded me as a coward, I would meet the same fate Jarvis met, but not for the same reason. I had heard that Jarvis was a brave man.

While my wound was being dressed several of my men came into the house, saluted, and sat down to watch the dressing. I passed cigarettes around. They dropped their little Spanish and commented in Indian about my white skin and long legs. They volunteered advice to the Indian and the old woman.

When the wound was dressed and the strings of flesh cut off, I stood up. I felt all right, but I had no trousers or boots to wear. I mentioned that fact. Two of my men immediately departed.

The old woman, at my command, had made some coffee and I was sitting there drinking it when my two men returned. They carried an assortment of boots and trousers.

"We had some trouble finding dead men who were shot above the trousers, Coronel," one of them explained, "so we had to take the trousers off of some men of the town. And we had to do the same with the boots."

Another took up the explanation: "Some of the men of the town were so rude they protested when we told them we wanted their boots and trousers for our coronel."

The first one continued: "Our coronel can now appear in public on the plaza without shame, although if I had such nice white legs I would not wear trousers at all."

One pair of boots fitted me well, and I chose a pair of trousers with little bangles on the legs.

"I thank you men," I said, taking some coins from my pocketbook and dividing them among the men. "Go and do as your lieutenants order. If you get drunk tonight no one will molest you. If anyone does, come to me and I will see that you are treated right. You are soldiers whom an officer can well be proud of."

They left and I gave the old woman a dollar for her trouble. Then I went to the comandancia, where I knew the general would establish headquarters.

When I reported to him the general said, "You did well, Colonel, and showed the true spirit of our army. You were wounded?"

"A slight flesh wound, General."

"You are aware that Colonel Jarvis is dead?" he asked.

"My men have so informed me, sir."

"A good officer," he continued, "and of your nationality."

"If I knew what portion of the States he came from," I said, "I would notify his folks, if he had any."

"I do not know that," the general said, "but he used to sing a song when he was drinking a little about cattle fodder along a river with a peculiar name."

"Was it 'On the Banks of the Wabash?'" I asked.

"That was it. Does that song give some clue to his residence?"

"No, General, that song is sung over the entire nation."

"Then perhaps we will have to let it go."

"I suppose so."

"Colonel Jarvis was a good officer," the general continued. "I was going to execute only five of the rebel leaders, but I have placed the value of Colonel Jarvis at twenty-five rebels. And I will shoot that many in addition to the five I intended to shoot. Have a drink?"

"Thank you, sir," I said as I downed the drink. "Colonel Jarvis was clearly worth twenty-five rebels. I think the General is no more than just."

I saw that our machine guns were placed within the comandancia, oiled and cleaned. Then, with two lieutenants, I explored the town, A clear, rushing stream bisected the town. There were few really large houses, as it was within the earthquake zone and two-story homes were not built. We were walking along when we met two infantry officers going from house to house. I asked why.

"We are seeking quarters for officers," one explained.

"We would like to secure quarters where there are senoritas," the other added. "After a campaign like this one likes to be entertained. The senoritas can sing to us and we can make love to them."

"What about your regular sweethearts in Guatemala City?" I asked.

"They will not know what we did in Esquipulas if we do not tell them," was the reply.

"I was intending to sleep in the comandancia," I observed.

"If you do," one of the officers cautioned, "you will be compelled to scratch fleas all night—fleas so old that they began to multiply when the Spaniards were here. If the Colonel will come back with us we will show you a home where there are six young senoritas."

"Can all six sing to a man at once?" I asked.

"Of course. We are going to room there, and there are two other rooms."

We walked back with them. We were introduced to the senoritas and sat and talked a while, the old mother hearing every word. From where I sat I could see across the rear of the house, built like all the homes in that country in the shape of the letter "U" with the rear portion open. Across a sort of alley I saw a woman tending some flowers.

"Who is that?" I asked. The woman appeared to be lighter than the senoritas were and she dressed better. "Who is the señorita?"

"Señorita—bah," one of the girls exclaimed. "She's no señorita. She's a widow and all of thirty."

I was tired. The attractions of the senoritas did not beguile me. I wanted something to eat and a place to sleep.

"I will leave my lieutenants with the six entrancing senoritas," I said. "I am in need of rest and I am going to ask the widow to give me a room."

"She has a large home," one of them observed.

"Has she been a widow long?" I asked.

"A number of years. It is charged she talked her husband to death."

"She will soon have grey hair," another put in.

"She is not native to this country, but an interloper," one girl declared.

The sun had set and darkness was coming on. I made my adieus to the senoritas and their mother and walked across the space separating the two patios. The woman was bending over a flower bed as I approached.

"Señora," I called.

She raised up and was not frightened as I thought she would be. It was evident that she had been watching and saw me approach.

"I am at your service," she said and smiled.

"I am an officer of the army and would like a good place in which to live while I am here," I explained. I gave my name and rank. The woman giggled like a young girl.

"I am astonished, my tall coronel," she said, "that you have come here instead of staying with the house of the six senoritas. I was not expecting anything as thrilling as this. I will entertain you to the best of my ability, my tall coronel. I will try to make you forget that you chose the home of a widow instead of the house of the six senoritas."

She called to a servant, who disappeared within. We walked toward the house.

"Have you been a widow long, señora?" I asked.

"For more than six years I have not felt a man's arms around me."

Señora Celeste opened the door and we went in. An oil lamp with several burners hung above a table being set for two.

"Excuse me, my tall coronel," the señora said, "while I dress more formally. I see my servant has placed wine on the table. Do my humble home the honor of drinking to its safety."

The wine tasted all right and I drank a small glassful. Presently an old servant came in with food and at the same time Señora Celeste came in from a room opposite. She had donned a formal dress, silk, black, beautiful. Around her neck was a string of pearls. I rose as she came near.

"Do I look pleasing to my guest?" she asked as she wheeled around, so that her dress spread out and I could see a pair of slim legs to the knees. "Am I, a widow, pleasing to the tall, norteamericano coronel?"

"You are beautiful, señora," I exclaimed. "You are seductively, ravishingly beautiful. You look just like some wonderful picture that has been brought to life."

I held a chair for her and we sat down. "You drank very little wine, señor," she observed.

"I do not care to drink much," I said.

The truth of the matter was the officers had warned me about drinking anything in the homes of the Esquipulas inhabitants until I was sure of their intentions toward us. It might be that the persons we stayed with had relatives or friends among those we slaughtered in the plaza that day. A few drinks of something that had been poisoned would get revenge. But now I did not believe the señora would try to poison me. Instead, she beamed on me.

"You do my home a great honor, Coronel," she said. "It has been years since I have had the honor of entertaining such a charming señor—and a gentleman who chose me rather than the six senoritas across the patio."

"Why has not the beautiful señora married?" I queried.

"How could I?" she pouted. "How could I, when there are so many virgin senoritas in the country? No man wants a widow when he can get a señorita."

"And you have had no proposals?"

"Several, my colonel. But I discovered in time that they came from men who wished to share what worldly goods I have instead of marrying me for love."

"It is deplorable that I am not in a position to marry," I remarked.

She smiled, then giggled. "The tall norteamericano colonel would choose me?" she asked.

"Without a moment's hesitation," I said.

We had finished and she invited me into another room for coffee.

"I do not drink coffee, my colonel," she said, "And while you are drinking I will prepare a little entertainment for the tall norteamericano."

She left the room and I sat in an easy chair and half-dreamed. Across the alley I could see the officers and the six senoritas and I could near their laughter. Their mother sat with them, according to Spanish custom.

Reaction after the battle had set in and I wondered why I really didn't stop in some place like this and live peacefully and indolently.

A huacamai gurgled softly to its mate outside the window. A burro drawing a cart passed in the street in front.

I felt old and tired and wanted to rest here forever. I was due to kick in, anyhow, and I might as well pass over right here as anywhere. The exertion of the day had left me without strength to do more than think. The entrance of the señora broke into my reverie.

She had changed costumes and now had on a fancy dress which came only to her knees. She carried a little guitar and while she danced she played a tune and sang a song about a lone woman weeping while her man went to war. When she had finished she bowed and I applauded.

"That is how I once danced in Valladolid," she explained.

"It was nice."

"Excuse me again, my coronel guest," she said and went into the other room.

She came in after a few minutes dressed in a filmy dress and not much else. In it she did a sort of slow dance to the music of a phonograph record the duenna had placed on a little instrument.

She used the skirts of her dress as a sort of sail. It was a sort of fan dance without fans, using a skirt instead.

"I danced that way in Madrid," she said when the record had run its course.

"You dance excellently, señora," I praised.

She left the room again and the old duenna went to answer the door knocker. She returned in a few seconds. "A soldier wishes to see his coronel," she announced.

The soldier hadn't waited to he announced. He followed the old woman in, saluted and sat on a chair. But only for a moment. He wasn't used to chairs. He sat on the floor in a corner.

"What is it you wish?" I asked. It was the same soldier who knew so many men in Quezaltenango, etc., and who had cut the leg off a companion to save him from the sting or bite of a ratita.

"The coronel must have his wound dressed again before he goes to sleep," he explained, "so that it will not become like the crater of a volcano." I think he meant gangrened.

"I thank you for thinking of me," I said.

"I have an ointment which will heal the sore gently," he said, showing me a little box of salve. "The apothecary said it would cost a dollar, but he gave it to me."

"Gave it to you?" I questioned.

"He was obstinate at the first of our talk. But when I told him I would cut off his head with my machete and take it anyhow, he gave it to me with many wishes for your quick recovery."

The señora came in again, in another costume, and danced. For quite a time, while I sat and drank coffee, she came and went, each time wearing a different costume.

At length I said, "The señora is entertaining and ravishingly beautiful. But now she must have become weary of the dancing. Will you tell your servant to bring a vessel of hot water to my room?"

"You wish hot water?" she asked in surprise.

"Today I received an insignificant little flesh wound," I explained. "I would like to have my man wash and dress it now and then sleep. I am fatigued."

"What!" she exclaimed. "The tall norteamericano coronel who thinks I am so ravishingly beautiful and who chose me instead of six senoritas, is wounded? And I have fatigued him?"

"You have entertained me, señora, as I have never been entertained before. But it is the long march and the fighting that have fatigued me. For the moment you made me forget my fatigue."

"You shall have the hot water in a moment and I will dress the wound myself."

My Indian soldier rose from his corner.

"I will attend the officer," he said

"He dressed the wound before and did a good job," I hastened to add.

"I will go with you," the widow said.

The widow, the old duenna, and two younger women watched the dressing of the wound. The salve the Indian applied to the wound burned a little. The operation was nearly over when two more of my men came in. They were just a little drunk.

"We came to see that the coronel was in good hands," one of them announced.

The Indian dressing the wound finished, and turned to the widow.

"Now give the coronel a drink of aguardiente," he said.

"I have none," she replied. "But I have wine."

"Do you think the coronel a baby?" he asked, with a tinge of contempt in his voice. "Would you offer a soldier a cup of goat's milk? The coronel drinks aguardiente."

"I am sorry..." the widow began, but the soldier who was in charge interrupted her.

"Go," he ordered the two who had come in latest, "and busque some aguardiente for our coronel."

They were turning to leave when I stopped them.

"I will give you money with which to purchase the aguardiente," I said.

"Why should they need money when they each have a good sharp machete?" the original soldier asked.

The men left the house without the money.

"I hope the coronel will be comfortable and sleep well tonight," the widow said.

"He will sleep well," the Indian replied. "I will sleep on the floor here at the door. If you disturb him in the morning before he wakes naturally you will be punished."

A few minutes later the other two soldiers came in with a garafone of aguardiente. I took a long drink and after that the soldiers each took one. Then they shooed the audience out of the room. I undressed and went to sleep in the bed. The three soldiers took another drink or two apiece and lay down on the floor.

13

The Executions

THE GENERAL HAD A HELLUVA HANGOVER when I reported next morning.

"Have a drink, colonel," he said. "Are you satisfied with your quarters?"

"They are excellent, sir," I assured him.

"We will not need the machine guns here anymore," he mentioned. "How is your wound?"

"Just a scratch, sir, but painful at times."

"Some of your men have told it about the town how you stood the pain while one of them cut flesh from the wound. It has raised you greatly in their regard. I know now you are fit to command."

"I have an excellent company of men, sir, although many of them are uneducated. It would not be well for an officer to show cowardice before uneducated men. And the dressing did not hurt more than if it were the pulling of a tooth."

"I understand," the general said. "Almost all men are brave because they are afraid to show cowardice. One can always bluff a man into thinking you are a brave man. I do so myself, because I am afraid to show cowardice. I can bluff everyone except my wife."

"A woman trusts her intuition, sir."

"A woman trusts no one. After she lives with a man a few years she knows just what he thinks, even when he says the opposite."

"I have not had much experience with women," I said.

"Before you are as old as I am, you will have had the experience. Have another drink?"

"I will send you back within a week," the general went on, after we had drunk. "In the meantime you will sit on a court which will try the rebel leaders. So that no one will accuse me of acting unjustly or illegally, I will detail three officers to sit as a court.

"I was intending to have five leaders shot as a certainty. Then there are twenty-five who will be shot for the death of Colonel Jarvis. You will understand your duty when you sit on the court, which will be much the same as the summary courts martial in your own country."

"I understand, sir," I said, "although I have never served on a court martial. In the United States Army I was a private, a man of no rank."

"The court will sit at ten o'clock," the general instructed. "With only thirty to be convicted, we should be through with the court routine and the executions by siesta time."

"How many will be tried, sir?" I queried.

The general filled his glass and my glass before replying. "Thirty, of course. Why waste time when all we need is thirty? Have another drink."

The trial lasted about thirty minutes and the executions occupied a little more time. Then I went back to the home of Señora Celeste, accompanied by three or four of my men. This time the men were content to let the widow do the dressing, while they looked on and commented. Anticipating such an event, several neighbors had come in. Three of the lieutenants having quarters in the home of the six senoritas, four of those senoritas, their mother and three or four nice fat, dusky senoritas from neighboring homes.

It was quite a show to them. It wasn't a thing that would happen again in a lifetime. They got to see a white colonel, one trousers leg entirely off, lying on a cot while his wound was dressed. My men sat on the floor watching every move of the widow. They still commented that if they had such nice white legs they would not wear trousers at all.

Ten days later, when I was ready to march my men out of Esquipulas, Señora Celeste, her two dusky girl servants, the old duenna and three or four neighbor girls with whom I had scraped an acquaintance, all kissed me and wept. The old duenna had been eating garlic.

One of my lieutenants fell a victim to a señorita's wiles, and she went with us to Guatemala City, where they were married. In addition, three of my soldiers had found girls they liked and had stolen them from their homes instead of giving their parents money for them. All were going through the legal ceremony as soon as we reached the capital. The privates' sweethearts, who were rather fat, wore men's clothing until we were safely away from Esquipulas, when they changed to dresses.

Guatemalan girls are well-built, especially those who live in small towns where all have to work. Even the lieutenant's fiancée marched with the rest of us. We traveled slowly and made the days short. We started about sunup, traveled until about eleven o'clock, rested and ate until about three, marched again until about sunset, when we camped for the night.

We made the trip back in three weeks exactly. I attended the wedding of the lieutenant, which was held in a church, and that of my three soldiers. I gave the lieutenant a $20 bill, United States money, and each of the privates a $5 bill, which was a great sum to them, as each dollar of the United States money represented $20 in Guatemalan currency. I still had a goodly portion of the money Amy Zubar and I had taken from the New York and Brooklyn natives on the lost ring racket.

There was a rift in the romance of one of the privates, however. On the march back to the capital, his girl became acquainted with one of the other privates she liked better than her original choice. Such affairs usually lead to a fight with knives and a killing, perhaps. This one didn't, however. The two principals played palo pinto for the girl, and the other man won her from the original lover. He, the original lover, was at the ceremony where his rival married the girl. They got drunk together after the ceremony.

14

The Survey

UPON MY RETURN TO GUATEMALA CITY, I was hailed as a sort of hero. I had been wounded and not killed. I had given all my men a few dollars each on our arrival home, and told them they were at liberty for a week. The Indian who had cut the loose flesh from my wound and several of his companions got drunk and bragged about how the norteamericano coronel had stood pain with the fortitude of an Indian. Their coronel, they bragged, also had nice white slim legs, even if he did persist in wearing trousers with which to cover them. This bragging of my men did much to enhance my reputation among the privates of the other outfits.

Nothing much was said about Colonel Jarvis. He had been killed. The Guatemalan soldier regarded a live colonel as worth many times a dead one. So I was in clover.

President Cabrera, himself an Indian, complimented me on my part in the battle of Esquipulas and told me to lay off duty until my wound had healed completely.

With the help of an American machinist down at the Central Railroad shop, I repaired the gun that had been damaged and it was good as new.

My brother officers, especially the younger ones, took great delight in kidding me about Señora Celeste. In telling the story of her conquest, they exaggerated her age and made her out a grey-haired woman. Some even went as far as to declare she wore a wig, had false teeth and a wooden leg.

Some of the married officers relayed the joke to their wives, who relayed it on until the exaggerations reached the ears of Señorita Sagusta, and one evening she mentioned, "Perhaps I should not see you again," she observed. "I have learned that you prefer old women with false teeth and a wooden leg, like the one at Esquipulas."

"If you refer to Señora Celeste," I retorted, "she was but thirty, had no wooden leg, and could dance a number of intricate and fancy dances. The only thing one could hold against her was the fact that she was a widow. Her home was a pleasant place for me to billet. Half a dozen of my men were there also, and they've seen her dance."

"Your brother officers tell it differently," she pouted.

"They tell it as a joke," I assured her.

"How soon are you going back to Esquipulas?" she asked, "to see this Señora Celeste?"

"I will go back to Esquipulas only when I am ordered to go," I told her. "Now let's quit this jealous foolishness and practice the American talk or you'll never be able to talk like they talk in New York or Kankakee."

"Do they talk the same in New York and this Kank—what you call it?" she asked.

"They can understand each other very well."

For several evenings she referred to Señora Celeste every time we were together, but as the joke became stale and the officers ceased telling it, the señorita apparently forgot the Esquipulas woman.

Surveys had been made to start construction of the Guatemala Northern Railroad from El Rancho to the capital, but that had been years before and the engineers' stakes had been lost or forgotten. One day, in conversation with the president and several other officials, I mentioned the fact that life in the city was getting monotonous and I wished another revolution would start so that I could see some action.

The men looked from one to another and the president said, "Perhaps we can give you some active duty other than that caused by a revolution. We are negotiating with foreign capitalists to complete the construction of the Northern Railroad into this city. Before we can deal with them intelligently and show them the route, we would like to have the stakes renewed and the route relocated. Can you use a compass and level, surveyors' instruments?"

Over in the Philippines my outfit, signal corps, had been in charge of rehabilitating the Manila & Dagupin Railroad. For labor we had used native convicts. I had learned to use a compass and level, under the tutelage of Lieutenant Brooks and Lieutenant Kirkland. And I had always had supreme confidence in myself. Anyhow, such an assignment would give me a chance to do something more than loaf around Guatemala City.

So I told the president, "I will be more than pleased to go out and do the work for you, sir."

I made out pretty well. The resident engineer of the Guatemala Central Railroad went over the field notes with me and coached me somewhat.

Those engineers who originally surveyed the route had put markers on stones or boulders instead of wooden stakes. After I learned that much I could find them.

The only trouble I experienced was the start at El Rancho. There the surveyors had put a marker on a big boulder. It was an ideal stone for a backlog, one might describe it, to a native cooking fire. So a native had built a flimsy house over the boulder. I did not disturb the house, but took the marker readings and went on. After that I got on famously.

My greatest trouble was in getting across barrancas. A barranca is a canyon. In the mountains between El Rancho and Guatemala City there were many of them, some more than a thousand feet deep.

At one point, where we ran up to the walls of a barranca, I had to send two men by roundabout ways to the other side so they could hold the pole while I sighted and signaled. Then I, with the rest of the party, traveled two days getting to the opposite side, where the pole party was. But when I reached there I could find no trace of a stone or stake marker.

So I traveled back. After I got across, in another two days' journey, I discovered a compass variation, caused, perhaps by a deposit of some sort of ore in the vicinity. I corrected for this and went across the barranca again. In all, I was about two weeks finding that stone, which had been marked years before.

But in Guatemala speed wasn't essential. If you didn't get something done today there was always another day coming. It took centuries and eons of centuries to throw up those mountains, the natives argued. So why should a little mortal like a man, soft as the mountains were hard, an infinitesimal little mortal, hurry? It was a good philosophy, but worthless in these days of hurry and bustle.

After all, it was a good life. We camped out and carried no baggage, and I never shaved. My whiskers were a bright red and stuck straight out like those on the faces of Bolsheviks in newspaper cartoons.

We ate on the country, but paid well for all we ate. As we got farther up in the mountains the nights were cold, and we usually found some sort of cave in which to spend the nights. If we were in a place where we would stay several days, the men would build a fireplace at the entrance of the cave. In this we would build a roaring fire and sleep comfortably.

The natives were friendly. All were as poor as Job's turkey, but what they had we could have, and welcome.

At one point on the route, where we camped near a village for a few days, we learned of a gold mine some distance up the canyon. We made our way up there, my six men and myself, and investigated. We found the mine all right, and two families were working it with wooden equipment.

"How much gold do you get out in a day?" I asked one of the miners.

"We do not count it by the day, señor," he replied. "We count it by the month. Last month we sent one of our family to Guatemala City with the gold we had and he brought back twenty dollars and eleven centavos and a sack of nails we needed. Of course his expenses for food on the trip cost nearly a dollar."

I lost interest in the mine. For four men, their wives and children, to work for a month for twenty dollars of that money was too much for me. It was about a dollar in United States money. But those families raised what they needed to eat right there in the valley and, like all Guatemalans, they did not work hard. Very little money satisfied those mountain Indians.

They were good people. One day, while sliding down the side of a mountain, trying to hold the level and the tripod and not break either, I cut my leg on a sharp stone. I had neglected to carry a first-aid kit with me. But the Indians were accustomed to having to deal with cuts and bruises.

An old woman fixed the wound with something she kept wrapped in a broad leaf, and in a day or two it was healed sufficiently for me to go back to work.

I carried quite a load of small coins, for every day I would give each of my men a coin with which to purchase food, usually tortillas and frijoles (corn cakes and beans). It would never do to give them more than one at a time, for if they got hold of more than one they would get drunk with the native drink, aguardiente. I carried a sack of small coins. I left them at our camp, in a house in a village, or anywhere else I happened to be, and never lost a cent.

I hadn't the archeological education to appreciate the ancient things before my eyes on that trip.

For instance, at one point the right-of-way for several kilometers had been surveyed along an old road, paved with stone laid in a sort of cement. Or perhaps the paving stones had washed off dust to form the cement. The natives told me the road had been there as long as the mountains. Landslides and washouts had destroyed some of the road, but in places for several kilometers it was as good as when it was built, in prehistoric times.

I learned afterward, from a professor in Guatemala City, that the road had been built, according to calculations and implements found along it, about the time of the birth of the Christians' Christ. He said stones that had been found along the route bore carvings similar to those made by ancient Egyptians.

I did not have the education to appreciate such things. But I did have the engineering knowledge to appreciate the work of the engineers who built that road. It had easy gradients, wide, even curves, and straight tangents, and today is part of the right-of-way of the Guatemala Northern Railroad.

Finally I got the stakes located to a point where the railroad right-of-way reached the paved road recently built by President Cabrera. From there on it was to use one side of the highway.

I took my notes, books and instruments on into Guatemala City, hiring an ox cart for transportation. I had been gone nearly three months.

15

Exiled

I REACHED GUATEMALA CITY late at night and got drunk treating my men. I lost consciousness sometime in the night and woke next morning in the cot of a caboose of the Guatemala Central Railroad. Someone had taken my boots and trousers, also what little money I had with me. The railroad conductor who had found me, and in whose caboose I slept, said I was the center of a crowd of natives, making them a speech. The natives had laughed because I was undressed. He got me away from the crowd and into his caboose.

One of my ears was cut badly, but the conductor bound it up with electricians' tape and it healed quickly. As I had not yet reported to the president and had been with my men all the time, the government officials, if they learned anything about the spree, never mentioned it.

A barber worked an hour getting off a three-month growth of beard, and I reported to my superior officer and later to President Cabrera. I had found every stake (or stone) of the original survey.

Then followed long days of idleness mixed in with machine gun drills, a look-in at the printing office, and a meeting with Señorita Sagusta almost every evening at some gathering or other. Our intimacy never went beyond the platonic. She was of a higher social caste than I, even though I was a colonel. Under my thin veneer of gentility and respectability I was still a hobo. I was more at home in a camp or bellied up against the bar of a low-class saloon than I was among the silver and fine napery of a banquet table.

Sometimes, while in a mild argument with some man high in the councils of the republic, I would find myself wishing we were in a saloon where I could take a poke at him because he entertained different ideas on certain subjects than I did. I had been trained by three years service in the Philip-

74

pines, to be a hobo, a tough, a man of direct action, the opposite of a diplomat. I would not do at all as the husband of an aristocratic young lady—a lady who could trace her lineage back to someone who may have crossed the ocean with Pizzaro, Cortez, or one of those old grandees who civilized the Indians at the point of a musket.

But the señorita was fun. She learned English quickly. After she had learned the usual polite style of English so that she could keep up one end of a conversation, I taught her the slang I knew. She mixed it in with the more gentile style. One day we happened to be leaving a room where three or four servants stood in the doorway. As I approached them I said, "Getta hell outta the way."

They moved aside, although they didn't know or understand what I said. A few evenings later, while Señorita Sagusta was walking across a room, two or three women stood in the way. "Getta hell outta the way," she ordered.

They moved, although they didn't know what she said. As they moved aside she looked around and winked at me.

There were other persons, however, who noticed and commented on our friendship. Finally, one of my brother officers spoke to me about it as we sat in our quarters taking a nightcap. He explained what numerous persons had said about what seemed to them to be a blooming romance.

"The younger officers have talked it over," he went on. "They have come to the conclusion that if you are in love with the señorita and want to marry her, they will see that no one prevents the marriage. You are of a different nationality, but that should make no difference. While you have been here you have been a good officer. Because you are a colonel you have not ceased to live with officers of lesser rank. So if you wish to marry Señorita Sagusta, we will assist you with any plans you may have."

I didn't want to marry anyone. There were lots of hills I hadn't climbed over. There were lots of curves I hadn't been around. I told the officer that much.

"Then it might be well to cease a close association with the señorita," he cautioned. "In our country constant association with a señorita can mean but two things—either a marriage or that you desire to make the señorita your mistress."

"I do not seek a mistress," I explained. "I'd cut off my right arm rather than make such a proposition to the señorita. She's like a little sister to me."

"But there is talk."

"I'll take a few days to think the matter over," I said. "I'll decide on some course that will quiet the talk and preserve the good name of the señorita."

The next afternoon I wandered into the San Marcos building. I chatted a few minutes with the manager of the Central Railroad, who had won his spurs on the Southern Pacific between New Orleans and Houston. Then I went to the office of old Welmyer, general manager of the Ocós railroad.

"How's everything, Mr. Welmyer?" I asked.

"Bad, very bad," he said.

I noticed he had a garafone of aguardiente and a glass on his desk, When a man started to drink in the middle of the afternoon in Guatemala City, he surely must have been in trouble. Most foreigners waited until the close of business before taking a drink.

"The man I had down at Ocós as master mechanic has quit," he went on to explain, "and he took several thousand dollars belonging to the coffee fincas. A steamer loaded coffee there last week, paid German gold for it, and this man took the gold and went across into Mexico."

It may be explained here that the master mechanic usually is the high man on most of those little coffee railroads down there. Usually there is an office man who does clerical work, but the master mechanic looks after the shops, track, and most of the business. In fact, a master mechanic is the boss supreme of most of those little roads down there.

"Who's master mechanic down there now?" I asked.

An idea had come to me that here was a way out of the trouble I was in concerning the matter of Señorita Sagusta.

"No one," Welmyer replied, "and there will be a steamer there about the first of next month. And there's a lot of coffee to haul down to the port."

I thought for a moment.

"Have a drink?" he asked. I took one, out of the same glass the old man had been using.

"If I asked for the job," I inquired, "would you send me down there?"

"You've got a good thing here," he returned.

"Being an army officer isn't in my line," I explained. "I'm sick of it. I'd like to go down to Ocós and do something."

"Well, if you went down to Ocós," Welmyer elucidated, "you'd have to do something. There's a number of your countrymen there—outlaws. They've run several young German resident managers out of Ocós. They live with native women. They boss the port. There is no law but what they say."

"So they may have killed your last master mechanic and got the money?" I inquired.

"They may have," Welmyer agreed.

"Doesn't the comandante give you protection?" I asked.

"He's afraid to do anything, even protect the young German residents I send down there. They go, stay a while, come back up here and threaten to kill me."

"Can I have the job?" I asked.

"If you want it. But if they run you out of the port, don't come back here and blame me. There's no law down there."

"I'm a good man with a gun," I boasted.

"You'll need it. Right now I'm standing the bill for a young countryman of mine who went down there and tried to fight back. They tortured him. He's here now in a hospital. He's lost his mind."

"Have you ever been down there?" I asked.

"Once, several years ago. I went down there from Champerico on a steamer. I stayed there ten days, till another steamer picked me up. I recovered three months afterward."

"Get drunk?"

"No. Wish I had, though. When a man's drunk he seldom gets the fever. I stayed sober and caught it."

"Want to give me the job?"

"Yes. How soon can you go?"

"As soon as I resign my commission. Tomorrow or the day after, maybe."

"You've got the job—if you can hold it," he said.

"I'll hold it," I assured him.

"Then have another drink. Sorry I haven't another glass, but my mouth's not diseased and that liquor would kill germs if there were any. Take a big one and I hope you'll live long enough to do something to that railroad. You've worked up a pretty good reputation here."

"Here's hopin'," I said as I drank.

"And remember," he cautioned. "Don't come back here and try to kill me if you fail to hold the job."

"I'll not fail," I assured him. "I feel a yen for some excitement. This job of being a colonel is too damned soft for me."

That night there was a gathering of officers and politicians—the usual thing. President Cabrera was in conversation with a group when I approached. He greeted me and hoped I was enjoying the best of health. He knew there wasn't a thing wrong with my health, but that was the usual greeting down there. I wished his health was of the best, which it was, and then made my proposition:

"You know how inaction palls on me, sir," I began. "Would you consider it ungrateful of me if I asked to be given permission to resign my commission so that I could go back to railroading, where there is plenty of work and excitement?"

"Have you any definite plans?" he asked.

"Señor Welmyer of the Ferro Carril de Ocós has seen fit to offer me a position as master mechanic on his railroad," I told him. "There is constant excitement in such a position—danger, too."

President Cabrera and those in the group with him exchanged glances. I knew as well as if they had told me that they were glad to see me go. It would prevent some sort of scandal. I had suggested a way by which the president could get rid of me without embarrassment. He was too much of a square-shooter to remove an officer who had saved his life just because of the talk about the señorita and myself. Yet I thought I detected a relieved expression on his plain face as he remarked, "Ocós is not a nice place, Colonel."

"I am not accustomed to nice places, sir," I argued. "That is why I wish to leave Guatemala City for a while. It is too nice here for me. I have been treated with too much consideration."

"Señor Daraga, the Comandante at Ocós, has been asking to be relieved for some time," one of the men with the president suggested. "Perhaps..."

"The very thing," the president exclaimed. "My young friend, tomorrow will be published the announcement that you have been appointed Comandante of the Port of Ocós and the district along the railroad. When do you wish to go?"

"As soon as possible, sir."

"I will arrange with the railroad to furnish you a private car as far as Champerico. There you can wait for a steamer going north," the president said, and continued, "and you may be sure you go with my greatest reluctance. I have long admired men from your country. But it has puzzled me for a reason why you and your countrymen wish to do everything today, to move, to push, to accomplish, to go on."

"It's the itchy foot," I ventured.

"I don't understand." The president looked puzzled and the others waited for me to explain. They probably thought it was some sort of disease.

"My feet itch," I explained. "That causes me to want to put one before the other continually. In doing so, I get over the next hill or around the next curve. Once there my feet still itch and I go over the next hill and the next. A man with itching feet can never stay in one place long."

The men laughed.

"An apt explanation," one of them remarked.

"Señor Daraga is one of the older officials of the republic," the president retailed. "He has accomplished many things in his day, but now he is old."

"Several of your countrymen, men of no character or standing, have given Ocós a bad name. You have my permission to proceed with a free hand. Any reports from Ocós other than those sent by you will not be read. If I do not misjudge your ability you will find a way to remedy the situation that exists there today."

"Thank you, sir," I said as I made my adieus.

Within half an hour everyone in the room knew I was going to Ocós and they knew why I had asked for the change. But not one of them mentioned Señorita Sagusta.

I believe they rather admired me for leaving the ease of Guatemala City for the hazardous life in Ocós. They did not know that I preferred the change and would have jumped at the chance regardless of the señorita. But they all shook my hand and wished me luck and told me how much they regretted my departure for the sun-baked little port of Ocós,

I saw Señorita Sagusta later that evening. I told her I was going.

"I once thought," I began and then hesitated. "That some time we might have a closer relationship and..." I did not know how to go on. "But it wouldn't do," I added.

"Perhaps you are right," she said. "Anyhow, I have you to thank for having taught me how to speak American as it is spoken in New York and Kankakee. I think I'll miss you a lot. You've been a peacherino," she added.

16

A Clipping

(NOTE: The following is reprinted from one of a series of articles that appeared in the *Mexican Herald,* Mexico City, describing the work of American hoboes in Central America. The publisher of that paper, an American named Hundson, hailing originally from Topeka, Kansas, ran a series of such articles occasionally for several years. I do not know the name of the author, or authors.)

AT THAT TIME, OCÓS WAS A HELL-HOLE. Situated three kilometers from the lower boundary of Mexico, bad men from that republic escaped across the Ocós river, which marked the border, got to Ocós and stayed there.

There were tales told of other American hoboes reaching Ocós and displaying what money they had. If it was any considerable sum, they disappeared and were never heard of again.

For some twenty years El Señor Daraga had been comandante of the port. No one respected either him or his orders.

His garrison consisted of a few barefoot soldiers, ill-clothed, unarmed, unpaid. For years the old gentleman had been asking to be relieved of his post so that he could spend the rest of his days on his farm up near the City of Quezaltenango. But a law prevented his quitting. The law forbade a public servant from resigning. He either had to be removed or die. So Daraga sat in the comandancia, drank far too much and let things go. The result was that Ocós had the reputation of being the worst little Sodom along the Pacific coast between Panama and San Francisco.

Kavanaugh rode down to Champerico in the special coach furnished him in Guatemala City. He reached that port late in the afternoon, paid his respects to the commander of the port—and then proceeded to get drunk.

The last seen of him that evening was when he was weaving his uncertain way toward his private oar, sidetracked down near the wharf.

In the morning he was gone. A hasty checkup revealed one thing—he had not gone out by rail and there were no steamers in port.

To get out of Champerico by any other method meant walking. It was established beyond doubt that he had not walked out of the port on the railroad. To get out any other way he would have had to swim or wade across a river infested by sharks if he went toward Ocós. To go the other way he would have to be ferried across the bay, and no boats had been used that night.

To get to Ocós following the beach, a man would have had to wade the shark-infested river. Then, when he got within a mile of Ocós, he would have to ford or swim another river—alive with sharks—and a bayou or arm of the sea. No man ever waded through either of these waters. Before a man had gotten fifty feet from shore the sharks would have torn him to pieces.

The comandante at Champerico waited a whole day and night, thinking perhaps Kavanaugh was sleeping off his jag in some native home. Then he telegraphed his superiors in Guatemala City, detailing the strange disappearance of the American. To which came the reply, "Kavanaugh reported from Ocós last night."

No wonder the officials at Champerico sat up in surprise. Just a week before, two natives had attempted to make the trip up the coast from Champerico to Ocós and had disappeared somewhere along the route. Either the sharks in the waters or wild animals in the jungle lining the beach had killed them. Now a slim American, not even armed as they could notice, had made the trip, apparently with no more effort than if he had been strolling the streets of Guatemala City.

Kavanaugh slept in the railroad shops across the bayou from the port the night he arrived. Next morning he called on Daraga and relieved the old man, much to the latter's joy.

The old comandante was furnished an engine and passenger coach to take him up to Ayutla that afternoon, leaving the young American monarch of all he surveyed—provided he lived.

Among the outlaws living in Ocós at that time was a man named Dineen, a former railroad man who had come all the way down in the social scale to living with native woman. As he was the biggest man, physically, in Ocós he was boss. He lived in style with three women. They supported him, carrying coffee sacks from the warehouses to the whaleboats when a steamer called at the port for a cargo.

Dineen was said to have killed several men in Mexico, which was his excuse for living in Ocós. He had fallen to the level of a peon, but what he said was law in that little port. He was boss. He laughed when he saw the slim young American who had come down to run the railroad and the port.

Kavanaugh checked over his office, looked over his little force of soldadas, gave them some money out of his own pocket, and inspected the round house and shops. Having completed his day's work, he strolled over to the Cantina del Barca de Oro for a drink and dinner. He had almost finished when Dineen walked in.

Without ceremony the boss of the port walked across the cantina to the table occupied by the new comandante and master mechanic of the Ferro Carril de Ocós.

Half a dozen other renegades followed and stood just inside the door. Dineen had promised them some fun.

"Hello, General," he greeted. "How's things?"

"Very well," Kavanaugh replied. "By the way, I understand you're a boilermaker. There's an engine over in the shops that needs new flues rolled in. Be ready to go to work at seven in the morning."

"I don't work," Dineen snarled.

"Then get out of this port by seven in the morning."

"Like hell I will," Dineen exclaimed. "I'll stay here as long as I want to. If you try any rough stuff I'll run you out."

Dineen's companions had edged closer. The new master mechanic didn't appear to notice them. He waited until he had finished his coffee before he spoke.

"Remember, seven o'clock, either the roundhouse or..."

The owner of the cantina told me about it afterward, as much as he saw of it, for a second later he had dropped behind the bar. Dineen raised a fist and lunged across the table toward the American.

Kavanaugh didn't even rise from his seat at the table. He slipped his right hand under his left arm, a revolver appeared, a shot sounded and Dineen dropped to the floor, clutching at his breast with both hands. Then Kavanaugh noticed Dineen's companions. He waved the revolver toward them.

"Pick up this skunk," he ordered. They obeyed.

Carrying the body between them, with Kavanaugh following them, they went out the door and were turning toward the hut in which Dineen lived.

"Here," Kavanaugh ordered again. "This way," and he motioned with the revolver.

"This way" led over the bayou bridge.

"Going to take him over to the shops?" one of them inquired.

"Keep going, you bastards," Kavanaugh said. "I'll do the talking here."

The cavalcade reached the center of the bridge.

"Stop," was the order. "Now, one, two, three, heave."

"You're not going to throw him to the sharks?" one of the men grumbled. "He may not be dead yet."

"Over he goes or you birds go, too," the new comandante ordered. There was a great commotion in the water of Ocós bayou as the body hit the water and the sharks fought over human food. In a minute it was all over.

Kavanaugh turned to go back, thought better of it, and turned toward the Americans.

"There's plenty of work over at the shops," he told the gang. "Be over there ready to go to work at seven o'clock tomorrow or get out of the port by that time."

Kavanaugh walked back to the cantina. The women of the place were cleaning the blood off the hard earthen floor. Kavanaugh sat down and ordered another drink and a cup of coffee. He did not appear excited. Finishing his drinks he walked over to the comandancia.

There was no more trouble. One of the gang reported for work at the shops the following morning. The others left the port.

Among the railroad employees at Ocós was a man named Pena Doros, who had lived for several years in the United States. He ran the switch engine and saw to it that the engines were fired up and ready to go out the mornings the trains operated. A friendship developed between the master mechanic and Doros. Doros had served some time in a United States militia outfit that had spent several months in Cuba.

Doros had not forgotten his military training. So Kavanaugh put him in charge of about fifty young men of the port. Doros drilled them in marching and the manual of arms, although the arms consisted of ancient and obsolete weapons, ranging all the way from a .22 target rifle to a German Mauser.

Kavanaugh requisitioned arms from the capital. As there had never been any soldiers to speak of at Ocós, the army headquarters at Guatemala City turned down the requisition with the notation that the former comandante had gotten along with the weapons he had.

Kavanaugh had served with the United States forces in the Philippines. He had first been issued the old Springfield rifle until the new Krag-Jorgensen rifle had been produced in sufficient quantities to supply the army.

Those old Springfields were weapons to be proud of. They were not long-distance shooters, but when a Springfield bullet hit a man it made a very small hole where it went in, but took out most of the body where it went out. So Kavanaugh diverted enough of the port collections to send to San Francisco for a hundred of these rifles, which he purchased for about five dollars each. Then Doros began to form a real company of soldiers.

The Guatemalan Indian hates shoes. His favorite footwear is a zapato, a sort of sandal held in place with a thong around the big toe of each foot and one around each ankle. Outside of this incongruity, Kavanaugh equipped his soldiers with distinctive uniforms of blue cotton cloth, purchased, as were the guns, with customs collections money.

It was a dandy little company of soldadas. Each man got his pay weekly. When a steamer arrived to load coffee the soldiers put away their uniforms and loaded coffee at the customary wage of fifty cents a day, silver. Within six months after Kavanaugh had taken charge of the port, every young man there was a well-drilled soldier.

"I had several men in that outfit who could hit a flying bird with those old Springfields," Kavanaugh told me afterward, "and there wasn't a man among them that wouldn't have gone to hell for me."

But trouble, political trouble, was brewing. Although Kavanaugh had remitted more money in a year than Daraga had in five years from port collections, he also made reports of the money he had used to purchase arms and ammunition. Some of the influential politicians at the capital wanted a cut, if there was one, on all money spent. This American at an out-of-the-way port was spending money and reporting it just like a book-keeper. They could not understand it. Finally, the big fellows prevailed on President Cabrera to send an officer down to Ocós to find out about things.

The officer detailed for that duty was Captain Leon Zuraba, who had served with Kavanaugh in the entourage of President Cabrera. Zuraba, aside from being an army officer, was an accountant.

He came across the mountains and was met at Pajipite by Kavanaugh, with a private car and about thirty well-drilled soldiers. Zuraba was brought down to the port in a car shiny and clean, over rails that permitted a smooth passage at a fair rate of speed. As a rule, the Guatemalan railroads were rough and no one could be sure of getting to a destination at any predetermined time.

Kavanaugh, having no superior officer except a German resident manager to whom he paid no attention, had put the track and rolling stock in good shape. Engines and cars were painted. Weeds and grass were cleaned from the track. The running time from Pajipite to Ocós was reduced from about eight hours to three or four. Things clicked on the Ocós road as they had clicked on the Iron Mountain out of Little Rock, where Kavanaugh had served his apprenticeship under his father.

At Ocós the remainder of the soldiers were drawn up at attention and presented arms to Zuraba as he left the car. They escorted him to the comandancia, where he was to stay during his visit to Ocós.

"My friend," Zuraba said to Kavanaugh that evening after dinner, "were I president I would appoint you commander-in-chief of the army half the time and minister of railroads the other half. What did you do to the thugs of your nationality who made life miserable for Señor Daraga?"

"I threw one of them to the sharks," Kavanaugh replied, as calmly as if he were detailing the fate of a dog. "The others decided to leave."

Zuraba had been instructed to investigate the situation at the port thoroughly. After he had audited the books and found them correct, he did his other investigating by drinking with Kavanaugh and loafing with him during the hot afternoons when the master mechanic had finished his work at the shops and roundhouse and assumed the position of port commander.

Zuraba waited for Kavanaugh to ask about the Señorita Sagusta. He knew, as everyone else at the port, that there were nights when the American drank too much, when he sat late on the comandancia porch and sang the only song he seemed to know, "I'll Take You Back Again, Kathleen," a song he probably learned from his Irish mother.

Then there were nights when he walked out to the end of the useless pier and sat there for hours gazing over the Pacific swell. While the young commander was out there seeking solitude, the natives stayed off the pier, although it was cool out there after sunset. The commander wanted privacy, they knew, or he wouldn't have walked away out there. The commander was thinking, and should not be disturbed.

The natives respected his privacy. He was their friend and they did not wish to do anything to disturb him.

He never mentioned the señorita who had caused him to leave the ease of Guatemala City for the sweat and dirt and disease of Ocós. He never mentioned her to his friend and companion. Zuraba was too much of a gentleman to ask.

After a month's stay in Ocós, Zuraba went back to the capital with glowing accounts of the American's success in governing the Ocós district.

Because he didn't know it couldn't be done in Guatemala, Kavanaugh had put the railroad in fine working order, had recruited and drilled a company of excellent soldiers, and made his district one of the most peaceful in the republic. Also, he had remitted more money from the port collection in a year than had been remitted in the five years previous. All this Zubara detailed in his report.

But that was not what the politicians up at the capital wanted. They did not like the manner in which Kavanaugh remitted the customs money to the treasury and accounted for every cent he spent on the port. As they do in the United States, the politicians wanted a cut of everything collected and spent.

17

Camandante

OCÓS, WHEN I REACHED THERE, resembled a place that had been criminally assaulted by a Kansas cyclone. Sometime before an earthquake had heaved up the beach about 40 feet, leaving the long iron pier high and dry. At the outer end of the pier where, before the earthquake, there had been about 40 feet of water there was now not enough to float a rowboat. To load coffee the steamers had to anchor out a couple of miles, and the coffee sacks were lightered out in whale boats.

At the time of the earthquake, the volcano of Santa Marie had erupted. It had erupted before, many times, but this particular time, instead of acting like a nice volcano and shooting its flames and lava straight up, it blew out the side nearest Ocós. The result was that the creeks and waterways in that district turned to lye as the volcanic ash settled on the waters. The inhabitants of Ocós were compelled to flee.

Three big warehouses stood on the beach to the north of the town, and were serviced by a railroad track running out to them. Across the bayou from the port were the railroad shops and roundhouse.

At the time of the earthquake a locomotive had been resting on tiers of crossties while the wheels were being trued and the boxes ground. When the quake came the engine toppled over and lay in a slimy morass. It was laying there when I took charge and no attempt had been made to raise it, no derrick being available.

The railroad could not borrow equipment from any other railroad, as it had no rail connections. The Ocós Railroad was operated from the port up to the mountains, serving a lot of coffee fincas, or plantations.

Every month or so a big black German steamer would anchor off port. Then for a few days everyone would be busy. Coffee went out to it in whaleboats, which could safely navigate the enormous Pacific swell.

Between boat arrivals the railroad operated leisurely, bringing down coffee and storing it in the warehouses. The steamers paid gold for the coffee when it was in the holds. Then it went to Hamburg.

As master mechanic, I ran the railroad. There usually was a young German there as resident manager to whom I paid no attention. None of these managers ever gave me an order. They were supposed to sign my monthly reports of business done, expenses, etc., but some months there were no resident managers there, so I signed the reports myself. After a time I got so I never even took the trouble to get the resident manager to sign a report. None were practical railroad men. They were sent there as a sort of check on the man who ran the railroad. They came and went. Ocós was a hot little hell, full of fever, mosquitoes and other insects too numerous to mention, even if I knew their names.

The railroad had been allowed to deteriorate until it was just two streaks of rust and no right-of-way, for the jungle had grown up to the tracks. It was difficult to get a train over it. The locomotive drive wheels would strike a place where the rails were overgrown with grass. Then they would spin around without getting any traction on the rails. The grass acted as a sort of oil that prevented the wheels from getting a "bite" on the rails.

I put natives to work clearing off the tracks. Then another gang followed them, surfacing. But weeds and grass grew so quickly in that moist hot atmosphere that before the grass-cutting gang had gotten five miles along the track, the grass at the starting place would be as high as it was before the cutting.

I decided to try something else. I had a whole ocean full of salt water right there at Ocós. I could get carloads of volcanic ash for the loading. So I tried a mixture of the two.

Using the salt water and volcanic ash I made a solution which I applied with a sprinkler I had made in the shops from old discarded boiler tubes. This sprinkler I placed on a flat car, with a large tank of the solution. Then all I had to do was to run the car up and down the tracks several times, sprinkling as we went along, somewhat after the manner of a street sprinkler.

That solution proved to be a good weed and grass killer. Within a month's time the vegetation between the rails and for two or three feet each side was dead and could be brushed off with brooms in the hands of the trackmen. After the rails were cleaned, I could pull a train of twenty little coffee cars and a passenger coach and make good time.

The Ocós Railroad (Ferro Carril de Ocós), like all the Guatemalan railroads, was of three-foot gage. One of our locomotives was from the Union Pacific, one from the Houston, East and West Texas and one from the Denver & Rio Grande Railroads. The engine lying in the swamp also was from the D.

& R. G. These engines had been sold into Central America when the roads changed from 3-foot gage to standard, 4 foot 8½ inches. The switch engine had been purchased from a Davenport, Iowa factory.

All the road engines had been purchased when they were junked by the former owners, so one can realize what we had to do to operate at all. But we did operate—with junk!

After I got things running well, I fell into a routine. I would go out to the shops every morning, stay there until noon directing the work, then walk back across the bayou bridge for lunch. After lunch I took my siesta. After that I did my duty as port commander.

There were cooking facilities in the building housing the commander's office, and I hired two mozos—an old man and his wife—to keep house for me. The stewards of steamers calling at the port sold me things I couldn't buy in Ocós, canned goods, such as tomatoes and the little fish—sardines.

To illustrate the absolute ignorance of some of those natives, I will say that as long as I was there I could never teach those two mozos to open a can of sardines with an opener I got off a German steamer. If I wanted a can of anything opened for a meal I had to open it myself.

I kept my aguardiente in a big safe in my office that could have been opened by a ten-year-old American boy by just turning a handle in one direction until it clicked and then turning it in the other direction until the door could be opened. Those two old mosos never could solve the mystery of opening that old safe.

I kept busy because I did not want to have time to think. I never realized how much I liked the company of Señorita Sagusta until I left her.

Several times I thought of going up to Guatemala City, marrying the girl and bringing her to Ocós to live with me. But I put that thought away from me. Ocós was not a nice place for a white woman. Besides, I valued my freedom more than I loved the girl. She had wanted to go to the United States and might have agreed to a marriage if I had promised to take her there. But I was fearful of the responsibilities marriage entailed. I knew I could not stay put for any length of time.

When a steamer was in port everyone was in a hurry. Siestas were forgotten, for the steamers had to be loaded and loaded quickly.

About once a week, usually on Sundays, I went up the road to the end and back, taking nothing but a locomotive and a fireman to fire it. I ran it myself.

The coffee fincas each had a spur track connecting their loading docks with the railroad proper. I would inspect these spur tracks and if they were in bad repair, I would order them fixed. I made it a rule that if the repairs I suggested were not made immediately the owners would get no cars to load.

18

Judge

BY VIRTUE OF MY POSITION as comandante, I was judge of the district, as well as police judge of Ocós, if there could be a police judge in a place where there were no police.

But there was very little crime in the district. Most of my minor cases were the result of a cock-eyed law they had down there. To make sure the native men and women would be ready for work Monday morning—for women worked as well as men—it was a misdemeanor to drink before noon of that day.

That law didn't compel the estancas, or saloons, to cease selling drinks Monday morning. They could sell as many as they had call for. The drinker was fined for buying the drink. I had a case or two every week. One I remember well, and it was a good sample of all of them:

A man had been arrested for drinking Monday morning. There was no question about his guilt, for when he was brought before me that afternoon he was still drunk. His wife had arrested him and brought him in, and was the prosecuting witness.

She gave her testimony in a shrill voice, punctuated by many gestures. In those little cases I never bothered myself putting a witness under oath. Anyhow, in any country, if a witness is going to lie, he or she will lie under oath as well as when not. I am not sure that Guatemala had a perjury statute.

"He spent seven centavos," the woman shrilled. "He spent seven centavos that I needed for food today! And my dress needs renewing. For seven centavos and twice as much in addition I could get a new dress from the Chino and now he spends seven centavos for drink and gets drunk."

"Did he beat you?" I inquired.

"Beat me? No, señor Comandante. I have carried coffee sacks for so many years that no man in the country has strength to beat me."

"If you had him at home now, do you think you could beat him until he was sober?"

"I would beat him until he could not walk for a week."

"Then I leave his punishment to you. If I make him pay a money fine it will mean that many days longer until you get a new dress from the Chino. Take him home and punish him well."

She jerked him out of the room and the case was closed.

I may say here that a Chinaman sold cloth and rice and a lot of other things in a store at the port. It was located in a large grass hut across from the comandancia. He compelled the natives to show their money before he showed his goods.

The Chinaman could speak a smattering of English, and often told me how he bought his wife from her parents about twenty years before for only fifty cents. She was somewhat pockmarked, but she was, he declared, a good cook and could tend store while he slept. They had two good-looking children and were a devoted couple.

I suspected the Chinaman of smoking opium, but I never found out for certain. I knew he never sold any or I would have had him run out of the district. I did not want any of the natives to become drug addicts. Besides, few of the natives could afford to pay for the drug, as all they made was wages for loading coffee and occasionally working on the railroad.

A dress like the woman wanted might have cost twenty-one cents or more and might be one that reached only to the knees, or it might reach to where the shoe tops would be had any of the natives worn shoes. But they didn't.

Those natives kept what clothes they had as clean as a society woman would. They were not ironed, as there was not an iron in port. They were washed in water at the edge of the bayou, out of the way of the sharks, and dried in the sun on the sand.

The native women were partial to short skirts, however, and as far as I could see, wore no underwear. But they were not immoral. Once married, they stayed married.

There was little major crime in the Ocós district, and the only crime of major proportions I knew of was committed by persons not resident in the district.

I had to deal with only one serious crime while I was there, and I got out of passing judgment by recalling an article I had read in a magazine.

A fisherman named Trazon lived in a hut up near the mouth of the Ocós river that marked the boundary line of Guatemala and Mexico. Trazon knew where salt could be found and did quite a business in marketing salt fish. Sometimes he sold quantities to ships loading coffee. He also sold to Mexicans across the river.

I knew him well. Occasionally I would walk up to his place in the late afternoon and spend a few hours with him. Before settling there he had been a sailor and knew many of the ports of the world. Ships he had sailed on had touched at New York and New Orleans.

Trazon had two daughters. His wife had died before I reached Ocós. All three were companionable persons, and the daughters had a miramba on which they would play tunes while I was there.

One day two foreigners, either Mexicans or other Central American nationals, came across the river, killed Trazon during a quarrel, and kept the girls prisoners for several days. Early one Sunday morning one of the girls escaped and came to Ocós and told her story. I got Doros and a few soldiers and we went up after the men. We caught them asleep and brought them down to the port.

I disliked taking the responsibility of ordering their execution. I had read an article in a magazine some steamer captain had given me about how women would make better jurors than men. So after breakfast I sent men out and they summoned six married women and six girls to act as jurors.

We gave the men a fair trial that Sunday morning. Then Doros, acting in the capacity of prosecutor, made a talk to the jurors something like this:

"The señor Comandante has left the punishment of these men in your hands. It is the custom in his country to let the people decide on the punishment for a crime. You have heard all the talk. I will give each of you two limes, a shriveled lime and a green one. Each of you will pass into the other room where there is a basket to the right of the door. If you believe the men should be executed for their crime, you will say it by putting the shriveled lime in the basket. If you believe the men should go free, you will put the green lime in the basket. Then throw the one you do not use in the corner so that no one will know how you have voted. Go in one by one and come out at once."

One by one the women passed into the other room and out again. When all had voted, Doros sent a boy for the basket.

All the limes in it were shriveled. The men had been convicted by a jury of women years before women were allowed to vote in the United States. This probably was the first jury trial held in Guatemala.

Doros and several soldiers took the two men to the railroad bridge spanning the bayou. They shot one and he fell into the water and the sharks tore him to pieces within a few seconds. The other man jumped from the bridge and tried to swim to the other shore, but the sharks got him before he had gotten ten feet.

I took the girls to lunch at the comandancia, where we talked over their future plans. They decided to continue the salt fish business. I made several trips up there after that and found them doing well. I gave them two revolvers old Daraga had left at Ocós and, as they were husky women, they could protect themselves. They were doing well when I left there.

19

Jungle Execution

THE YOUNG GERMAN RESIDENT MANAGERS came and went. They couldn't stand the heat and stink and living conditions. Before they came they pictured a tropical paradise, with cool drinks, dancing girls and all that.

Instead of the tropical paradise they pictured, they found a humid, dirty, mosquito-infested little port set on the sand of the beach. All drinks they got were tepid, or really hot. The pictured houris were husky Indian girls, many of whom could shoulder a sack of coffee and carry it to the waiting whaleboat as well as a man. There were few beauties among them.

So the young German resident managers sweated, fought mosquitoes, slept in a tightly-closed room if they hadn't brought a screen with them, watched the sun sink in the Pacific Ocean, and cursed the man who sent them down there.

I paid little attention to those German resident managers, as they were not practical railroad men. It was the duty of these men to go out to the steamers and check the sacks of coffee as they came aboard, while I checked them as they were loaded into the whaleboats at the warehouse. But this arrangement was reversed, as the young Germans were afraid to venture out through the high surf in those old whaleboats.

As a result I would delegate the German to check the coffee into the whaleboats while I went out to the steamer. There I would delegate one of my men to check the sacks as they came aboard while I drank beer with the captain and mates. They had iced beer. In Ocós we took our beer tepid.

Sitting on the hot beach checking sacks usually proved too much for the young Germans. One died of sunstroke. Generally half an hour settled them and they would turn the checking over to a native and seek the shade.

I think it was the third or fourth resident manager who came after I got to Ocós that made a good story, if I had had the nerve to publish it. That is, his fate made the story.

I hadn't heard a word of English or seen a white face for several months when Welmyer telegraphed me he was sending another victim. I was anxious to see a white man again, so I took a locomotive and a passenger coach up to Ayutla for him.

The bird could speak English very well, but little Spanish. He had lived in New York and Baltimore and was a baseball fan. He knew all the big players and could even quote their averages.

When he deposited his credentials with me, as comandante, he said, "I do not know of the railroad one damn thing. I think I loaf. You run the railroad. You got some pretty girls here who do not wear many clothes, ain't it?"

"There are a few pretty ones here," I agreed, and then cautioned. "Let them alone. If you fool with them, you get in bad. If you marry one, you'll never be able to bring her up to your level, and she'll bring you down to hers. Fight shy of them."

"I like pretty girls," he said with a laugh. "I always liked pretty girls. Bremen, New York, Baltimore, Panama—I always had a pretty girl."

"Lay off 'em here," I warned, "or you'll find yourself dead some nice warm morning."

He laughed and changed the subject.

He had been there about a month when an American machinist who was working in the shops to make a stake to get down to Panama called my attention to the German.

"That Dutchman's going to get a knife in his guts pretty soon," he mentioned to me one morning. "He's trying to make a girl the natives say is Pancho's girl, and they say Pancho's hell with a knife." (Pancho was a worker in the shops.)

"The Dutchy will have to look out for himself," I said. "I've warned him, but he seems to know it all. Did you hear Pancho threaten him?"

"No, but I've heard some of the others talking about it. I've heard them guying him about the Dutchman taking his girl, and you know that's poison talk."

"Pancho hasn't paid for the girl yet, though," I remarked. "She isn't his until he does."

"No, and the Dutchy can afford to pay twice what Pancho can pay, and perhaps has done so already."

"I could send the Dutchman out of the district," I suggested.

"Damn 'f I would," the machinist said. "Maybe things have gone too far already. Those young spigs are joking Pancho about the German baby he'll inherit."

The German went up the road with me the next Sunday while I was trying out an engine. I had raised the engine the earthquake had upset, put wheels under it and was trying it out. I had raised it by cribbing; just a few inches at a time. I was afraid the boiler had been damaged by salt water and would not hold a full head of steam.

I ran the engine myself and the German rode in the cab with the fogonero (fireman). Coming back I let the engine coast and spoke to the young man about native girls.

I call him a young man, but the fact of the matter was he was about my age. But he had not been hardened by three years in the Philippines. I looked at least ten years older than he did.

"You'll get into trouble sure as shooting," I cautioned. "Pancho will put a machete through you some night." I spoke in English and the fireman did not understand what I said. He was a friend of Pancho.

"I'm not afraid of a dozen Pancho's," the German boasted. "These greasers don't know how to fight."

"If they were greasers," I explained, "I'd say go on and do as you please. But these people are Indians and have queer ways of getting even with a white man."

"Oh, you've been down in this hot country so long you've lost your manhood," he hooted. "If I had your position here, I'd have a girl for every day of the month."

"I may have lost my manhood," I agreed, "but I haven't lost my caution. If you're so damned anxious for a woman, why not try a young widow. There's four of them in port. They're crazy for a man. Every time there's an American working here I have to run them out of the shops because they pester him."

"I don't like widows," he said.

One night, shortly after that conversation, I got a telegram from a coffee finca which had promised to load ten cars with coffee next day asking that I postpone sending a train up its spur because a heavy rain had weakened a bridge.

There was a telegraph instrument in the shops and I had one wired into the comandancia, but there was no one at the shops at night who could receive a message. I wanted to let Doros know about the change in plans, as I had ordered him to have two road engines ready to go out at six o'clock in the morning. With the change in plans we would need but one.

Although it was after ten o'clock, I walked across the bayou bridge to the shops. Doros lived in a lean-to at the rear of the roundhouse with his wife and two children.

To get to the bridge from the comandancia I had to pass the railroad station. The resident manager had living quarters above the station, which were reached by an outside stairway. As I passed I saw the silhouette of a man and woman sitting on the top step of the stairs. I thought it might be the German and a girl, but I did not appear to notice them, and walked on.

I did not see the German next day, but there were many days when I did not see him. But on the second day I received a telegram from Ayutla saying there were some things there for the resident manager, and I went over to see if he wanted an engine sent up for them.

The door to his quarters were unlocked and I went on in. It was about 8 o'clock and his bed was made. I knew the old woman who cleaned his rooms didn't get there till later and I wondered about it. I was going down the stairs when I met the old woman.

"Where is the Alaman?" I asked. (A German is an Alaman in Guatemala, and Germany is called Alamania.)

"I do not know, señor," she replied. "Yesterday he was not here either."

"When did he leave?"

"I do not know, señor. Yesterday his bed was not disturbed, for he was not here."

"I wonder if that fool Dutchman went bathing and a shark got him?" I said in English. The woman did not understand and looked at me in surprise.

"If the Alaman comes, tell him the comandante wishes to speak to him," I instructed her. Then I went about my business.

The man did not show up for a week. Neither did the girl he was after. I sent a message up to Guatemala City telling Welmyer of his disappearance. But the government line beyond Pajipite was not working and the message lie at that point awaiting line repairs. At length I spoke to Doros about it.

"Something has happened to the Dutchman," I remarked one day.

"I think so, too," Doros replied with a shrug. "And his girl is gone as well."

"Have you heard anything about it?" I asked.

"Only that Pancho was angry with him for taking his girl, and Pancho has many friends," Doros replied, and added, "The German had no friends."

"Then it might be advisable to question Pancho and his friends?" I suggested.

"It would be useless," Doros said. "Just a waste of time. They would pretend to know nothing and we have no proof that the missing man has not left on a visit."

"But he couldn't have gotten out of here except by rail or on a boat. There hasn't been a boat out of here lately. And he isn't a man that would walk up the track when he could get an engine and coach whenever he wanted to."

"That would make no difference to Pancho and his friends. He didn't walk away nor did he ride. But I will listen closely and perhaps I can find a clue."

"Do so," I said.

After about three weeks wait I got a message from Welmyer. The government line had finally been put in working order.

"I will send a resident manager when I get one," the telegram read. "Have no news of Brausch."

So his name was Brausch. I called all those young Germans Otto. It was easy to remember. Besides, a name meant nothing down there.

One afternoon about sunset I was watching Doros drill his company of soldiers. I just had had a few drinks and was feeling fine. As he swung the company around at "right forward, fours right," I clapped my hands to applaud, for those boys were really good.

After another example or two of good drilling Doros brought the group to a company front, they ported arms in salute, Doros raised his sword as an American officer would have done. I acknowledged the salute and he dismissed the company. He then came to where I stood.

"If you will go with me, sir, as soon as I have changed my uniform to working clothes, I think I can show you where the German and Pancho's girl are."

I waited while he went to the round house and changed clothing. He came back with a lantern, as the sun had set and there was a very short twilight there.

We walked north to the warehouses. We went to each door as if we were inspecting the guards stationed there. Then we walked down to the water. It was now dark. Doros and I walked down the beach, the waves lapping at our feet. We walked for about a mile, then turned into the jungle. Once in the jungle, Doros lit the lantern.

"I think this is the place," he said.

We walked into the jungle for perhaps half a mile. Suddenly Doros swung the lantern upward and stopped. He pointed.

It was the Dutchman all right, but I wouldn't have recognized him if it hadn't been for his shoes and some of his clothing. He wore toothpick shoes and they were still on what was left of his feet—the bones.

Tied back to back, with the tree between them, were the two skeletons, their bones picked clean. One of the girl's legs was gone, probably having been taken by some prowling animal. But the thongs that bound them to the tree held her upright. The Dutchy's bones were all there, and when a breeze came in from the sea his leg bones swung to and fro, causing a slight rattling sound in his shoes.

I knew what had been done. The two wayward persons had been tied to the tree and molasses or some sweet syrup poured over them. The ants and other little creeping insects had done the rest. They had been punished, Indian fashion.

I looked a little while, perhaps a minute. I became sick to my stomach and gagged. Then we walked back out of the jungle to the beach. As we came out of the jungle Doros extinguished the light by jerking the lantern and we walked home on the sand down at the edge of the water, the waves lapping at our feet.

At the warehouse we again spoke to the guards, to make them think it was merely a routine inspection. It was my habit to walk out any time of the night and see if the guards were awake. If I had found one asleep I would have run him out of the district. I never had to run one out.

When we reached the comandancia, I asked Doros in. I set a garafone of aguardiente and two glasses on the table between us. We drank. We drank again.

After two or three drinks my stomach settled. I began to feel good again. I asked, "What would you suggest, Pena?"

"We inspected the guards at the warehouses tonight," he said with a smile.

"I think you are right, Pena," I agreed. "We inspected the guards at the warehouses tonight and found them all awake and alert."

"Si, señor," he said. "It is best."

That was the end of that resident manager. His fate was never reported. I did not want a scandal and an investigation by German diplomatic officers in my district. The Dutchy had brought it on himself.

I was glad I was girl-shy.

20

Railroading

I HAD THE RAILROAD in tiptop shape. I could send a train out and it could go to the end of the line, switch the loading tracks of the fincas along the road and get back to Ocós the same day. Before I rehabilitated the road the same trip had required two or three days.

One day a Pacific Mail steamer from San Francisco unloaded some freight for the port and among the articles was a gasoline engine, the first one I had seen. It was a two-cylinder opposed motor, a great deal cruder but on the same plan as the ones now used in very small airplanes.

The finca owner who had ordered it refused it for some reason or other, so I fell heir to it, as a law forbade the shipment of usable machinery out of the Republic of Guatemala. This law was promulgated to prevent companies from dismantling and shipping the machinery of manufacturing plants to other countries.

I put in a lot of time working with that gas engine. Finally I got it running. Then I looked around to find some place to put it so that it would prove useful.

We had a light passenger coach in the shops that had once been a San Francisco street car. It wasn't more than twenty feet in length. After experimenting at odd times for a couple of months I had it attached to the wheels of that car and it worked like a charm.

After I got it running I used the car for inspection trips or when I had occasion to take coffee money up to the finca owners.

I could have taken passengers in it, but the Ocós Railroad did not cater to passengers. Few cared to use the road. No one who could help it ever wanted to come to Ocós. We never had a schedule of passenger fares.

Once I issued an order that no Chinese should ride in passenger coaches, but I did this on the advice of a ship's surgeon, because he said there was danger of bubonic plague and that Chinese carried it around.

This rule was never enforced because there was but one Chinaman in the district—the merchant at Ocós. The only time I ever remember hauling him was one day when he went up the line to purchase some hens.

That day he couldn't ride a passenger coach because we didn't haul one. On the return trip he rode a box car in company with his chickens.

Because I charged him no train fare he gave the old mozo woman who kept house for me a new dress with spangles on it, worth probably fifty cents of that money. He gave me a young hen which the mozo woman cooked by patting an inch or two of mud on it and then baking it, mud and all, for about half a day. It tasted good and she didn't have to pluck the feathers. They came off when the mud, baked hard, was broken before the chicken was served.

21

Missionaries

MISSIONARIES GAVE ME SOME TROUBLE. If trouble started up the line and they anticipated danger they would come down, pronto, trying to get out of the country and into Mexico. I would send them back to Limones, where a boatman would take them across the river and they could walk on up to Tapachula.

In many cases they were broke when they reached Ocós, and I would lend them money with which to purchase food on the way up. They invariably took my name and address and promised to send me a check as soon as they could, but they must have lost the addresses, for I never got back a cent.

Up around San Felipe embryo revolutionists were always cropping up and raising trouble, but they never did any damage. They were more of the bandit class than real revolutionists. They made a lot of fuss for a few days, then government troops executed a few and things quieted again.

After I got my company of soldiers organized and drilled, these bandit-revolutionists fought shy of the district along the railroad, for my men had the reputation of being able to hit a flying bird with one of those old Springfield rifles.

Then one day, one of those bands raided an estanca at a little place above Ayutla, where there was a German finca owner who had a lot of coffee gold. They got the gold, wounded the German, and came down the railroad to hold up another place. In Ocós we were notified of the raid by telegraph and I sent Doros and 10 soldiers up to see what was happening.

Doros and his men caught the robbers and tied up those they did not kill. The bound men were put in charge of three men with orders to watch them while Doros and the rest went up to see how badly the German was wounded.

Those three soldiers of mine were weary and did not relish watching those prisoners, eight, as near as I know. So they took them to the side of the railroad right-of-way and tied them to trees, after which the soldiers went to sleep. Then Doros returned that night with the engine and car he went up on. The soldiers were still asleep, but the prisoners were dead. There are a million species of little crawling insects in the jungle which feed on human or any other kind of flesh if the flesh can't move and fight them off.

Doros brought the sleepy soldiers to me, but instead of punishing them I congratulated them for tying the prisoners, but docked them a week's pay for going to sleep. This incident was repeated from person to person all through the district and those adjoining Ocós. The consensus of opinion was that my soldiers had been taught to take no prisoners.

That is why everyone within reach of the Ocós district knew that if my soldiers captured a bandit it would be the end of that particular bandit.

One self-styled bandit general, Zelaya, made it a sort of habit to start revolutions. None of his revolutions ever clicked, however.

Zelaya was a Mexican, but revolutionized in Guatemala. He'd start a revolution and when it petered out he'd slip over to Mexico and await another effort. He had men who watched for shipments of the coffee gold and I think his efforts were directed mostly to getting a whack at it.

About once every three months the coffee finca owners would gather the money they had received for their coffee and send it up to San Francisco to a bank. They invariably sent it by Pacific Mail steamer and not by a coffee tramp.

I usually made the trip up with a regularly equipped train and got the gold from each finca owner a day or so before a steamer was due on its regular trip north. To signal it we made a big fire and covered it with green leaves to make a black smoke.

The steamer captain, seeing the smoke, would anchor off the port and I would go out in a whaleboat, deliver the money to the purser, take a separate receipt for each sack, and drink a bottle of cold beer with the mates or captain. In addition to this, the steamer officers usually gave me a few old magazines.

I often wondered why the coffee planters did not send their money back to Hamburg by the coffee tramps or just take checks on some bank in Germany. But they didn't. It was gold on the coffee sack, so to speak. Then the gold was sent up to San Francisco.

The time I met the other kind of missionaries was on one of my trips to get the gold. I had telegraphed the fincas that I would be after the money they might wish to send. I used a steam locomotive. Behind it I coupled a flat car on which I had mounted three machine guns. Behind these cars were two box cars, and then a passenger coach. Thus equipped, I went up. If the steamer was on schedule it would be along the following day.

If an American hobo happened to be working at Ocós I took him along on a trip like this. But Ocós was hot and feverish and dirty and stinking, so Americans or Europeans did not stay there long. And there wasn't a resident manager there at that time. The last one had got a touch of sunstroke and tried to commit suicide, so I had sent him out.

I got the money they had farther up the line and came on down, getting more from each finca owner.

It was nearly dark when the train reached Limoncite. I was to have been met there by a finca owner with his gold shipment, but he was delayed and I went over to the estanca for dinner.

I had heard Zelaya was on another revolutionary spree and had my men watching. I had information furnished me by telegraph that he was making for the Ocós Railroad. He had passed through San Felipe three days before, while the San Felipe garrison was hunting him in another part of that district. I knew what he was after—the finca gold.

I was eating my dinner when one of my men came in and told me two missionaries were approaching. A few minutes later, another man came in and told me they were outside, waiting to see me. My men were holding them until I gave my permission for them to enter. They had no permission to enter the district and it was dark. After dark one had to show what he was or take the consequences.

I had expected the usual slim, middle-aged missionaries with their holier-than-thou attitude and wordy mouths.

"Let the missionaries come in," I ordered, as I went on eating.

Who should walk in but two young women! By the way they walked I could see they had been riding burros for several days. By the way those girls walked I could see they didn't care much what happened to them so long as they didn't have to ride those little mules again!

22

El Señor Diablo

ONE OF THE FEMALE MISSIONARIES might have been in her early thirties. The other about twenty-five. They weren't bad-looking, either, but I didn't like missionaries. I didn't like missionaries, either male or female, and the womanly charms of these two didn't make me change my opinion a bit.

So I inquired, "What do you want here?" Unconsciously, through force of habit, I had used Spanish.

"I am resident missionary at San Felipe auxiliary mission," the eldest began in Spanish.

I interrupted, "Say it in English, sister. Your university Spanish is rotten."

She drew herself up to her full height, about five feet four, and began in English, "I am resident missionary at San Felipe and Zelaya..."

"I know that, sister," I interrupted again. "Zelaya went through San Felipe and is headed for the coast. We may tangle with him before we reach Ocós tonight. I suppose you want to go down with us?"

"Yes, sir."

"Who gave you permission to come into my district?" I asked.

"We feared Zelaya and..."

"You people come down to Guatemala to try and teach the Indians to quit a religion that was old before the birth of the Christians' Christ and join up with a bunch of shouting Protestants and then, at the first rumor of danger you run, eh?"

The youngest girl, who had taken no part in the talk, but had just been looking around, chimed in, "We come and go as we please. There's a United States gunboat at Amapala and..."

"A helluva lotta good it'll do you," I said.

She flared up—and looked real pretty. "You're exactly what the natives call you," she exclaimed.

"And what do the natives call me?" I asked.

"El Señor Diablo—the mister devil—the man who threatened to cut off the ears of an officer who was sent down here to investigate your actions."

"That's right, sister," I laughed. "Down here one must forget many of the refinements of our so-called civilization. It's either brute force or you find yourself dead—but I run the railroad and the district."

I called the woman who ran the estanca. "The senoritas are tired and hungry. Get them some food."

The girls were still standing. "Sit down, ladies," I invited. "As bad as they make me out, I'll not bite you if you sit at a table with me. I'm sure you're hungry."

"I could eat anything," the younger one said.

"When do we leave?" the eldest asked.

"Just as soon as a finca owner gets here with a shipment for Frisco," I replied.

Those girls surely were hungry. I noticed they were uncomfortable and asked the woman to get them a cushion apiece. She brought the articles.

As she did so the youngest one laughed and remarked, "I'd almost be willing to be captured by Mr. Zelaya if I was sure I'd never have to ride a little mule again."

"The car you'll ride down in isn't very comfortable, either," I explained. "It has no windows and the seats are of hard cane. If it had windows we couldn't shoot through them. What I mean is that the glass is all gone and insects can enter and annoy you."

The eldest girl looked up, fright in her face. "Will there be shooting?" she inquired.

"There may be," I replied. "If there happens to be shooting, get down between the seats and keep away from the windows. You'll be safe."

"Unless they capture us," the eldest added.

"When they capture us, I'll be dead," I asserted with a lot of pride. "I'd rather be dead that have the reputation of having a phony revolutionist like Zelaya pull anything over me."

"Are you an American?" the youngest asked.

"I served three years in the United States Army and was born in the states," I replied.

"We had heard many stories about what you were before you came here," she said.

"And believed them all?"

"From the way you have received us, I am inclined to believe all they have said about you," she affirmed.

I motioned to the estanca woman to fill my glass. She did—with aguardiente.

"Are you an alcoholic?" the eldest asked, looking daggers at the glass.

"I drink some," and then went on to explain, "If a man ever gets cold sober down here he dies of the fever."

"Medical authorities differ as to the efficacy of alcoholic beverages in preventing tropical fevers," the youngest remarked. "In some cases..."

"What do you know of medicine or the tropics?" I interrupted.

"I am a medical student," she said. "One more year at university, an internship, and I'll be a full-fledged physician."

"Then you're not a holier-than-thou?" I asked.

"If you're trying to ask if I'm a missionary," she said in a tone of voice intended to wither me, "I may as well inform you that I am not. My sister is resident missionary at San Felipe Mission. It seems that you have forgotten polite language, El Señor Diablo."

"I use it very little here," I confessed. "I know a few words of Indian and can speak Spanish. I haven't heard a word of English for a long time. An occasional hobo comes through and stays a while, but not often."

"Can we secure quarters in Ocós?" the eldest queried.

"I can put you up in the comandancia."

"If your wives do not object?" the youngest suggested.

"So they've got me running a harem, eh?" I observed. "Why the only woman around the comandancia is so old she remembers when the Spaniards ruled this country."

One of my men came in just then to tell me the finca owner had arrived. He came into the lighted room and blinked. He saw the girls and laughed.

"Ho, ho. So the comandante is starting a harem? Ha ha."

He was a big fat sweaty German and the Spanish coming through his beard was rotten.

They're missionaries," I explained. "They're running from Zelaya."

"For the start of a harem they're a good beginning," he said, laughing. Both his belly and his beard went in and out when he laughed.

23

We Fight Zelaya

I CALLED ONE OF MY MEN and told him to see the senoritas went directly to the passenger coach. I wasn't sure how much of the German's Spanish they had understood. My reputation was not of the best, according to what the girls had said, and I did not want them to fear I would start a harem with them.

After the girls left the German counted out his gold. I placed it in a canvas sack, put a car seal on it, wrote his name and address on a shipping tag, and gave him a receipt. We had a drink together and I looked at my watch. It was almost 11 o'clock. I should have been in Ocós before that time.

We had to be careful on the trip down to the port. The engine had no headlights and if those bandits got between us and the port they could take a rail out and ditch us.

I had two men with reflector lights ride the pilot and we slogged along at about five miles an hour. It rained constantly. I censured myself for waiting so long for the last bag of gold. It might mean disaster. We might lose the gold to the bandits and we might be massacred.

I didn't go back to see how the girls were faring. I hadn't brought them there and wasn't particularly concerned about them. When girls of that age go gallivanting around the tropics lots of things could happen to them.

I rode the engine and sometimes the cars with the machine guns on them. Just behind the gun car was the boxcar in which the money was kept. I had put a man on guard there. He was a stolid Indian who could be trusted to guard that money with his life, just as long as I told him to do so. My gunners were sleeping under the tarpaulins which covered the guns.

I had made my way over to the cab of the engine and was sitting on the fireman's seat when one of the men riding the pilot swung his lantern. The engine stopped within 10 feet. I went out on the running board at the side of the boiler and slid down beside him.

"What did you see?" I asked.

"Something moving on the track ahead."

I walked back in the dark to about fifty feet ahead of the engine and called to the engineer to come slowly. By the light of a lantern I examined the rails. Sure enough, someone had started to loosen the bolts that held the fishplates, where they held two rail ends together. As I leaned over to examine the place I heard the "ping" of a bullet over my head.

"Let 'er go," I called to the engineer. "This won't ditch us."

We passed the spot without lights. As we did so, I heard another shot, farther back. I thought of the one light I had left on in the passenger coach. There was a light at each end of the coach, but I had lighted but one.

"Go back and put out the light in the passenger coach," I instructed a man. "Tell the senoritas we were shooting at mosquitoes."

He returned with a few minutes.

"Were the senoritas fearful?" I asked.

"One was," he replied.

"And the other?"

"There was no other."

I was wondering if I hadn't better go back and find out what had become of the other girl when we approached a little station and the lanterns swung again. This time a rail was out. So I concluded Zelaya had divided his band into several small parties with the intention of one of them copping the gold if the others failed.

I had no time to go back to the passenger coach. In fact, for the next half hour I was so busy I forgot all about the girls until I ran into something that startled me.

Behind the little railroad station building stood an old shed. Wood was piled around. Occasionally I bought fuel for the locomotives there. As we were replacing the rail by the light of lanterns a volley of shots interrupted us. Two of my men fell. I got a little wound in the fleshy part of my upper leg. But I let no one know it. We extinguished all lights.

I made my way back to the flatcar where the machine guns were placed. My gunners were sitting there, awake and alert.

Another burst of shots came from the direction of the woodshed. This time it raked the machine gun car. It got two of the gunners and the other one rolled off across the car and disappeared. I did not know whether he was killed or just scared.

I reached the first gun and let go a burst of shots. I could see nothing moving at which to shoot, so I merely swung the gun back and forth, raking the woodshed. Finally, for I had forgotten my machine gun training in the excitement, my gun jammed. I crawled to the center gun.

I had just swung it around when the third gun blistered out. Its bullets swung through the shed, silencing the gun there, and then swung on around. In the dim light I could see the station sign on the end of the building grow a little line of holes diagonally across the lettering. I know I had no man at that gun, but someone was operating it. The man I had stationed there had been killed and was lying across the car nearby.

I crawled across the interval separating the guns and jerked a ponchoed figure to its feet. It was the youngest girl.

"A holier-than-thou, by God!" I exclaimed. "Who in hell taught you to operate a machine gun?"

She jerked her shoulder from my grasp. "You're as big a brute as they say you are," she spit at me.

"Who taught you to operate a machine gun?" I repeated.

"A militia officer whom I dated at the university," she replied, and then added, "but he was a gentleman."

I laughed. "Sorry I can't be a gentleman down here," I told her. "I think you've put that gun out of commission. But why did you pepper the station?"

"Just because I wanted to," she explained, and I let it go at that.

There were no more shots from the shed. I called to the engineer to relay the information to the workers ahead that they might light lanterns again so as to see better in replacing the rail. I examined the men on the car and found them dead. I could see nothing of the one who had rolled across the car and fell to the ground.

I put a new bandolier into the number three gun and, after notifying the men ahead that I was doing the shooting, I raked the shed again, using short blasts. But I got no reply. Everything out there was silent except for the sound of insects. A sleepy huacamaier called to his mate. A jackal or some such animal howled in the distance. A big body moved in the water at one side of the track.

Presently one of my men came up and told me the track was fixed, and I called to the engineer to proceed as soon as the tools were loaded.

While they were loading tools I got off the flat car. The girl was standing near the edge of the low car and, without asking her permission, I reached up and lifted her off and waited for the money car to pull up. The man I had stationed in there as guard opened the door when I called and I told him to go back and ride the passenger coach down.

I lifted the girl into the money car. Rain had ceased and beyond Santa Marie volcano I could see dawn creeping on. I opened the opposite door so that the fresh air could come through.

The girl was arranging her skirts which I had disarranged while carrying her.

"You say you're a medical student?" I asked.

"I am."

"Can you dress a wound and not faint?"

"Of course."

I took out my knife and slit my trousers leg and exposed a rather ragged wound. She started.

"I thought you'd faint," I taunted.

"I'm not fainting," she asserted.

"Can you dress it?" I asked.

"Expertly," she replied. "Am I supposed to tear my dress to pieces to provide bandages?"

"There's a first aid kit on top of those sacks," I said, as I pointed. "There's water in that keg in the corner. Sure you know how?"

"Sure thing," she said. "It's good practice for me. If I had my instruments with me I'd like to amputate both your legs and, perhaps, your head."

I lay on the floor, wound up, while she pulled a sack of limes over and used it for a seat. She cut a piece of flesh from the wound and looked at me, smiling.

"You don't cringe when I hurt you, do you Mr, Devil?" she remarked.

"If I cringed every time something hurt me," I told her, "I wouldn't be El Señor Diablo. I'd be somewhere up in the States, wearing a thousand-mile shirt."

"I don't understand."

"You wouldn't," I assured her. "You've never sunk that low and never will."

"And now you are..."

"Boss of a few hundred natives who'd go to hell for me."

"I wonder what became of Zelaya?" she asked.

"You may have killed him," I suggested.

"If I didn't he'll be mighty angry with you," she said.

"Not at all," I explained. "Zelaya wasn't after my hide. He was after about five thousand dollars in German gold I have in this car. If I gave him that he'd fall on my neck and kiss me."

"Wouldn't that be better than have you shooting at each other and killing people?"

"No," I said. "Those people trust me with their gold. I'll see it on the steamer if I'm alive."

The sun was rising behind Santa Marie and visibility was good. We stood in the doorway and breathed in the fresh morning air. Within a couple of hours the heat would be stifling.

"Don't you ever want to go back home, El Señor?" the girl asked.

"I could go back to the States," I replied, "if I wished. There's nothing against me up there. But you don't know what a boost it gives one's ego to be a boss, even if it is being the boss of a few natives. Always before, in the army and in my work in the states, I've been under someone. Down here I'm boss. It's great."

"I suppose it is," she mused aloud. "But I couldn't stand the dirt and heat and filth that is commonplace down here."

"It's like olives," I returned. "You've got to acquire a taste for it."

The whistle of the engine announced our arrival at Ocós. The sun was just above the peak of Santa Maria. I leaned out as the train swung around the curve going into the yards and signaled the engineer to pull on across the bayou bridge. Pena Doros caught the train as it passed and I told him to have the smoke fire built so that we could signal the steamer to stop.

I took the girls to the comandancia and after coffee I showed them into my bedroom so they could get some rest. As I closed the door after showing them the room, I remarked, "Sorry I can't give you a key so that you could lock yourselves in. But I have no key. And there's no lock on the door, anyhow."

"Don't let that worry you," the younger one countered. "I neglected to mention back there that I used to date the intercollegiate boxing champion and he gave me a lot of pointers in the art."

24

The Missionaries Keep House

THE STEAMER SHOWED UP that afternoon and I called the girls and told them to follow me up to the warehouses, where I would have a whaleboat ready. Then I got the gold and walked up, two of my soldiers carrying it. The girls followed within a few minutes. When they were in the whaleboat I asked the younger one, whom I knew now as Frances, if they had money to pay for their passage. They had.

We boarded the steamer and I told the skipper I had two passengers for him. I thought he would thank me but instead of thanks the skipper exploded. He wasn't taking any passengers from any port down there where there wasn't a physician stationed to give them a clean bill of health, he asserted.

It was true that those little ports bred a lot of fever, but I hadn't thought anything about it until now. I wasn't familiar with the passenger health regulations of the Pacific Mail Steamer line.

The girls could go across into Mexico, he said, to Salina Cruz, the nearest port where there was a physician, or down to Champerico, and board a steamer, but he would accept no passengers from Ocós.

I did not argue with him, but the girls did, and he got the best of the argument. I delivered the gold to the purser and got his receipts for each bag. Then I went topside to hear the arguments, pro and con, about taking passengers from Ocós.

"If I took you on here, without a health permit," he explained, "my vessel would be quarantined for 30 days on its arrival at San Francisco. Tying up a vessel like this one for that length of time would mean a loss of thousands of dollars to the company. If I caused anything like that there'd be a new master on this vessel and I'd be looking for a job."

"Could you notify the authorities in the United States that we are here in Ocós and in danger?" the eldest girl inquired.

"I could, but I won't," the captain replied. "This port is as safe as home as long as that Irisher runs it. Don't let a snake bite you and sleep in a screened room."

The eldest girl looked at me doubtfully. The youngest looked at me and winked.

"Now I'll have to ask you to go ashore," the skipper concluded.

We got into the whaleboat and came back to the comandancia. It was along about 4 o'clock and I had had no luncheon or cold beer. Usually the steamer captains treated me to a couple of bottles of cold beer whenever I went aboard, but this time the girls were there and he forgot to do so.

I called the mozo whose wife kept house for me and told him to have his wife prepare dinner.

The eldest girl interrupted. "If we are going to stay here for any length of time," she said, "we should make some other arrangements. Isn't there any other place where we can stay?"

"None. Isn't this all right?"

"But we are taking your bedroom."

"I'll sleep in the office. It's well screened."

"Then I don't like the appearance of that mozo. He's dirty. And his wife is so dirty I'd rather not eat what she prepares in the way of food."

"Can you cook?" I asked.

"Of course."

"Then go to it, if you wish."

"Have you any American food at all?"

"Only one thing—sardines—and I think they come from Norway. And beans, of course, which could be classed as an international food."

"I'll try, anyhow," she said. "Come on, Frances."

I called the mozo and told him about the new arrangement. I suggested he and his wife take a paid vacation while the girls were there. I even paid him in advance, well knowing he would spend that and I would have to pay him again. While I was talking to him I could hear sounds of an argument in the kitchen. The mozo's wife and the eldest girl were having it hot and heavy. I told him to go in and tell his wife they could leave.

After a few minutes they came back, carrying some personal effects.

"If the comandante will permit me to say a word or two," the old woman began as they were passing out.

"Say what you wish, señora," I replied.

"The younger one will make a nice companion, señor," she said, "But before you sit the older one on your knee, try doing the same with a wildcat. Then you will know how the older one will treat you."

"I have no intention of having either one of them sit on my knees," I protested.

"El Señor Comandante is a sly one," she said as she turned to leave. "Sending the mozos away while the pink and white senoras are here. But beware the older one. When I told her you'd prefer her sister every time if she did not mend her temper she threatened me with a stick of wood."

The older one took charge and really cooked some good meals. The younger one loafed around the port, bought native dresses and wore them, much to the mortification of her sister, for they came only to the knees at a time when long dresses were the style. She doctored the sick, visited the warehouses, made eyes at the young men, taught the children how to play ring-around-a-rosy. Once a day, for about a week, she dressed my wound, under the critical eye of her sister.

One day I suggested to Frances that she ditch her native clothes, and she said, "When in Ocós, señor, do as Ocosians do."

"But your sister is..."

"Between you and me, señor, I'm about fed up on this missionary business. I'm going home pretty soon to begin the Fall semester at university. There's a man coming out—a man Agnes is going to marry."

"Another missionary?"

"Another missionary. He gets his greatest thrill sitting in front of the fire reading the Bible. I don't know what he'll do for a fire down here in the hot country. He'll have to sit before something else."

"And the man you marry must be otherwise, eh?"

"Yes. I want a man who will swear when he is angry, and who'll enjoy an occasional knock-down-and-drag-out. I want him to be a doctor, too, so that for want of anything else we can have an occasional argument about some phase of materia medica."

"I wouldn't fit into your scheme of things, then?" I asked, smiling.

"I'm afraid not," she replied. "You're a bit too uncouth, too uneducated."

"I'm sorry," I said.

"I knew you'd be," she returned, "when I put on these native clothes. That's to repay you for the way you treated us the night we first met you. But I must tell you that you disappointed me."

"How?"

"I'd heard much of the tough El Señor Diablo. I pictured him as a big man, perhaps six foot ten, and weighing 250 pounds. And here you are a..."

She hesitated and I prompted, "A what?"

"A stripling of 150 pounds—a man that, if you were dressed convention-ally, could pass as a professor of domestic economy in a girls' school."

"But I run the railroad and the district."

"Perhaps," she mused, "but you'll never run me. I believe I could best you in a fist fight."

"You might, at that," I agreed. "Perhaps, after all, we'd better not marry."

"I wouldn't marry you on a bet. Agnes said last night she thought you had designs on me."

"Meaning what?"

"That you would try to make me stay here with you—sans ceremony. She said it was the result of me wearing these native clothes."

"I'll be glad to get rid of you—and your sister most of all."

We did not hear from Zejaya again, although I sent telegrams to every point I could reach in the district asking for information about him. We had either killed him, or he had gone back across the line into Mexico.

So, after they had been with me about three weeks, I told the girls I would take them up the road and see that they got burros and mozos to make the trip back to San Felipe Mission. They were not enthusiastic about riding burros again, but it was the only way out, as they could not board a steamer to go down to Champerico and go up by rail.

"Must we ride those little mules again?" Frances asked.

"You might walk," I said.

I took them up the road next morning on my gasoline car. At the little station where we had the fight, nothing would do Frances but to get out and examine the woodshed. A lot of dark stuff that might have been blood was scattered about, but there were no bones or other evidences of a fight.

We ate dinner at the estanca where I first met them, after I had arranged for mules and mozos to be ready early next morning.

"I'm rather sorry to see you go," I remarked as we sat at the table. "I'll miss you for a while."

"I believe if I stayed here another month I could vamp the terrible El Señor Diablo until he would eat out of my hand," Frances said.

"Frances!" her sister exclaimed. "Remember we are ministers of God and must show it by our actions and speech."

"And run when danger comes," I took pleasure in adding.

"You do not understand Agnes," Frances explained. "She was raised, you might say, in an atmosphere of religion. We were orphans and were reared by two different families. I lived with the family of a physician. Agnes was raised in a parsonage. Now you can understand the difference in our opin-ions about different things.

"Good bye, Señor Diablo. If you ever come up to the States look me up. You have my address."

I rode my little gasoline car down to Ocós. I missed the girls. Especially the meals Agnes had served.

25

Over the Next Hill

I HAD BEEN IN OCÓS nearly three years when three entirely unrelated things caused me to leave.

First, old Welmyer sent down a new resident manager.

He wasn't a German, but an Englishman, about 40 years old. He had a wife and three dusky children. His wife was a Mexican. With him came a young man, brother of the wife.

The Englishman, named Hylton, criticized everything I had done for the Ocós Railroad. I had spent too much money in rehabilitating the railroad and rolling stock, he asserted. He interfered with my management of the mechanical department of the road to such an extent that we almost came to blows.

An American hobo machinist came along and I put him to work at the usual ten dollars a day, Guatemalan money. Hylton protested, saying native wages were enough for any working man. At that time we were paying natives fifty cents a day, but they were poorly skilled.

This American stayed for two weeks and I told Hylton to pay him the ten dollars a day or I'd have my men throw both him and his brother-in-law to the sharks. Hylton paid.

Hylton's brother-in-law wanted a job in the shops. As he had no skill I gave him a job sweeping out and helping the laborers. He protested doing this sort of work and I had him kicked out.

I soon realized I could never get along with the new resident manager. He lost face, too, when he decided to go up alone after the money that was to be shipped up to Frisco by the finca owners.

Evidently those German finca owners did not like him or did not trust him, for they made excuses and put off sending the money until about time for another steamer, when I went up with him. I signed the receipts for the gold that time.

Second, the trouble I was experiencing from the capital.

The republic demanded and collected one dollar in gold from the coffee fincas for every quintal of coffee shipped. (A quintal is a Guatamala standard of about 225 pounds.) I collected and remitted everything above what I used for port expenses.

The former comandante, Daraga, had allowed certain finca owners to get by with paying only a portion of the money due. I collected every dollar and accounted for it. I collected money due from former years. Just after the earthquake and eruption of Santa Maria many of the finca owners were in bad shape financially. They gave notes of hand to Daraga against future shipments. I collected what was due on all those notes by a dint of persuasion and cajolery.

Those finca owners weren't dishonest. They merely put off paying the government as long as possible. I collected all those back export taxes and did it in a way that none got angry with me or sore at the government.

In fact, every one of those finca owners remained friends of mine to the last. All the time I ferried their gold down to the steamers my receipt was as good as the gold.

But the politicians at the capital didn't like my way of running the port. Several army officers and a number of government officials were sent down from time to time to check on me. Every one of them made a favorable report with the exception of one.

This fellow took a delight in criticizing all my actions. He even went so far as to hint that I had murdered the German resident manager who disappeared.

When I could stand it no longer I furnished him a train up to Pajipite and told him if he ever came into my district again I would have his ears cut off. He made a very bad report of my office when he got back to the capital. He asserted that I ought to be shot for threatening his ears.

Third, I got tropical fever.

So did many of the natives. I shipped the natives who came down with the fever up the road nearly to the frost line where the fever would freeze out of them, but I had to stay at the port.

I hadn't anticipated getting the fever, for I drank as much as ever. I had no quinine, which a white man should take in such a place. I could eat little or nothing.

Every night I tossed with a fever. I would go out of my head, so to speak, and wander around the port until the mozos caught me and brought me back to my bed.

I became so weak I could hardly walk the quarter mile separating the shops from the comandancia. I didn't have the energy of a petrified snail. At times I felt so badly I seriously considered jumping into the bayou and letting the sharks finish me.

I sent numerous telegrams to President Cabrera begging him to remove me so that I could go to my own country to die. I didn't bother notifying Welmyer. I left that up to Hylton.

Hylton and his family got the fever, also, and he moved up to the slope of Santa Maria, where he established temporary headquarters.

I suffered for more than two months. Many of the port inhabitants died, regardless of what I could do for them. I laid the epidemic to a visit of some Salvadorians whom I hired for a week or so while two coffee steamers were loading. They had carried the fever into the port, I thought, because three of them died there before any of my people became ill.

One day we made a smoke and stopped a northbound Pacific Mail steamer, and I went out to see if I could see the ship's doctor and get some medicine. The captain called down from the deck and ordered me to keep clear of the vessel, for if I came aboard they would be quarantined at San Francisco.

I knew then that word had gone up and down the coast that fever raged at Ocós. The little port was poison.

Finally a new comandante came in. I sent a train up for him. He rode down and we checked the office. Next morning I left Ocós.

26

Kissing the Brides

PRESIDENT CABRERA HAD SENT me a letter by the new comandante telling me my commission as colonel was to be made permanent, although, according to law, I had been removed from my post at Ocós. He suggested I come to Guatemala City to recuperate. If I didn't care to do that, the letter stated, he would like for me to keep him informed of my whereabouts. I didn't want to go to Guatemala City. There were other places I hadn't visited. I would go somewhere else.

One of my trains took me to Limones. Almost all the inhabitants of the port went with me to see me off, and they were hours bidding me goodbye. Finally, about noon, a boatman took me across the river and I started to Tapachula on foot. I could walk a quarter mile and then have to rest. Several times, when I sat down to rest I fell asleep for an hour or so.

I was El Señor Diablo no longer. I was not the commander of the port. I was no longer master mechanic of the Ferro Carril de Ocós. Now I was simply another American hobo, fever-stricken, palsied, short-winded. It would not be long, I knew, if I lived, until I would again be wearing a thousand-mile shirt, eating in hobo jungles, riding freight trains, wondering where my next meal was coming from, but knowing I had the ingenuity to get that meal.

I was not homesick for Ocós, but I knew I would miss my Indian friends there. I had grown to like the stolid, copper-colored people of the port, and I knew they liked me. I had tried to be a sort of father to them and I think I succeeded. Every person living in Ocós and along the railroad was my friend.

It was nearly sunset when I met two Mexican rurales who rode up and halted me. They dismounted and we sat in the shade of a tree and talked.

I told them about the fever in Ocós and about my anxiety to get to Tapa-chula where I could get medical attention. I was carrying a bundle and they asked me what was in it. Clothes, I told them, and they did not search it. I had a bottle of aguardiente and we took a drink together.

They rode on, after instructing me about the road. There was one road, they said, that apparently went to Tapachula, but didn't. If I took that one, they said, I would eventually come to Tuxtla Guiterrez, where I didn't want to go. I must be sure, they said, to take the other road, which would lead me to Tapachula.

One of them asked me if I knew El Señor Diablo who lived in Ocós and of whom they had heard many tales. I told them El Señor Diablo had vanished. No one would ever see or hear from him again.

Those rurales were nice fellows. I had heard hoboes speak of the brutal-ity of Mexican rurales, but the two I met were gentlemanly and polite. We wished each other many kinds of good luck when we parted.

I think a man can make a stranger a friend or enemy by the manner in which he approaches him. If you laugh and treat the stranger like a friend he usually will reciprocate. If you are hunting trouble and are pugnacious you will be accommodated.

I spent the night under a great tree whose branches furnished shelter from the rain if any came. I was still feverish and dreamed I was back in the states. One time I woke when I heard my sister call me to breakfast. I rubbed my eyes and looked around. Then I remembered that my sister and her husband had been living in Galveston when the great flood came, and were never heard from again.

Came daylight and I walked on.

If one takes a journey leisurely as I had to do, it gives one a chance to meet interesting persons he would not meet otherwise. I walked half a mile or so and then rested. Soon after sunup I had walked a little and then rested my back against a tree. An old man and a young woman came along and I said the usual "Buenos días."

They stopped and chatted awhile. They were father and daughter and were going nearly to the Guatemalan line to seek some herbs said to grow there. I was ill? Could I manage to get to the next village or should they help me? I thanked them and we parted.

Later in the morning while I was sitting on a stone in the shade of a tree two men rode up. They were dressed in the Mexican best—sombreros, tight trousers, decorated short coats and all that. They stopped and asked about my health.

So I was suffering from fever? It was too bad. Could they do anything for me? Would a peso help me on the road?

I told them I was well supplied with money, and I was traveling very slowly as befitted my weak condition. They were on their way to Tuxtla Guiterez, they said, as they bid me goodbye.

A herdsman caught up with me. He was driving three cows. Not being in a hurry he sat and rested with me for the greater part of an hour. I still had the remains of a garafone of aguardiente, which we drank. From his saddle-bags he brought a few tortillas and a couple of pieces of dried meat and we ate and drank and parted with many protestations of friendship. He told me of a village about three miles distant, a little off the main road, where I could get accommodations for the night. He was going by there, he said, and would tell an old woman friend of his, who lived in the second house to the right as I entered the village to prepare something for me.

I slept in that village that night and the old woman let me sleep in a hammock in the back yard of the house. In the morning she cooked two eggs for me and refused the money I offered her, telling me she had a letter from her son who was working on a railroad up in the states and made $1.15 American money every day, and had two pairs of shoes with soles on them. So I left a Mexican dollar on her table when she wasn't watching.

All that day I walked and rested, walked and rested. Later in the day a young man riding a horse caught up with me and slowed the pace of his horse to my walk while we talked. He offered to take my bundle to the next village and leave it with the jefe politico, an official something like a mayor in the United States.

I felt so tired and worn out that I let him take it. He was out of sight before I remembered that my money was in the very center of the bundle. Perhaps, I began to fear, I would never see it again. But when I reached the village and asked the jefe politico about the bundle he gave it to me. The young fellow had been as good as his word.

A few incidents like this has led me to believe an old banker who told me that ninety-eight percent of the people were honest, and he never did business with the other two percent.

At sundown the next day I reached a little village in which a celebration was being held. I drank with the men in the estanca and joined the crowd on the plaza. There I learned the celebration was because of a number of weddings being performed. It appeared there was no resident priest there, so when the priest came through a wholesale wedding was celebrated.

After the ceremonies there was a dance by music furnished by two men on a homemade marimba and all the single men took turns dancing with the brides. After each dance the single man dancing with the bride would drop a coin into a little sack each bride wore on a ribbon suspended from her neck by a ribbon.

I could not dance, so I merely kissed each bride and dropped in a coin. This action of mine caused much merriment as it was not the custom to kiss brides.

After this was over I took the grooms over to the estanoa and treated them. To still any jealous feelings they might have felt I told them it was the custom in my country for men to kiss brides, always in the presence of the guests.

I also told them how lucky they were in getting such beautiful and healthy-looking brides. Instead of being jealous they invited me to their homes and told me their homes were mine as long as wished to stay. But I did not accept any invitations.

I slept that night on a scaffold which was used for drying beef, vegetables and what have you. It was high enough off the ground so that prowling animals could not get at me.

With the coming of dawn a drove of little black monkeys, each about the size of a kitten, invaded my sleeping place. They climbed all over me. They would sit and chatter a quarrelsome chorus at me, run across my body, pull at my hair. I tried to shoo them away but they wouldn't shoo.

Finally I had to get up. As none of the villagers were awake, I walked on without saying farewell. The monkey family followed me for nearly a mile, swinging from limb to limb on the trees above the trail.

Three days later I reached Tapachula, Mexico.

27

Information About Corsets

TAPACHULA WAS AND IS, quite a city. It had an ice plant, operated by a surly American who became friendly after he learned that I was paying my way and not panhandling. He was a lonely bachelor in a country filled with comely young women.

If a man wanted a wife from the lower classes all he had to do was to make certain financial arrangements with her parents. If he wanted a wife from the higher classes he had to court her in the presence of all her relatives, for a while and then make the financial arrangements. As the ice plant owner was from Alabama, he classed all dark-skinned women as Negroes and would have nothing to do with them. He became real friendly with me.

"Go and get you a coupla dozen bottles of beer," he said. "I'll put them on ice and you can come down any time and drink them, real cold."

But I didn't care much for beer when I could find something else to drink. It always seemed to be a sort of belly-wash, in my opinion.

The Japanese-Russian War was on then, and a little daily newspaper in Tapachula, El Sud de Mexico, featured big headlines on the front page. The paper was all of four pages, four columns to the page, and sort of freakish. Sometimes half a column would be perfectly blank.

I wandered into the office. Two or three men were setting type out of cases, among them a man who introduced himself as owner, the others as his son, and two more as sons-in-law. Right there in the middle of the office was a perfectly new Canadian linotype.

"Why do you set type by hand when you have a linotype?" I inquired, after introductions.

"Something is wrong with the machine and we know nothing about it," the owner explained.

"Care if I look it over?" I asked. "I'll be in Tapachula a while. I used to know all about those machines."

"If the señor wishes. I have made but one payment on the machine and will not make others if it is to stand idle just for us to stumble over."

I was weak with fever, but I looked over the machine, made a few adjustments, had one of the men clean the coal oil burner and turned the machine over by hand.

By then it was siesta time and I went back to the hotel where I had stopped the night before, lay down, and slept a few hours.

All the guests in that Tapachula hotel slept on the second floor, men, women and children. There were no partitions, but partitions were not needed as there were no lights up there. To secure more privacy I took my cot out through a hole and slept on the roof the first and second nights I was there. There was more fresh air up there and not so many snores.

The next morning I went back to the newspaper office, put on the power, lit the oil burner and tried the machine out. Before noon I had it working perfectly.

After I got it working I asked if anyone there could operate it. Everyone could, I was told, as long as the machine functioned. Even the old man who cleaned up about the office had learned to operate a little. The barber next door, and the policeman who loafed around the plaza could do a little on the keyboard. That was what had put the machine out of order. Too many amateurs had tried to operate the machine.

I refused to take pay for my work and next day the owner insisted that I make his home my home while I was in the city. I accepted his invitation, and found a nice family group, and a good many members of it. It is the habit of married children in Mexico to continue to live with parents if they wish.

In the family and living in one house were the owner and his wife, the two older daughters and their husbands, and four younger daughters who were not married, the youngest being about seven and the eldest about seventeen or eighteen. There also was an infant, a grandchild of the old couple.

It took a lot of food to feed such a mob, but everyone appeared to be happy and living well, especially after I had fixed the linotype which made it easy to get the paper out.

Each day the paper received 100 words over the government telegraph line about the war in Russia. These 100 words were skeletonized so that, with true Yankee ingenuity, the owner could fill the front page of the paper with war news, occasionally using his imagination for details that were not in the 100 words.

Usually, when a foreigner enters a Mexican home of the middle or upper class the women of the house treat the guest as a stranger and never become familiar with him, regardless of how intimate he may be with the head of the house.

But in this home it was different. I was a man of the same trade as their father and husbands. I was a member of the linotype clan. So the women treated me as one of the family right away.

The mother gave me a drink of something very bitter which she had made herself and which, she said, would strengthen me and prevent recurrent periods of the fever. She never let me forget to take a dose before every meal while I remained in her home. I told her an army doctor had given me only a short time to live, anyhow, so why take medicine? But she lectured me as she would one of her daughters and I took the bitter dose before each meal.

After dinner the first evening, the unmarried daughter brought out copies of several American and Canadian magazines and proceeded to question me about the advertisements therein—especially those advertising corsets. All the women gathered around while I tried to explain the uses of the garment.

Pictured in one advertisement was a woman with a very slim waist, with nothing much on but the corset. The women compared their waists with that of the woman pictured and began questioning me.

"Did they start using corsets when they were very young so they could have slim waists when they grew older?"

"How did they get them on?"

"Did it require the services of another person to get one on and buckled tightly?"

"How long would a corset last, if it were used all the time?"

"Could a girl run with a corset on?"

"Could one corset be purchased and used by several members of the family?"

"Was it worn while the wearer slept?"

"Was it uncomfortable when wearing a corset to sit down or recline on a cot?"

"How could one scratch if a flea happened to get under the corset?"

I could answer several of the questions but not all of them. I was rather girl-shy and therefore did not know how a corset was put on. In fact, I had never seen a corset on a woman. I had observed them, casually, in show windows.

Girls may have worn them while they slept, but I was uncertain about it. I was not sure how long a corset would last, and I didn't know whether one was uncomfortable while its wearer was sitting or reclining. In fact what I didn't know about corsets would have filled a large book.

Several of the women commented in undertones about how strange it was that I knew so little about corsets when I knew so much about a linotype.

I stayed with those folks three weeks, during which time I instructed the men in the mechanical mysteries of the linotype and answered hundreds of questions about corsets and other articles of feminine apparel worn by the women in the great country above the Rio Grande.

Then, with the good wishes of all the family, I walked north. I was bound for Tonala, the southern end of the Pan-American Railroad.

I had intended leaving at dawn, but I had to bid goodbye to each member of the family. After I got to the plaza I had to take a drink with the barber next door to the print shop, the policeman, and several other acquaintances I had made during my stay there. At length, about ten o'clock, after it had become good and hot, I got off. Then there happened to be a man with an ox cart who was going a few miles in my direction and he insisted in giving me a ride as far as he went.

Almost every family in that portion of the Mexican republic owned a Singer sewing machine—one of those little ones turned by hand, which could be fastened to a table. There was a Singer agency in Tapachula and from this agency I purchased a lot of small supplies—needles and the like.

I purchased a little horse for $20 Mex, so small that I could extend my arm and it could walk under it. It was a good little creature. I named it Billy and that name stuck for a day or two until I found I had the wrong gender. After that her name was Adoline.

28

Snakes

I HAD A LITTLE MORE than twelve hundred silver dollars, having changed my Guatemalan silver into the Mexican peso at the rate of five to one. I had some German gold and did not change it, as it was par anywhere. All this money was quite heavy so I put it in a sack and Adoline carried the sack, the metal being divided into equal parts, half in one end of the sack and half in the other. In addition to this she carried what few clothes I had, my Guatemalan colonel's uniform and a few private papers.

From Tapachula to Tonala there was a reasonably good trail, over which hung the government telegraph wire, hung on trees and occasionally on poles where there were no trees.

There was a village every few miles and I made it a routine when I reached one, to go to the intendencia, sometimes in a real building, sometimes in a grass or adobe hut, tell the jefe politico my business, which was repairing sewing machines, and ask permission to stay all night in his village. I wasn't compelled to ask his permission, but it made him feel important to think that I would do so. Then I would throw my money sack into one corner of the room, out of the way, and go about my business, which was buying food for myself and Adoline.

The intendente's wife usually needed a needle or two. Others would come around to buy a needle or to get me to make some little repair. My money lay undisturbed. I didn't worry about its safety. Those people, poor as any on earth, were honest.

To be more exact, they were poor only from the standpoint of a person from the United States and accustomed to our standard of living. They had plenty of food. They didn't need many clothes. They farmed a little, raised a few horses, and some raised goats. They could raise and gather two crops of corn or beans a year. They had all they wanted, but they seldom saw a dollar and were not at all envious of me, a Gringo with a sack of pesos.

No one could eat pesos, they argued. Now if a man had a thousand goats he would be rich. The goats would furnish a lot of milk and could be butchered for meat. But after all, one intendente told me, if a man had even a hundred goats he could not dispose of that much milk and he would have too many to butcher, which was a laborious task. So why have that many goats to look after? This comandante had eight, with three more coming at foaling time, so why want more?

I met with two adventures on this trip.

The first was late one afternoon when I was following a sort of trail through a swamp. The trail was but a path of water through the jungle. Adoline was leading the way and she stopped suddenly—so abruptly, in fact, that I almost fell over her.

When Adoline stopped suddenly that way I knew something was radically wrong. Her usual technique for stopping was to gradually reduce speed until there was absolutely no forward movement.

I looked ahead and saw there was a huge snake hanging across the path. It was in the trees about eight feet from the ground, its head on one side of the trail and its tail on the other. I could see neither the head nor the tail, however.

It was about an hour before sunset and I didn't want to spend the night in the swampy jungle. But Adoline was afraid to pass under the snake. So was I.

I hunted around, got some sticks and threw them at the snake. For a time it did not move, but finally, after I had thrown sticks for half an hour or so and was about to give up and go back, it slowly drew its body back into the trees at one side of the path.

It backed up, because when its head appeared over the trail it swung it back and forth as if trying to see where the missiles were coming from.

Adoline stood her ground and so did I. After the head had disappeared I waited a while and then pushed Adoline to get her started. She moved a few feet, but was fearful. I got in front of her, made a run for it and passed the spot at top speed where the snake had been. Then I turned to call Adoline. But I saw her coming, plodding along at her usual gait, about a mile an hour.

She passed the spot where the snake had been without looking right or left. She evidently had forgotten all about the reptile and was intent on following her master, as it was getting along toward feeding time.

I learned that night from a villager that those big snakes were absolutely harmless, having no poison glands. They live on birds and insects.

The other adventure was three or four days after the big snake scare. With Adoline, I had started from a village just before sunup. The trail led through a large prairie, and it was just a narrow path beaten down below the grass surface by barefoot natives.

I had heard of the ratita, a venomous little black and yellow snake that made its home on Southern Mexican and Central American prairies. Its bite or stings, according to the stories I had heard, would cause certain death after the victim's body had swollen to more than twice its usual size. But I wasn't thinking of it that morning until I felt a sharp sting on my right ankle.

I had made almost all of that trip barefoot as I had only one pair of shoes and shoes like Americans wear cannot be purchased in Southern Mexico, or couldn't then. I wanted to save my shoes for the time when I reached the end of the railroad and met other foreigners. Natives wear zapatos, a sort of sandal.

I felt the sting and looked down at my bare ankle. A small red round spot showed, in the center of which was a smaller round white spot. Then I happened to remember what I had heard about the ratita.

I had been bitten and would die. I walked on until I came to a big rock at the side of the trail. I sat on that, got out paper and pencil and began to write my name, age, nationality and other particulars. I made a sort of will, leaving my money for the benefit of Adoline, to whom I had become attached.

29

Adoline Finds a Home

AS I WROTE, I COULD FEEL myself beginning to swell. I really could detect a slight enlargement of my legs, bare below the knees. I could feel my body gradually swelling. Instead of feeling fear I wondered just how I'd look after I had swelled. All my life I had ranged in weight from 140 to 150, and being six feet tall such weight made me slim. If I swelled to double my usual size I would look like some of the big men I had envied.

A native came along, carrying a big bundle on a tump strap. I hailed him.

"I am in trouble, señor," I called. "I have been bitten by a ratita."

"Then, of course you will die, after you swell up like a dead horse," he said, not much interested.

"Have you ever seen a ratita bite?" I asked.

"No, señor," he replied. "But why worry? If you die this year you will not have to die next year. We all must die."

"Look at this," I invited, extending my foot.

He took my foot in his hands, peered at it closely, and then reached with the nails of a thumb and forefinger and plucked something from the center of the red spot, which had now grown to the size of a dollar.

"It is not the sting of the ratita, señor," he said. "It is but a grass thorn. You may not die yet."

I was so relieved I could say nothing for a few moments. The native put his tump strap in place and was leaving when I called him back.

"Here, señor. Take this and drink to my health at the next cantina." I held out a dollar.

He shook his head.

"It is not for me to have a whole peso," he explained. "I would be imprisoned for robbing someone if I showed so much money. Now if the señor has some small coins..."

I gave him all the small coins I had, more than a dollar's worth. I pushed Adoline to get her started.

I was happy. Half an hour later I looked down at my ankle. The spot and the swelling were gone. I tore up my will making Adoline my heir.

A healthy man could have walked from Tapachula to Tonala in a week. I made it in thirty-one days. Adoline rested when she got tired and happened to find a spot of grass she liked. Sometimes I had to push her several times to get her started if the sun was hot and we happened to stop under the shade of a tree. Nights I slept in a hammock I had purchased, and she would stand with her head over me and sleep, too.

One portion of the journey took me across a level prairie for half a day. Little wild animals I took to be antelope came right up to us and investigated. One got behind Adoline and licked her rump. She let go with her hind legs and kicked the animal. After that they kept their distance, but followed us for several miles.

I ate at little villages along the trail. Baked iguana is good and tastes something like breast of chicken. Iguana is a large lizard which sometimes grows to a length of three or four feet. The smaller ones are the best for eating, a native woman informed me, as the meat of the older ones gets tough with age.

Beans and tortillas and corn cakes were the universal food, however. There were no hotels in the little villages and one made a round of the houses to find one which served meals. A meal might cost from a centavo (cent) to twenty-five cents. In many instances, where the native was sociable, there would be no charge. In such a case I gave the children a few centavos.

The journey was slowly killing the fever in me. I slept well, the sleep of a man physically weary. I was out of the mosquito zone and that helped. Then I gave some credit for my recovery to the bitter medicine the newspaper owner's wife in Tapachula had given me. As I was leaving she gave me a bottle of the stuff, but I threw it away as soon as I got out of town.

So I reached Tonala. I surely was glad to see the railroad yards, the roundhouse, the locomotives. I went to the restaurant operated by a Chinaman for supper. There I got the first piece of pie since leaving New York!

The railroad men were almost all from the Union Pacific and were good fellows. Several of them had their families with them.

After supper I walked down through the yards and noticed a locomotive with a set of the new-fangled valve gears, a gear that caused a great deal of speculation when they were first introduced into this country. Two men were standing near the engine.

"When did you get the Walschaert valve gear away down here in Mexico?" I asked as I went nearer to examine the layout.

"Have you ever worked this monkey motion?" one of the men asked.

"No. But in my luggage I've got a book of instructions on it."

"Want to sell the book?"

"I don't think so. Having trouble?"

"A little."

"I'll go get the book and see what's wrong," I said.

I went over to the Chinaman's and dug into my things for the book. Adoline, waking after a hearty meal, followed me back to the engine.

"What's that?" one of the man asked with a laugh.

"Looks like a new kind of rabbit," the other remarked.

"That's Adoline," I explained. "Just now she's causing me a lot of thinking. Now that I'm going on up by rail I don't know what to do with her. If I can't get someone to take her and treat her right, I'm going to kill her, painlessly. I don't want her mistreated. She's a friendly little animal."

"Say," one of the men exclaimed. "I've got two kids, six and eight, that'll make a pet of that little hoss. Want to sell her?"

"No. But if you have time we'll go and see how the children like her."

Adoline had found a home. Early next morning I walked over to where the children lived. One of them was on her back, while the other led her around by carrying a panful of cornmeal mush.

"Why don't you both ride?" I asked.

"We tried to," the oldest child replied, "but she wouldn't move. She just went back to sleep."

"Get on," I told her, "and I'll show you how to move her."

With both children on her back, Adoline went to sleep without moving. I got behind and pushed. She started and gave the children a ride. The parents came out and after the children had ridden for a while I was invited in for breakfast with the family.

"We should pay you something for that little horse," the mother suggested.

"Take care of her and she belongs to the children," I said.

"How are you fixed for money?" the engineer asked.

"I've got more than twelve hundred dollars, Mex," I replied.

"And you're going to carry it on up?" he asked again.

"I suppose so."

"Don't do it. From here on up there's lots of men—mostly Americans—who would kill a man for ten dollars. Where is your money now?"

"The Chinaman at the restaurant is keeping it for me."

"He represents a bank in the City of Mexico. He'll sell you a draft and you can carry that safely."

"Draft any good?"

"Good as gold. You can trust a Chinaman in a legitimate business transaction. Most of us railroad men here buy drafts from him and mail them up to that bank."

The Chinaman charged me $11 for that draft. And what a draft it was. Just a big slip of red paper with hieroglyphics painted on it. The Chinaman looked me over critically while he did the painting.

"This draft will be good in the city?" I inquired. "Will they know it is me without my signing this draft?"

"Him good. You get money."

"How about identification?"

"Nobody get money but you. They know you is you when you show paper. Paper tell what you look like."

I had kept out enough to do me to the City of Mexico, and I pocketed the red piece of paper.

About ten o'clock I walked over to see how Adoline and the children were getting along together. The children were asleep on cots swung between trees, close together. Adoline was standing between the cots, asleep. I did not disturb them.

30

More Trouble

THE TRAIN LEFT ABOUT eleven o'clock. All the way up I rode the locomotive and at stops the engineer and I studied and adjusted the new Walschaert valve gear until, by the time we reached San Geronimo, we had the engine "cutting steam" perfectly, which meant less fuel and more power.

"Want to sell this book?" the engineer asked as we coasted to a stop at San Geronimo.

"Keep it," I told him. "I can get another one. You can't."

At supper that night my money was counterfeit as far as spending it was concerned. We slept in the passenger coach that night. After breakfast next morning the conductor said, "I've wired headquarters of the Tehuantepec Railroad for a pass for you, as a railroad man seeking employment. The agent of the Tehuantepec will give it to you when it comes."

That afternoon the agent handed me a telegraphic pass without starting point or destination on it. So I could use it anywhere on the road.

I got as far as Rincon Antonio that night. It was the division point between the Atlantic and Pacific terminals. In the railroad restaurant that night the third-trick train dispatcher told me he would like to go across the country to where it was said there was good fishing, and would I work for him a few days? His shift was from midnight to eight o'clock in the morning and there were few trains to handle. So after a session with the superintendent during which he tested my knowledge of handling trains, I took the job.

I had kept out enough money to do me to the City of Mexico, but during the five days I worked for the dispatcher I had to pay for meals, although I slept in a vacant caboose. So when my regular returned and I was released I was broke.

Getting paid for a few days' work on a railroad is a slow task, involving a lot of red tape. I waited two days and then got sore about the matter. I went up to the judge of the district, an old, very polite Mexican, and old him my troubles.

"In Mexico the laws provides that a worker's wages are due when the sun goes down," he said.

I knew that, but it hadn't been applied to the railroad, so far as I knew. I thought the old man would expedite payment, but I was not prepared for what he really did.

The judge sent a few soldiers down to the superintendent's headquarters and arrested him, took him before the judge, who said, "The law of Mexico provides that a worker's pay is due when the sun goes down. You did not pay this man when the sun went down. The soldiers will take you to jail until this man is paid up to sunset tonight."

They hauled the superintendent off to jail.

This wasn't what I wanted at all. It was not the fault of the super, but the red tape in the general office in the City of Mexico.

I went around among the railroad men in Rincon Antonio and told them the facts. Finally the man who operated the restaurant at which the railroad men took meals furnished the money I was paid and the superintendent released. The judge charged me fifty cents for court costs. I could have made the super pay the court costs, but I had already gotten him into enough trouble.

I still had my pass, but it was unnecessary. Railroad men carried railroad men without passes or money.

I changed railroads at Santa Lucretia, took the Vera Cruz & Pacifico to Vera Cruz where I ate the traditional fish head at eleven o'clock one morning. Everyone in Vera Cruz eats a fish head at eleven o'clock. It is a sort of tradition down there. After eating one I found I could do without fish heads for a long time to come. I inquired, but no one could tell me what they did with the rest of the fish.

My money gave out at Puebla, one freight division out of the City of Mexico. My father had at one time been superintendent of that railroad, the narrow-gage, but the labor turnover had eliminated everyone who had been there in his time.

I got into conversation with a Mexican the night I reached Puebla. He had interests in and around Tapachula. We conversed about that city and he took me to dinner.

Early next morning a freight engineer permitted me to ride with him into the city. I reached there late at night, walked clear across the city from San Lacaro station to Buena Vista station, across from which is the Dos Republicas hotel.

The Dos Republicas hotel, I knew, was patronized by men from the United States exclusively—railroad men, oil men, mining men, and men who make an uncertain livelihood gambling or betting on the horses. I went in there, a rather pathetic figure, for I wore tropical clothes and looked seedy. I had not shaved for a week.

I explained to the bartender that I was temporarily broke, but had a draft on the Chinese bank that I couldn't get cashed until it opened in the morning. I even showed him the draft and asked if he would stake me to a room for the night. He listened to me and then let out a shout.

"Here's a new kind of panhandle, boys," he called out. "Here's a bum with a Chinese laundry ticket he says is worth eleven hundred dollars. What do you think of that?" And he laughed uproariously.

For half an hour or so those present made sport of me, although several of them included me when they set up drinks. But not one of them would lend me a dollar for a bed that night. I couldn't sleep outside, for it gets cold in the city after sunset.

Finally I walked to the door, held it open, turned and called, "Laugh now, you rats, you scabs, you skunks! I'll see you again when I'm on top of the world."

One or two of the men started toward me and I slammed the door and ran. I slept that night in the seat of a locomotive in the Mexican Central Railroad roundhouse.

Sometime in the night a peon engine wiper shared his poor lunch of tortillas and carne with me. Then the fever caught me and for several hours I lay in the seat of the locomotive, unconscious, delirious. It was daylight when I came to myself.

I walked slowly to the Zócalo, a huge park in the business portion of the city. It was cold outside, but the cold seemed to drive the fever from me. I sat on a bench in the park, waiting for nine o'clock, when the banks would open. I was very drowsy, but one can't sleep in a park in the City of Mexico. A policeman will run you out if you do.

I sat and watched the street cars pass. At that time the funerals in the city were conducted by street car. That is, the body and mourners were taken to the cemetery in specially equipped street cars. I watched several pass. I wondered if I would be carted out in one soon. Perhaps the doctor at Honolulu was right. Just then I felt as if I didn't care much if I lived or died. I heard the clock on the corner strike nine. I got up to go to the Chinese bank.

31

Fever—and on North

AS I WALKED TOWARD the bank I was beginning to get a little dubious about my piece of red paper, for I knew if payment was refused I would have no recourse. In the time of President Diaz a man who raised a fuss or created a scene in or near a financial institution was given short shrift. Diaz was for the big man and the hobo was tolerated only as long as he stayed out of sight and ran the railroads and did the mining.

I once stopped and was about to throw the red paper away and try going on up north on the bum, for I was not physically able to work. But I mustered up the courage to present the slip at one of the tellers' windows in the bank. The young man behind the window looked at the paper and motioned me to the next cage. The second teller looked me over closely.

"Your name?" he asked. I gave it.

"Why my name?" I asked. "It couldn't be on that piece of paper. Or is there a Chinese character representing the name of Kavanaugh?"

"No," the clerk said in perfect English, "but I wanted to determine if you were really the American who purchased this draft."

"And now you know?"

"Your hesitancy in pronouncing your name checks with the other facts given in your description written here." (I have a slight stutter in pronouncing certain words, among them my name.)

"How do you wish the money?" the teller asked.

"Give me two hundred dollars and keep the rest to my credit," I told him. "And when you communicate with your countryman down in Tonala, thank him for me."

It cost me about a hundred dollars to get dressed decently. I got a room at a native hotel and slept most of the day.

It gets very cold in the city after sunset, but after I had eaten I walked over to the Thieves' Market. There I spoke to several stand keepers and told them I would be at a certain entrance for a while. I knew enough of the lower-class lingo to assure the men I was not an officer.

I stood at the entrance I had mentioned for a few minutes and one after another young men came to me and introduced themselves. I told them to wait until I had ten men.

These young men were well dressed, shaved, and looked like young business men except that they inclined to the rather loud dress. In Chicago or Kansas City a few years ago they would have been known as torpedoes, or gunmen. Instead of a gun the Mexican torpedo carries a knife.

I gave each of them five dollars, which was good pay for what I had in mind. Walking down to the Dos Republicas Hotel I gave them instructions. On the way down I took them into a bar or two and treated. If a man happens to have conscientious scruples against doing something unlawful, they desert him when alcohol enters his stomach. Alcohol deadens conscientious scruples.

I had planned well. There were about a dozen Americans in the Dos Republicas barroom, and the same bartender was on duty. I bellied up to the bar.

Four of my torpedoes ranged themselves beside me. The others took their stations as I had instructed. The bartender came over to serve us. He did not recognize me right away.

"Give us some drinks," I called in English, and added, "and make it quick, you lousy rat. And see what those scabby friends of yours want. I'm paying for the drinks tonight. I'm paying for the drinks out of that Chinese laundry slip you laughed at last night. The drinks, pronto!"

Instead of serving the drinks the bartender edged over toward the telephone at one end of the bar. He never got near it. One of my torpedoes was standing right there, a smile on his face and a knife in his hand.

Several customers started for the door. My men were between them and the door, knives in their hands, smiling. The customers turned back to the bar.

"He's crazy as a loon," one of the men remarked. "Better serve him. He's got enough men here to murder all of us. I'll take a little whiskey."

Everyone drank and I paid for it all. My men quietly changed places so each of them could get a drink. My torpedoes were enjoying the drama or comedy. There was a fat man present, and I remembered he had been in the group the night before. One of my torpedoes said, loud enough for all to hear:

"I wonder if my knife is long enough to go through the fat on that man?"

I bought three rounds of drinks, all the time telling the Americans what I thought of them, their mothers, and other things. Then I gave the sign and the torpedo nearest the telephone cut the wires and we left. True to their instincts of self-preservation, my men backed out.

Those inside were afraid to come out and by the time they did my gang had scattered and I was well away from the place. I was down at the Mexican Central Railroad roundhouse. I hunted up the peon who had shared his lunch with me the night before and gave him a roll of ten-cent coins I had secured especially for him.

Then I walked down a side street and took a drink in every cantina I came across until I got so full I didn't remember anything.

I woke next morning in bed with a couple of children in a private home of the lower class. Someone must have put me to bed. I found I had little more than a dollar left and laid it on the floor as I crept out without waking anyone.

I was very sick for several days after that spree. When I had recovered enough to travel I asked the doctor about going up into the cold country.

"You made a mistake in coming up here in the first place," he said. "The altitude is too high. If you will take my advice you will go down to Vera Cruz and catch a boat for New Orleans. The ocean air, away from mosquitoes, will help you. Then stay in New Orleans for a while. After that it will be safe for you to go up as far as you wish."

"You think I'll croak, anyhow, eh, doctor?" We were speaking English. "The doctor in Honolulu said I would. Or do you know the meaning of the word croak?"

"I received a portion of my medical education in the United States," the doctor replied. "I am well up on American slang. You'll die when your time comes. You've abused yourself. No man in your state of health should drink alcoholic liquor. But do as I say about going north and there is hope for you."

Let me digress a little. That doctor, Señor Estevez, was killed at the same time President Madero of Mexico was murdered. When he treated me he was a young physician just starting practice in his profession. He served his internship in Johns Hopkins hospital in Baltimore, Maryland.

I secured a draft for the balance of my money from the Chinese bank. This time it was in the usual draft form, printed in English on a New Orleans bank. I thanked the clerk and the official who signed the draft after the clerk had filled it out.

I have dealt with the Chinese several times," I remarked to the official, "and find them far above my own countrymen in honesty."

"No country has a monopoly on honesty," the official said as he signed the draft.

I mailed the draft to myself in care of Dago Pete in New Orleans. He ran a cheap lodging house in Exchange Alley, just off Canal Street. I had never been there, but had heard a lot about him from other hoboes I had encountered. He would keep my mail until I called for it, even if it was months.

In connection with the lodging house he operated a sort of clearing house for skilled hoboes. When a firm in one of the Latin republics of Central America needed a man of a certain caliber it would send to Dago Pete. He usually could furnish the right kind of man.

One story told about Dago Pete may have some truth in it. For years it was told and retold around many a jungle fire:

One night a well-dressed man came into Dago Pete's place and walked up to the window where Pete sat. Pete was his own clerk and sat in a little wired cage having a small window. The newcomer asked, "Remember me, Pete?"

"Yes, You were here five years ago and you owe me forty cents."

"Those men you sent me out with were mining men away up on the Aroyo Railroad in South America. They had a good mine and we worked it intelligently. They had no money so I took my wages in a share of the mine. We had to work like hell and fight like hell to hold it after we got it producing.

"Last month we sold it to a syndicate for just three million good old American dollars, which we divided among the three of us. So I came in to pay you your forty cents."

The man flipped a bill across the opening and turned to leave.

"Just keep the change, Pete," he said. "You did me the greatest favor possible by sending me out with those two men."

The man left and Pete glanced at the bill. It was a thousand-dollar bill. Methodically he put it into his till, with a few dollar bills.

32

"Don't You Like Our Grub?"

AS SOON AS I MAILED my draft to New Orleans, I took a train down to Vera Cruz. The Munson line steamer wasn't due for several days, so I loafed around the city.

One day I fell into conversation with a man who proved to be second mate of a sailing vessel about to leave for Biloxi, Mississippi. The vessel had brought down a cargo of pine timber, sawed 12x12, to Panama and was going back for another cargo, picking up what freight it could at Gulf ports.

I went aboard and interviewed the captain. Yes, he said, he would take a passenger, but he wasn't sure when he would sail or when he'd reach Biloxi. He would charge me $20 for passage. While the ship was lying at Vera Cruz I could eat and sleep on board.

They set good meals on that ship. They filled their plates and ate huge meals. At the first meal on board I ate but little and the first mate noticed it. He flared up.

"Don't you like the kind of grub we serve?" he asked angrily.

The captain spoke before I could explain.

"The man's been sick," he told the mate. "Tropical fever."

"Come from the south?" the mate asked.

"Porto de Ocós, on the Pacific coast of Guatemala," I replied.

"I've sailed by there several times and heard about it," he said. "Helluva little hole."

"Helluva little hole," I agreed.

"You'll be all right after a week or two on a windjammer," he went on. "When you can eat as much as I can you'll be good as new."

"If you like anything in particular that we don't serve," the captain added, "tell the cookie. He's good."

We sailed three days later, having taken on a load of cocoanuts and other things that wouldn't spoil if the ship was delayed.

I had read stories of the brutality of hard-boiled sailing officers and feared what was to come. I had handled men myself and found it best never to use brutality. I never worked a man who disliked me when he quit, and I have never worked for a boss I couldn't go back and work for again if he needed men. So I waited, intending to go below and stay there if there happened to be fighting.

But on that trip I never heard a word spoken above the ordinary conversational tone. The mates and skipper were seamen, of course, and I think the men were, for they went about their duties without many orders being given. We were becalmed for a couple of days and the men put in time painting the ship, but they worked leisurely, singing and joking each other while they plied their brushes. They quit work in plenty of time to wash and clean up for meals.

There were no alcoholic liquors aboard and I missed my drinks. I happened to mention this fact to the first mate one day and he laughed. He had been checking up on my appetite each meal and figured the percentage of my health gain by the amount I ate.

"I don't claim we're prohibitionists here," he explained, "but we just don't stock liquors. I take a drink or so while ashore and that goes for the skipper and the second. No one would have objected had you brought a supply aboard. But we forget it while at sea."

"I've been accustomed to having my drinks in the tropics. They say drinking prevents fever."

"I know that," the mate said. "I sailed the Sierra Lone coast a year and it was either quinine or whiskey. We kept a supply of quinine aboard."

"I had no quinine," I told him.

"So you had to take native booze."

Early one morning a tug warped us up against a lumber pier at Biloxi and I caught an L&N train to New Orleans. The trip had helped me.

39

Scotching a Revolution

BEFORE NOON I WAS at Dago Pete's in Exchange Alley. He handed me my letter. I opened it and showed him the draft.

"Will you help me get this cashed?" I asked. "You are the only one here who knows me. I'll pay you well."

"The saloon at the corner of the Alley and Canal Street will cash it for you," he said. "I'll phone them right away."

Before nightfall I was a gentleman again. I rented a real nice room, the first one with private bath I ever occupied. I spent a lot of my time the first day or so just running the hot water and sitting in it. I gave Pete a dollar for his trouble. His rooms, about 4x6, with a cot, cost only fifteen cents a night. For the time being, I was above that sort of lodging.

I loafed. The fever was slowly going out of my system and I felt that death was far away.

I got in the habit of walking down the levee as far as Chalmette, where I found a saloon and restaurant operated by a French woman. She sat up good meals and I usually ate my midday meal there. Then, after a drink or two, I would walk slowly back to the city. The walking helped me gain strength.

Quite a number of foreigners ate and drank at the French woman's place. Gradually I began to make acquaintances. Several of the men spoke Spanish and I could speak it. After a time, after sizing me up from all angles and finding me just a harmless hobo, they confided in me.

Four of the men, I learned, had been sent up from Guatemala to purchase arms for a revolution they were going to pull against the government of President Cabrara. I listened to their talk for days. After they had hinted that if I had the nerve to face a term in a federal prison if I was caught, they could make a highly remunerative deal with me, I volunteered to help them.

I did not mention, however, that I was a colonel in the Guatemalan army and that President Cabrera was the best friend I ever had. The only thing I feared was that someone would show up who would recognize me as El Señor Diablo.

I was willing to take almost any risk to do a favor for President Cabrera.

It seems they had tried to purchase arms, and after they had bargained for two thousand rifles, the seller became frightened when Secret Service men came around asking questions—and the deal was off.

They had bargained with a ship master to take the arms down, but he got cold feet when a Secret Service officer visited his vessel a number of times.

They let the information slip out that the arms were to be paid for by a group of New York capitalists. These capitalists wanted a more pliant man in the president's chair in Guatemala so the group could secure juicy franchises in the republic.

Cabrera was stubborn when it came to selling franchises. He was the only president in all the Central American republics at that time who never maintained a bank account in Paris, London, or New York against the time he would be compelled to flee his country. He preferred his country to be a little backward rather than give it to foreign capitalists to exploit.

I suggested a plan by which the guns could be gotten away from New Orleans and into Guatemala. I would buy them piecemeal, I elaborated, in small lots, and bill them as pick handles. Ship them to Livingstone, where little attention was paid to what was unloaded there, and then on inland. Or bill them to Panzos. The latter billing would require the boxes to be unloaded at Livingstone and shipped by boat to Panzos. The boat could be detoured and never get to Panzos.

We talked the plan over. A man came down from New York and we held conferences with him. To make my plan a success, I declared, I would have to have cash money. I would deal in no checks or drafts or anything that could be traced. Teddy Roosevelt was president at that time and he would bear down hard on anyone attempting to unseat another president in the Western Hemisphere by force of arms.

Then came a week of frantic telegraphing between the parties in New York and those in New Orleans. Finally the whole plan was passed over to me, with an American from New York and a man from Guatemala sticking around to see that I didn't decamp with the money.

I hired a warehouse and bought ten guns. They met the requirements of the men watching me. Then I bought a lot of boxes in which to pack guns. Each box was labeled as containing twenty-four pick handles. I had a special stencil made for that purpose.

The second or third day at the warehouse a man with a star on his coat stopped the American and began asking questions. The American ran. Half an hour or so later the same thing happened to the Guatemalan.

After that I ran the scheme alone. To tell the truth, I had contacted the Guatemalan consul and between us we had put up a job on the revolutionists.

The officers who kept watch on the warehouse were men hired from a private detective agency and had no police powers at all. But the revolutionists were afraid of a long term in Leavenworth.

The firm of J. B. Camors & Company was astonished when I ordered enough pick handles to build all the railroads in the world. But they got them and I boxed them. When all was ready, I shipped them to Morgan City, Louisiana, west of New Orleans. A vessel chartered by the man from New York was waiting below that port.

The loading was tedious. Men with stars on their coats lingered around Morgan City as they had New Orleans. So I had to attend to every detail myself.

A number of oyster luggers operate out of Morgan City. They go down Berwick Bay to the oyster beds empty and return loaded. I hired the oyster luggers to take my pick handles down to the steamer waiting near a lighthouse near where Berwick Bay empties into the Gulf of Mexico.

Finally every box of pick handles was stowed in the hold of the chartered steamer. Then I told the skipper to get going before he got into trouble.

I made it back to New Orleans with the captain's receipt for so many boxes of pick handles to be delivered at Port Livingstone.

No one on earth would want to ship pick handles to Guatemala. They could be had out there for about four cents each, and are. But the captain of the chartered steamer might not have known that. Anyhow, the last I saw of that steamer was when it was heading out into the Gulf.

According to my figures, I had bought, boxed and shipped two thousand Remington rifles and a lot of ammunition at a cost of a little more than $35,000. I had received cash and had paid cash for everything I purchased. The real figures, if I had revealed them, would have disclosed the fact that I had bought a lot of pick handles and boxes which cost me about $2,000.

When I had paid the Guatemalan consul a little and settled my hotel bill, I had a balance of almost $20,000. In addition to that, I had saved my friend, President Cabrera, a lot of trouble.

With a draft in my pocket for all that money I faded away from New Orleans. I had to fade away to keep healthy.

34

Discover a Singer

I KNEW IT WOULD not be healthy for me to remain in New Orleans after that shipment was delivered and the revolutionists had found out I faked them. Once the deception was discovered I would be a marked man and would either die of lead poisoning via a bullet, or maybe by a knife in my guts. So I left New Orleans and left no forwarding address.

I found satisfaction in the fact that I had done a favor for my friend, El Señor Don Emanuel Cabrera, president of Guatemala. I wrote him, detailing all the facts in the case, and mailed the letter at some station between New Orleans and Memphis.

I had more money than I knew what to do with. A hobo doesn't value money like a home guard does. With all that money I was no happier than when I had none. My greatest thrill was in the thought that I had scotched a revolution and gotten a lot of money from New York capitalists, who would have used their power to scrape the Republic of Guatemala clean of its resources if they had succeeded in deposing Cabrera and installing a president who would do their bidding.

I didn't know what to do with my money. I couldn't possibly eat 20,000 steaks. I needed an overcoat, which might cost thirty dollars, but I didn't need 1,500 overcoats. If I took fifty drinks and day and ate ten times a day I would only kill myself and there would still be some of the money left. Since I had reached the United States, I had almost ceased drinking at all. Probably the dry spell on the sailing steamer had cured me of the habit. After a time I dismissed the subject of what to do with the money and went to sleep in the Pullman bound for Chicago.

Winter was coming on and the cold air in the north would drive away the remaining effects of the tropic fever. The first thing I did when I got to Chicago was to purchase the heaviest overcoat I could find. After that I deposited my draft for $18,000 in a bank.

It's surprising how friendly the employees of a bank become when a man deposits $18,000 in one lump. The teller at the window where I made the deposit left his cage for a moment and spoke to a man outside the railing. After my deposit was cinched a uniformed officer touched me on the shoulder and told me Mr. Something-or-Other would like to make my acquaintance. I wondered if I was in for trouble over my activities in New Orleans. I remembered those New York capitalists might be linked with the Chicago bank. But it was too late to get out now. I determined to bluff it out, come what might.

I went back to the big man's desk and talked a few minutes. He was interested in Central America to a certain extent, but he was more interested in selling me some stocks and bonds.

"Teddy Roosevelt will be elected this fall," he said, "and things will hum in a business way. Ten thousand dollars invested in copper right now will almost double in ten years."

I thanked him, but did not bite. I'd prefer to spend the money otherwise. If I thought I was going to die anyhow I'd try to eat and drink all I could and leave the rest to some home for dogs. I've always liked dogs.

I put up at one of the best hotels in the city. The wind blowing off the lake was too cold to make walking a pleasure. So I went to shows. I went to one so many times that one night when one of the actors was a few seconds late in appearing and the others had to ad lib a few words I noticed it right away.

I had attended a show one night and was in a lunchroom eating midnight lunch, when I fell into conversation with the man seated next to me. I noticed his union button and told him I was a telegrapher.

"I'm with a brokerage firm here," he explained.

"It's a snap—only five hours a day and I get seven dollars a day for it."

I didn't know what a brokerage firm was and said so.

"Come up tomorrow and I'll show you," he said, and gave me a card with the address of the brokerage firm on it.

During the time the market was active he walked about on a narrow platform before a big blackboard that covered one side of the room. On the blackboard he marked down stock quotations as they came in over the telegraph sounder.

To do this efficiently enough to hold the job one had to memorize about 300 code symbols. Each stock had either one or two letters designating its name, and the operator had to be familiar enough with the code symbols to mark up the quotation in the proper column instantly.

For example, the ticker would click "GN124" and the operator would mark $1.24 under the column headed "Great Northern." Within a split second's time another quotation of a different stock would follow. Once in a while an operator had a few seconds idling time. But usually he would have to mark up steadily and swiftly, to keep from getting behind and missing out on a quotation, for hours. One error and the operator was out of a job—forever, as far as brokers' offices were concerned.

Because the board room was warm and I hadn't anything else to do I sat there day after day and learned that code. I risked fifty dollars occasionally and it may have been my business acumen or it may have been just luck, but I never lost it. Neither did I gain anything. I specialized in what they called industrials. I would buy and the stock would go up. Then I would sell. Next day I would buy and the stock would go down. Then I would sell. It was just like shooting craps or what they designate in different portions of the country as Baltimore billiards, galloping dominoes, and what have you.

And all the time I was learning that code.

After a time I got so I could work for that man when he wanted off, especially on Saturdays, when the markets closed at noon in New York and an hour earlier in Chicago, due to the time zones. I never charged him for taking his place because I was learning something.

One day he showed me a message from a brokerage firm in Columbus, Ohio, asking for an operator. I wired the firm and got the job.

I liked that Columbus job. I got six dollars a day for about five hours work.

The operator whose place I had taken because he wanted to go to New York put me wise to another source of income. I could go over to the Western Union office and work a "hot" wire for about two hours in the evening if I could hit the ball. I could, and so I worked there and got three cents for outgoing messages and two cents each for incoming messages. I usually handled about a hundred messages in the two hours. About nine o'clock I quit and gave over to a regular man who didn't have to be so swift. But during those two hours I never had time to smoke a cigarette or take a drink of water.

So my income ran about $10 a day when railroad passengers conductors worked for about $120 a month, and linotype operators, a high-wage trade, worked in Columbus for about $21 a week.

I needed a quiet place to stay, for I had an idea for a piece of railroad signaling equipment which would prevent collisions. I wanted to install a drawing board and perfect my idea, then sell it.

The Western Union manager told me of a private home near where he lived that occasionally rented rooms and served excellent meals. One afternoon I walked out there and met the housewife. Like all women who ran boarding houses she had seen better days.

I listened to her account of what her family had been and all that and finally we made a trade. She had a sitting room and bedroom on the second floor that I could have for $30 a month, payable in advance, and where were my references? I gave her the name of the Western Union manager and paid my $30 and that made me solid with her. I was to pay extra for the meals I ate. The next afternoon, I moved in with my drawing board, my trunk and my chattels.

While I was arranging my things she came up with her two daughters, nice girls, to whom she introduced me. I bowed to them and then forgot them.

I usually came back to my room about four o'clock and worked at my drawing board or read until dinner was served at six. The second or third afternoon I did this, after I had been in my room about an hour, I heard someone singing in the other upstairs room.

The singer had one of the most beautiful voices I had ever heard. She was singing a religious song. "I'll go where you want me to go, dear Lord. I'll be what you want me to be..."

I heard her singing often after that. I thought it probably was one of the two daughters, as there were no feminine guests. One afternoon I asked the landlady, "Who is the singer of the family? I hear her nearly every afternoon."

"I'm sorry she disturbs you," she said quickly. "I will..."

"She does not disturb me. On the contrary, I like to hear her sing. I've paid five dollars to hear worse singers. It is one of your daughters?"

"No. That's my niece, Hortense. She sings in the church choir and practices afternoons when she has nothing else to do."

"I'd like to meet her."

"You may. I'll introduce you."

The woman smiled a wry smile. "She's a good musician. My husband was very fond of her and sent her to the best musical instructors, but when he met financial reverses he could not do more for her. Now all she does is direct a choir and sometimes acts as accompanist when noted singers come here for a recital or concert. As far as making anything of herself, she just hasn't the brains or getup."

"I'd like to meet her," I repeated.

"You shall, and I know you will agree with me that she will never make a success of her education, which cost so much."

I followed the woman across a hall and into the apartment in the rear. The sloping roof made that apartment ceiling so low that one could not walk erect in about half of it. There was a bed, a washstand and an easel holding music.

The girl blushed when I was introduced, and I found out afterward it was because she wore what was then called a Mother Hubbard.

She was an attractive girl, about my age. But there was something about her attitude that reminded me of a dog that has been whipped. She looked to me like she had been whipped many times—mentally, I mean, not physically.

After the introduction the landlady left the room and I stayed a few minutes, complimenting her on her singing. I could see she wanted me to go, but I stayed.

Finally she said, "I'll have to go down and help with dinner, if you will excuse me."

"I'd like to see you oftener," I said, with my hand on the door. "Do you ever go out—say to a show or something like that?"

"Oh no, I couldn't do that," she exclaimed.

"Why?" I asked, half way out the door.

"I'm afraid Auntie..." she hesitated, and I closed the door and went to my room.

In those days a man couldn't call on a girl in her room, but I made shift to see Hortense several times a week, even for a few seconds. Then something happened that put a new light on the whole thing.

35

Rehabilitating Talent

ONE NIGHT I NEEDED some notes I had in my trunk. I unlocked it, got out the notes and neglected to lock it again. In the trunk I had my two bankbooks—one from the Chicago bank with about $18,000 deposit, and the other from a local bank, in which I had about $500.

The next afternoon when I went into the trunk again I noticed the bankbooks had been moved about in the tray, and I knew that whoever had cleaned the room that day had investigated my financial standing.

I dismissed it as the natural curiosity of the woman who had cleaned the room. An unlocked trunk is always a temptation in the boarding house. Usually, through the medium of unlocked trunks, the servants in the house know about as much about a boarder's financial and business affairs as the man himself.

That afternoon a traveling operator panhandled me for a meal and I fed him and took him to the Western Union office to work the Chicago wire for me that evening and thereby make a few dollars to help him on his way. After I had squared him with the manager I took several drinks, the first since coming to the city, and then went to my room and lay down, awaiting dinner. But I fell asleep, and it was probably ten o'clock when I was awakened by voices in the room below me, the sitting room of the family.

"...and he has a lot of money and would make a good husband for either of you," the landlady was saying.

"He's stuck on Hortense and hardly ever speaks to either of us," one of the daughters said.

"Then we might get him to marry Hortense and then she could pay us the eight hundred dollars she owes us," the old woman said. "That would be a great help right now."

"Hortense said he asked her to go out with him several times," one of the younger women remarked.

"I'll talk to her about that," the mother said. "If she married him she could pay us the money she owes us and we would be through with her.

"She has no clothes to go out in—nothing but her best dress."

"You could lend her some, if he asks her again," the mother concluded.

I let them talk on and sneaked out and got something to eat. Next morning I explained that I had been detained downtown the night before.

Knowing what I had heard, I made it a point to leave my door open that afternoon and when Hortense came out to go downstairs I stopped her.

"There's a good show in town tomorrow night, Hortense," I said. "I don't work Saturday night and I wish you would go with me."

"I might," she said, hesitatingly. "I'll ask Auntie and let you know tomorrow afternoon."

I knew the old woman had been working on the girl after she had inspected my bankbooks.

I took Hortense to a show every Saturday night for three weeks. Away from her aunt she expanded and was not the shrinking violet she was at home. She could discuss other things beside music, of which I knew nothing.

"Haven't you any ambition to go on up in your singing, Hortense?" I asked her as we sat in a restaurant after the show one Saturday night. "Wouldn't you like to go to New York and become a great singer?"

"I have the ambition, but not the means," she said. "I thought once..."

"Before your uncle crashed?"

"Yes."

"Your aunt told me something about that," I said.

"What you need is a business manager—someone like me. I have rehabilitated a railroad and I think I can rehabilitate a singer."

"I don't know what Auntie will say and..."

I interrupted. "I understand there is a certain financial obligation which compels you to stay under your aunt's thumb. If I settled that financial matter, could I act as your manager?"

"I owe Auntie $800, but I couldn't take it from a stranger."

"Why not call it a loan?"

"I am not sure..."

Again I interrupted. "All right, we'll call that settled. I'll pay that debt and you're to put yourself in my hands. Before I am through your name will be in big lights in front of a theater. A man that could rehabilitate the Ocós Railroad can surely put a singer like you on the road to fame. I'll pay your aunt tomorrow."

"But I..." She was going to protest, but I paid no attention.

As we walked home Hortense said, "Auntie told me to do what I could to get you to marry me, but I dread marriage right now."

"How old are you?"

"Twenty-four."

"Ever had any proposals?"

"One, when I was sixteen. The young fellow told me he'd kill himself if I didn't elope with him."

"And he did?"

"No, he postponed his suicide and then forgot all about it. When I last heard from him he was married and the father of two children."

"Well, now that I'm your business manager you must do exactly as I tell you. Will you promise?"

"If it is nothing degrading."

"On the contrary, it will be uplifting—at least in a financial way."

"I'll promise, then."

"And instead of this shrinking violet air you assume, cultivate an aggressive, compelling personality. I've never weighed more than 150 pounds in my life, yet I've bluffed a score of men that could have broken me in two."

Wednesday nights, after prayer meeting it was the rule that Hortense train the choir for about an hour. The Saturday after I had paid the aunt $800 I called on the minister of that church. He wasn't a bad fellow. I told him I was business manager of his choir leader."

"Miss Freeman is a very estimable young lady," the minister said, non-commitally.

"She has been coaching and training your choir for a long time, hasn't she?" I asked.

"She has," the minister agreed and added, "she has made the choir what it is now—one of the best in the city."

"But she draws no salary?"

"No, of course not. We have never seen fit to pay her. All she does she does from a desire to help the church."

"I'm now her business manager and hereafter, if she continues the work she has done, her salary will be $25 a week, payable every Wednesday night."

"Impossible," the minister exclaimed.

"I understand you draw a salary of $3,000 a year, aside from being furnished this parsonage."

"You are correct."

"Well, Miss Freeman has more talent than you have and..."

"But we cannot do it. There is no comparison between the work of Miss Freeman and the work I do."

"Can you recall the thirteenth verse of the third chapter of John?" I asked.

"I can't say that I do, offhand."

He reached across his study table for a Bible. I laughed.

"Never mind," I told him. "I don't even know if there is a verse and chapter of those numbers. I just wanted to test your knowledge of what you're teaching—the Bible."

"Do you realize you are becoming somewhat insulting?" he asked with dignity.

"I'm sorry," I said. "I didn't mean to be insulting. But there is no need going any farther with this talk. Either Miss Freeman gets a check for $25 every Wednesday night or she sings no more in your church. She's been knuckling down to everyone for years. Now she's got a hard-boiled manager and she's going to get paid every time she sings or coaches or makes use of her talents in any manner."

"You are rather hard-boiled as you term it," the preacher remarked.

"I learned to be in the army, and after that I ran a district and a railroad down in Guatemala where I became case-hardened. I'm here to see that Miss Freeman gets what's due her."

"I'll have to see the stewards of the church and put the matter up to them."

"How soon can you see them?" I asked.

"Tomorrow morning, after."

"May we—Miss Freeman and myself—attend and sit in the meeting?"

"I would be pleased to have both of you present."

36

Ready for New York Lights

WE ATTENDED THE MEETING of the church stewards after the Sunday services. It was held in the pastor's study. The stewards, or maybe they were called trustees, were of widely different classes. A banker, forceful and arrogant, who wanted to run the meeting; a hardware man suave and business-like; a real estate man, ditto; the young manager of the water plant, inclined to be somewhat frivolous and sarcastic; and an old retired gentleman who said nothing.

I had cautioned Hortense not to say anything, but refer every question to me. The meeting was a little stormy for a Sunday meeting, but it ended the way I wanted it to end. I never realized before that there was competition among the churches, but learned it there. After I sensed this competition things went easy. By deducing a lot that I hadn't known before I got what I wanted.

As we walked home from church I said, "Number one!"

"What do you mean?" Hortense asked.

"I mean that's number one settled," I explained. "Who else has been using your talents gratis?"

"There's a symphony organization here for which I usually act as accompanist when they import some singer. Where some artist has no accompanist I usually act in that capacity. I learn quickly and with but few rehearsals."

"No pay?"

"I never thought of asking for any."

"Hereafter it'll be $10 a night or symp, or whatever you call it, and more if there are rehearsals."

"As you say," she agreed. "I still don't see how I'll ever repay that $800. It seems such a large sum."

"Forget it. You are just an experiment with me. I want to see if I can rehabilitate you like I did a railroad down in Guatemala."

"You've sort of purchased me."

"Yes."

"And I don't know what you're going to do with me."

"Neither do I, right now. Speaking railroad language, you need a thorough overhauling."

We were late for Sunday dinner. The others were leaving the table as we came in and went upstairs.

In those days, girls were clamped in tight corsets and I had an idea of how much it hurt them when, on Sundays, they were clamped tighter than ever. As we went to our respective rooms I told Hortense, "Pardon me for being a little personal, but go into your room and ditch that corset. I'm going to look after your health as well as your financial affairs."

She looked at me in surprise. "Why, Mr. Kavanaugh. No gentleman has ever..."

"I'm not a gentleman. I'm your business manager. I can't manage a singer who is sick. Go in there, put on something a little more comfortable and come on down to dinner."

"But I eat in the kitchen."

"Not any more. You'll eat right by my side. Go on in there and do as I say. If you're not out in five minutes I'm going in after you and then there will be something doing for sure."

Within three minutes she came out, dressed in a sort of house dress. We went down to dinner.

The Negro maid came to service me. "Where's Miss Freeman's place?" I asked.

"Well, sir, you see she usually..."

"Hereafter I sit at the head of the table, and Miss Freeman sits at my right," I said. "Now get busy."

"But, sir..."

"If Miss Freeman isn't served right away, right here, there'll be someone in the hospital for the next six months, wondering what happened," I said.

"Yes, sir," the maid said and proceeded to serve us.

The governing committee of the music club was not as hard as the minister and trustees of the church. I made them a business proposition and they were liberal enough to discuss it. We made an excellent financial contract with the organization.

"I've often wondered why Hortense didn't make her music pay her," one of the committee said to me after we had completed negotiations. "She is a natural musician and deserves better than she has been getting."

"I'm only interested in developing a talent," I explained.

"And then you'll probably marry the talent?"

"That is in the future," I said. "I never look very far into the future."

Occasionally there were social gatherings on Sunday night to which we were invited. At these gatherings, of course, Hortense made no change for what singing she did.

After a month or so she grew, so to speak, expanded, imbibed some of my aggressiveness. She could laugh at things as I did. She could order her dinner at a public eating place without a tremor even if the waiter did resemble the nth power in dignity. She imbibed my nerve and could send a dish back with as much sang-froid as a sophisticated matron. She even grew mischievous at times.

One night we were guests at a gathering after Sunday evening services and she sang several songs, religious songs, of course. At length she rose from the piano, despite the appeals of these present for another song.

"I'm tired of singing," she said, "but if you wish I'll recite for you." She stood with one hand on the piano, winked at me and began:

"I stood at eve, when the sun went down,
By the grave where a woman lies,
Who lured men's souls to the shores of sin
By the light of her wanton eyes.
Who sang the song the siren sang
On the treacherous Lurley Heights,
Whose face was as fair as a summer's day,
Whose heart was as black as night."

It was "Ostler Joe." Mrs. James Brown Potter had created a sensation when she recited it before a New York audience a few years before.

I watched the reaction of the audience with some misgivings. When Hortense reached the place where "Joe, the baby, died that winter, and the man was left alone," several women wiped their eyes and one of the men blew his nose. When Hortense had finished there was a moment of silence and then applause. Those people were not too straight-laced. They appreciated an artist, even on Sunday evening!

"Where did you learn that poem and why did you recite it on Sunday evening?" I asked as we walked home. "Didn't you know it wasn't exactly the thing for Sunday evening?"

"I found it in one of your books while I was cleaning your room," Hortense replied, "and I just had a curiosity to see the reaction of these people."

"You got a good reaction," I agreed, "but they might have thrown us out."

"That would be a new sensation, wouldn't it?" she said. "I've got that thrill coming to me yet—the thrill of being thrown out of a place."

It was along about the middle of March when a noted singer was guest artist at the municipal music festival. Hortense spent a day or so rehearsing and acted as her accompanist. I met them at the close of the concert and asked the singer to accompany us to a late dinner before time to catch her train. One of the big hotels had opened a dining room with shaded lights, waiters who served noiselessly and the food was good. I had reserved a table.

"Why do you not come to New York and try for fame?" the singer asked Hortense, while we were waiting for our coffee. We had been interrupted several times during the meal by parties coming over to congratulate the singer. No one thought of congratulating Hortense.

"Why do you not come to New York and try for fame?" the singer repeated, as Hortense looked at me for reply. I pretended not to hear the question.

"I'm afraid my manager will not let me go," Hortense replied, and the singer turned to me.

"Would you have an artist hide her talents under a bushel basket out here in what we call the steeks?"

"I was intending to take her there soon," I said. "If I should send her there, could you help her get a start? That does not mean she will come as a beggar. She will have funds with which to pay her way."

"I would be glad to do so," the singer said. "And if she could sing as well as she can..."

"With the exception of yourself, Madame," I interrupted, "Hortense is the best singer in the United States."

"I would like to hear her sometimes," she said, glancing at the clock, "but just now I have little time and..."

There was a piano on a raised platform in one corner of the room.

"There's a piano over there," I interrupted again. "You can hear her sing right now and yet have ample time to catch your train."

"But the hotel management might object," the singer cautioned.

"To hell with the management!" I exclaimed. "Come on."

The singer chuckled. "Your manager is so forceful," she remarked to Hortense. She chuckled again."'To hell with the management.' What would he do if they tried to prevent us singing?"

"He'd probably clean out the place," Hortense said. "And I'd help him."

"He is so forceful," the singer repeated. "Is that why you luf him?"

"That is why he is my manager."

At that time it wasn't ladylike to cross a public dining room alone, so I offered my arm to the two and escorted them to the piano. The singer acted as accompanist and Hortense sang several old songs. Instead of throwing us out the manager came up and congratulated the ladies. Finally we went back and finished our second cup of coffee.

I saw it was nearly time to get the singer to her train, so I called a waiter.

"Please bring me a check and call a hack," I ordered, within a minute the manager came to our table.

"There is no check," he informed me. "You and your party are my guests. You have given us a thousand dollar entertainment for nothing."

He turned to the singer. "I am delighted to know that you have dined with us this evening," he said, "and I hope to have the opportunity of serving you again."

As we were leaving he put his hand on my shoulder. "Any time you and Miss Freeman care to come here you will be my guests and I trust you'll come often."

I had a word with the singer before she boarded her train.

"If Miss Freeman should come to New York soon, could you sort of look after her until she got a start?"

I certainly will," she said. "Write and let me know when she is to come. I will meet her at the train and see that she meets the proper people."

37

Box Cars Are Ripe Again

IT WAS THE MIDDLE of March and I realized that before long warm winds would blow up from the south, box cars would be ripe, and my feet began itching. Hobo nature would compel me to see around the next curve—over the next hill. It would not be long before I would pull up stakes and go somewhere, and I did not care where.

I was making what was then a good income. I could call many of the leading citizens by their first names. I was welcome in many of the best homes in the city. I was manager of a coming singer, but the call of the road was beginning to urge me to move, just as the sun, slowly traveling northward, was urging the daffodils from the ground. I had to go.

The life of a good solid citizen palled. I would dream at night of sitting on the little seat of a machine gun tripod and spitting bursts of bullets at shadowy forms back in the jungle. I would dream of the locomotives at Ocós and how they threw sparks high in the air in early mornings, when we were getting them ready to go out. I could see the sun come up over Santa Marie and set in the waters of the Pacific. I would dream of jumping up when a bugle blew reveille, jumping into my clothes, and going out to answer the roll call.

I would be changing clothes and think of the uselessness of trying to be civilized and what is known as "refined." In Columbus I put on a clean fresh shirt every morning, and if I went anywhere in the evening I changed again. But I longed for the days when I had but one shirt and wore it until the sweat caked it and the caked parts broke in two like cardboard.

I had sent in the blueprints and specifications of my railroad block signal to a company whose specialty was manufacturing railroad equipment of that kind. I was sure the device would yield me at least a million dollars.

I hadn't the faintest idea of what I would do with a million dollars if I had it. I couldn't buy a million T-bone steaks with it. I couldn't eat that much if I lived to be an old man. I had several suits of good clothes, and my salary was enough to do me.

But I wanted the product of my brain and ingenuity to yield me a million dollars. I figured that if I got a percentage on the sales of the device I would soon be rolling in wealth. I had no reason for wanting to roll in wealth or anything else.

One day in late March I got a letter from the manufacturing company. In the same mail came a letter from President Cabrera of Guatemala. The manufacturing company offered me a thousand dollars for all rights to my patent, or, as I hadn't got the patent yet, but only applied for it, they would assume the expenses in getting it, provided I would assign it to the firm. I was disgusted. I knew I couldn't peddle the device to each individual railroad company. That would take years. So I wrote and told them to send the check to be deposited to my account in the Chicago bank.

With Hortense leaning over my shoulder I translated the letter from Cabrera. It read:

"My dear Colonel: I received your letter telling me about the revolution and what you did to prevent it, and I thank you. I also received the letter you sent later, giving your address. The revolutionists who were in Guatemala and expecting to receive the arms and ammunition have been eliminated."

I explained to Hortense that meant they had been backed up against an adobe wall with a firing squad in front of them. The letter continued:

"I would like to see you again and assure you that if you ever return to Guatemala you will receive a welcome becoming to a gentleman who has saved my life and the life of my republic."

"That shows the difference between men," I explained to Hortense. "Here is a company who will make millions off of my patent, and I have to be content with a lousy thousand dollars. If I really needed a thousand dollars I could cable President Cabrera and I'd get it within twenty-four hours."

"And you've worked so hard on that patent," Hortense consoled.

"It isn't the work I regret," I explained. "I don't mind working. But my brain originated it. My brain perfected it. I might as well have no brain at all if I have to sell its product for so little."

"There's no other way to sell it?" she inquired.

"No." I studied a moment. "Let's leave here and go to New York, Hortense."

"I am ready when you say so."

"Hadn't we better marry before we go?"

"I'd rather not, my nice man."

"But what will people say?"

"To repeat one of your pet expressions, 'To hell with what people say.'"

"I don't want to compromise you in any way. We could marry here and then part."

"As long as we know we have done nothing wrong, I see no reason to try to make excuses," she said.

"Write that singer, then. I'll get a man to take my place."

By return mail Hortense received a letter from the singer. "I have secured an apartment for you next to mine and it will be ready for you when you get here," the singer wrote.

It took me a week to get a man to take my place and I stayed with him a few days to make sure he could handle the job. My employers had treated me royally and I did not want to put them in a hole.

As we watched the scenery rush past as the train bore us toward New York, Hortense put her hand on my arm and asked, "When we get to New York—then what?"

"I'm not sure yet."

"You will go on and desert me?"

"Not if you'll marry me."

"I do not wish to marry yet."

"Perhaps you are sensible."

"But if I ever want to marry I will let you know, no matter what part of the world you may be in."

"Perhaps it is best. I'll not even let you know where I am."

"I could trace you by writing to the president of Guatemala."

"You might, and then again I might be around the world from him."

"But I could trace you."

"Perhaps. You've been a good scout, Hortense, to put up with me. I think you've learned to take care of yourself."

"I have. But I'll miss you."

"And I'll miss you. But it's all in a lifetime, anyhow."

We reached New York on a blustering morning. The singer met us and took us to the apartment she had secured for Hortense. It was just across a hall from that of the singer.

"I will leave you now," she said. "This evening I am having a little dinner—six or seven persons I want you to meet."

There were ten persons at the dinner—all artists but myself. I realized that if Hortense associated with such persons I would be out of the running altogether. I was dressed as a gentleman and I knew which forks and spoons to use for what.

This was but a veneer, however. Underneath my fine clothes I was still a hobo, a man with itchy feet. Polite conversation didn't interest me.

They talked of composers. I had heard of Beethoven, but the other names might have been names of insects for all I knew. Hortense could discuss them intelligently. I couldn't. All the conversation about the table was above my head.

But I comforted myself with the thought that I could adjust Walschaert valve gears to make a locomotive cut steam evenly. I could take a linotype apart and rebuild it. I could cut my initials in the side of a wall with a machine gun.

As far as music was concerned I knew nothing. My musical education had ceased about the time "Give My Regards to Broadway, Remember Me to Herald Square" was a popular song. I didn't know the author of it, but I could whistle it with but a few sour notes.

We tarried a few minutes after the others departed. The singer wanted to talk over business matters.

"And what is your business manager going to do in New York?" she asked.

"I resigned that position today," I said.

"He wants to go somewhere and shoot a few revolutionists or rehabilitate a railroad," Hortense put in.

"I thought perhaps you would marry him," the singer remarked. "I noticed when I dined with you out in the steeks that you liked to hold hands and defer to each other in little things, and that is a sure sign of love."

She pronounced the last word "luf."

"She won't marry me and I won't marry her because she is an artist and I am a hobo," I explained.

"He was colonel in the Guatemalan army," Hortense added. "He rehabilitates railroads. He took me and rehabilitated me like he does railroads."

Next morning I came over from my hotel and breakfasted with Hortense. After that we visited a bank, where I made a deposit for her. She was so excited at being in New York that she never noticed the amount, until late that afternoon while we were seated in her apartment. She had sorted out some of my clothes and put them away, for I was going to travel light. She was putting some of her effects into a drawer when I heard her sobbing.

"What's wrong, Hortense?" I asked.

"This is our last day together," she said, "and we've had such grand times."

"You'll soon make new friends and forget me," I said with a laugh, but there was a lump in my throat.

"I'll never forget you," she said. "You've raised me from a shrinking, fearful girl to one who can look the world in the face and tell it to go to hell. But you shouldn't have given me so much money."

"I have more in Chicago," I said.

"Is that where you are going?"

"That will be my first jump."

"And from there?"

"No one knows. There's lot of country I haven't seen yet."

"Europe, perhaps?"

"Not for me," I said emphatically. "Europe's too common. Every time a citizen of this country gets enough money together to make a trip he or she goes to Europe to be goldbricked by the remnants of a moldy and decadent civilization. You'll find persons right here in New York who think we're fighting Indians in the West, but who know Paris and London and Berlin like a book. No Europe for me."

"But you'll keep in touch with me?" she asked.

"It's not necessary. You've been a good little girl. You've cooperated in maintaining my reputation for rehabilitating things. I'll leave no forwarding address. Just forget me."

"I'll never forget you. I believe if you asked me just now, when we are parting, I would marry you."

"I'll not ask you. Remember last night at that dinner party? Everyone could discuss music but me. You'd soon be ashamed of me."

She began to cry.

"Didn't I teach you never to cry about anything?" I asked.

"I know, but..."

"I might not care, but it looks like you haven't my cast-iron in your makeup after all. Are you going to kiss me goodbye?"

"Yes," she said, after drying her eyes on a very small handkerchief, "and I'm going to cry myself to sleep tonight and the night after and perhaps many other nights. I don't care what you think."

"Goodbye, girlie," I said, starting for the door.

"Goodbye, my nice man," she said, her lips trembling. "I'll meet you again sometime."

I didn't realize then under what tragic circumstances we would meet again.

Turn of the century
vintage Linotype Machine

Guatemala President,
Manuel Estrada Cabrera

Mamie with step siblings: Joe and Ida Radotinsky

Mamie, baby Mary Frances, and Frank, circa 1916

H. H. WINDSOR
EDITOR AND PUBLISHER

POPULAR MECHANICS MAGAZINE
WRITTEN SO YOU CAN UNDERSTAND IT

CHICAGO   December 27, 1918.

J. L. PEABODY
MANAGING EDITOR

Frank Kavanaugh,

1830 N. 12th St.,

Kansas City, Kans.

Dear Sir:

I am enclosing two dollars for your story
on Natural Gas for Motorcycles. We expect to use
this material soon.

The other two suggestions have been turned
over to our Shop Notes Department, and you will
hear from them direct in a day or so.

Thanking you for submitting these items, I am

Very truly yours,

Managing Editor

JLP/LS

Enc chk $2.00
12/28/18

December 27, 1918

FORM 4-18-30—15M

CABLE: ADDET

FICTION HOUSE, INC.
Publishers
220 EAST 42nd STREET
NEW YORK

J. W. GLENISTER
President

J. B. KELLY
Treasurer

June 9th, 1931.

Mr. Frank Kavanaugh,
1857 27th Street,
Kansas City, Kansas.

Dear Mr. Kavanaugh:

We found "Bill Grubbs and the Hong Kong Chatter"

an amusing short. Shall we send you a check for $25 for it?

Now that you've broken the ice, come again!

Sincerely,

John F. Byrne,
Managing Editor,
FICTION HOUSE INC.

JFB*DM

June 9, 1931

169

Mary Frances and C.J. ("Brother"), 1936

Grandkids Larry and Sue Cooper, 1944

599

TAPS

United Spanish War Veterans

Camp No. 6   Dept. of *Kansas*

Grabolas

To Department Adjutant
Department Historian

4 – 23 , 19 46

Cremated 4-25-1946

Dear Comrade:

I deeply regret to report on the death of a member of this Camp as follows:

Name and highest rank in U. S. W. V. *Frank Kavanaugh*

U. S. Service *Private 2nd Texas* Co. K   Ship _____
(Highest rank)

Reg't *2nd Texas*

Married or Single *Wife Marie Kavanaugh*
If married, state name and address of widow

Number and age of children _____

Place of birth *Dallas Texas*

Place of death *1858 North 29 St. K.C. Kas.* Date of death *4 – 23 – 1946*

Buried in (*Cremated*) Cemetery at – *Ashes in Urn*

with military honors (yes or no) _____   *4-24-46*

Grave in charge of *Burial in charge Moldors Camp U.S.W.V. Camp No. 6*

Located in Kas. City Kas Yours in F. P. and H.,

Born Galveston Texas 1876.   *William Leaton*
Adjutant (Historian).

This notice is NOT TO BE SENT to National Headquarters except in case of the death of a Past Commander in Chief, Past Department Commander, Department Officer, Camp Officer, or Comrade of an Unattached Camp.

United Spanish American War Veterans
Found on Ancestry.com

38

Gunman

WHEN A HOBO WISHES to leave New York without going to the trouble of purchasing a ticket and boarding passenger cars he goes to a place where a four-track railroad runs under a number of bridges. The bridges carry the usual street traffic.

Anyway, the railroad tracks run in a deep cut. For the life of me I couldn't locate the place now. A hobo with whom I had a drink in a greasy saloon put me wise that this was a good spot to catch a train.

All you had to do to catch a train there was to wait on one of the bridges until a passenger train came along. Then you let yourself down from the bridge and if you were lucky you landed on the top of a passenger coach— and stuck there.

I don't know exactly what would happen if a man failed to hang on after he had landed on top of the passenger coach and was jostled off. Chances are he would rate a five-line story in agate in the newspapers with the added information that his body was picked up in a basket and the pieces were at the morgue.

I dropped from a bridge to the top of a Pullman coach, the last one on the train, and succeeded in hanging on, as there are several pipes that run the entire length of the roof of a Pullman.

I made myself as comfortable as possible on top of the Pullman coach and was riding fine when we passed a telegraph tower. The tower operator saw me, waved at me and yelled something I did not get. Then he leaned over the telegraph table and began sending a message.

I sensed what that meant. He was warning the railroad police ahead to be on the lookout for a hobo riding the top of that train. In hobo parlance what I was doing was called "topping the plush." I knew I would have to unload. I didn't want to be arrested by railroad police. They had a bad habit of beating up hoboes before they chased them off railroad property.

The train stopped a minute or two later and I looked ahead. We were at another tower. I saw a man I spotted as a railroad "bull" or officer coming down along the side of the train. On the other side came another bull. I slid off the rear end of the car and ran. One of the hulls yelled at me. I ran faster. I found a path leading down from the tracks to where a switch track on a lower level crossed a street by means of a bridge. Underneath the bridge were three small boys, newsboys, matching pennies. They looked up as I ran toward them.

"Where can I hide, kids?" I inquired. "The bulls are after me."

"Get right up there under the end of the bridge and crouch down behind the end bent," one of the advised, and I had barely hidden in the corner where the end of the bridge contacts the surface when the bulls came running through.

"See a man running through here?" one of the bulls asked.

"He went that way," one of the boys said, and he pointed down the street. They ran on.

I waited there, crouched in a very small space, for several minutes. Finally the bulls came back through, panting. They passed and a boy called, "You're all right now, 'bo."

As I crawled out one of the boys queried, "What did you do, mister, croak a guy?"

"No," I replied. "But I've got to get out of town and I was topping the plush."

I took those three boys up the street and threw a big feed into them, probably the best meal they had had since they were born. They told me the best way to get back to where I could top a passenger train again. I wasn't going to let one little failure keep me from getting to Chicago that way. Because it was after dark when I made my second attempt it proved successful, even if it was a little more dangerous.

Bock beer signs were being placed in front of saloons along North Clark Street. Boys were flying kites along the lakeshore front or anywhere else that could be utilized to get a kite up. Workmen were tearing up pavements. Spring was coming up from the south.

I drew enough money from the bank to do me a few days and just loafed. All winter I had been active and hadn't had much time to do absolutely nothing. Now I did it—for a few days. Then it soured on me.

A telegraph operator told me the Santa Fe Railroad was shipping men west to desert stations but I would have to pass an examination as to my ability right there in Chicago, and that the man who passed me was hostile.

I had heard of the hostile attitude of the little bosses on the Santa Fe toward men hunting jobs, but I tried him.

He wasn't much older than I, but he had a hard-looking face, as if his heart was made of ice.

The interview, as far as talking, was brief. He asked me my name. They didn't care much for the past records of the men they sent to desert stations. Then he took me into an inner room where there were a number of men working at telegraph tables. He went up to one.

"Let this man try out a while," he said.

I listened to the sounder while he was saying that and knew what was to come. Some station was sending in car reports—initials and numbers of car, contents, and destinations. It was conglomeration of figures and letters, hard for a man who happened to be a ham. But I was just off a broker wire, so it wasn't hard for me.

For half an hour I sat there and took it. The operator who had given me his place went over to the water cooler and smoked a cigarette, but the man with the congealed heart stood there and watched me. I finished two such reports when he tapped me on the shoulder.

"That's enough, 'bo," he said, and he motioned the regular man to come back. We went into the front office.

He sat down and reached into a drawer for his book of passes. Then he looked up. "What's that name?" he asked. I told him.

"I didn't ask for clearances," he said, as he wrote the pass.

"I wouldn't put my hand into my pocket for a clearance to show for a desert job," I said.

"I know you hoboes," he said. "You won't handle any company money out there, anyhow. Ten to one you've worked out there under another name before. But you can telegraph. That's all we ask. Your train leaves at 6:15 tonight. Be on it. If you peddle this pass and get drunk we'll send you to Joliet for two years. So get going."

I've forgotten what station I was supposed to go to, for I never got there. I got off the train at Kansas City and never got on again. On the trip down I won seven dollars off the three Pullman porters and the coach porter, and with their dice, too.

Kansas City was, and is, a nice city. Down across from the Union Station I fell in with a man who was selling farm machinery and we had two or three drinks together. He wanted a Turkish bath and I went up town with him and got one, too, my first. But I got out sooner than he did and never saw him again.

I went back to the Union Station and stood in a line of persons who were buying tickets. The man in front of me said "Fort Smith" and shoved a $10 bill across. I said "Fort Smith" and shoved a $10 bill across. Then I went out and got on a train.

Fort Smith was the seat of one of the most noted federal courts in the country. It held jurisdiction over all that country known as the Indian Territory, home of many bad men, but many good ones, too.

Garrison Avenue, the main street of Fort Smith, had forty-one saloons along its mile length. They were not patronized so much by residents of the city as by visitors, witnesses, deputies, and all that.

Some man I met at the station directed me to a saloon where I could get a good drink and a meal at the same time. I entered, looked around and saw a man I knew. I had met him in Honolulu. I went over to him.

"Say, corporal," I asked, "did you ever meet the Chicago cop, number 315 wasn't it, and knock hell outa him?"

He recognized me.

"I never got closer to Chicago than I am now," he said. "Why'n'll ain't you dead? You're ruining the reputation of that castor oil manipulator that was out in Honolulu."

"I just didn't die."

"Violated the Articles of War, eh, by not doing as a commissioned officer said you would."

"I didn't want to go out and shoot myself just because he said I'd die."

"What're you doing now?" he asked.

"Nothing."

"Want to join up with me?"

"Sure thing. What're you doing? Train robber?"

(Train robbing in the Indian Territory was quite an industry just then.)

"Hell, no! I'm a deputy United States marshal. I hunt criminals."

"What'll I do?"

"You'll be my posseman."

"What's a posseman?"

"First assistant to a deputy. Like as if I was a sergeant, God forbid, and you was a corporal."

"I'm in. Soon as I eat we'll start."

"We'll start tonight."

"Clicks with me."

"I had a good man—half breed but..." he hesitated.

"But what?"

"Damn fool went and got himself shot."

"Dead?"

"Anybody'd be dead with six .44 slugs through him."

"Too bad."

"Such things happen out in the territory."

For most of that day we sat under the shade of a tree down near the waters of the Arkansas River and talked. We remembered the story about Jimmie Pendexter who was found cut into quarters because he tried to make love to a Mohammedan girl; of the Gugu art of throwing a bolo through a man; of the time the bird from the Twenty-First had thrown a glass through the mirror of McCarty's saloon, and lots of the same things we had talked about in Honolulu years before.

Harry Callahan did not drink much. About one o'clock we went up to the wagon yard and fed his horses, and then went on and got a drink and dinner. Then we came back to the river's edge and sat on the other side of the tree, for the sun was changing to the west.

Harry had heard a song in a vaudeville show some time before that had affected him greatly, and he said the words came to him every time he was pouring a drink out of a bottle. He sang:

"Oh, father, dear father, come home with me now,

The clock on the steeple strikes eight.

There's nothing to eat at home but pie,

And the cook has gone out on a skate."

It was almost sunset when we left the river and went back to the wagon yard, where we fed and watered the horses again. Then we went to the saloon where he had parked his guns. We went up Garrison Avenue a little way and found a pawnshop.

We haggled with the man there, and finally, when we walked out, I had a .38 caliber Colt on a .44 frame, a gun just like that carried by Callahan. He had two rifles. Now we were armed.

For two or three hours we wandered up and down Garrison Avenue, looking for someone. At last we found them—a half-breed and a whiskered, tough-looking white man. Harry pointed them out to me.

"Bootleggers," Harry explained. "I want you to tail them and find out where they're going and when they leave. They know me, but they don't know you. I'll be down at the wagon yard."

I followed those men for an hour. They visited several saloons which I did not enter, but waited outside.

It was just pure luck that got me the information I wanted after all. They went into a saloon from which a door opened into a restaurant. I went into the restaurant and ordered a chili. I was eating it when they men came in. They seemed to be acquainted with the waiter.

"What'll it be, boys?" the waiter asked.

"Chili and a cuppa coffee," one of them said.

"Thought you'd be leaving town by now," the waiter went on as he served them. I appeared not to notice them.

"We're leaving an hour by sun," the white man said. The Indian drank his coffee and said nothing.

"Muskogee?"

"Not that far this time, The Chocs are dancing above Featherstone."

I had heard all I wanted to. I paid for my chili and went out to find Callahan. We saddled our horses and rode across the river, west.

We stopped at a little ranch about sunup for breakfast. Callahan was a great eater. He explained the reason. "Sometimes a deputy gets killed, and I've always had a horror of dying hungry."

Along about the middle of the morning we came to a place where the road descended into a creek—a sharp curve. We hitched our horses down the stream several hundred feet, sat down and waited.

It was about noon when we heard them coming. They rode around the sharp bend in the road, leading a pack horse. They hadn't a chance the way we were placed. Callahan held a rifle on them while I got their guns. Then they tied their horses, sat on a fallen tree and the palaver began.

"How many ye got?" Callahan asked.

"Fifty quarts," the white man replied.

"Too many for us. We'll have to break a few."

"Coat us $40."

"Bad stuff."

"Good enough for the Chocs."

"Mebbe so," Callahan agreed and went on. "We'll take the stuff and your guns. I'll leave your guns with the postmaster at Featherstone. Go back to Fort Smith and try some other district next."

All the while we were sitting there that half-breed had eyed me, and I could see murder in his eyes. He recognized me as the man who had tailed them for a deputy marshal. In his eyes I was a million times lower than a deputy. I was a spy, a stool pigeon, a man without principal.

"Don't we get anything back at all...?"

I was sitting with my back against a big tree, my gun was on my lap, cocked, ready to fire. I heard someone moving in the brush behind me.

Callahan had heard the same thing, but he never turned his head to see what it was. Those men, had we turned our heads, could have leaped across the interval separating us and got our guns. Callahan, calmly as if he were speaking to friend, asked, "Know my partner?"

They didn't know me, so they said nothing. "Allow me to introduce the Spavinaw Kid." I bowed.

The Spavinaw Kid must have had quite a reputation. I upheld it by doing absolutely nothing.

"The Spavinaw Kid has the reputation of shooting what's in front of him," Callahan remarked, "before he turns to see what's behind him."

The noise in the bushes behind me became nearer and louder and I was almost on the point of leaping up and shooting when the underbrush parted and a big shaggy dog came in view. He looked at the four of us, hesitated a second and then came and lay at my feet, looking up in my face, his wagging tail kicking up the dust.

I breathed again. The tension was over.

39

Fatal Bullets

THE RESULT OF THE PALAVER was that we sent the half-breed and his white partner back toward Fort Smith, sans guns and booze. True to his word, Callahan left their guns with the postmaster at Featherstone.

That night we sold the confiscated booze to the Choctaw Indian dancers for $3 to $5 a quart. The demand far exceeded the supply.

As soon as we had disposed of our stock we rode on. We were bound for Tahlequah. When the dog got tired of walking, we carried it before us on one of the horses. And it was lucky we did so, for it was the means of saving our lives a few days after.

We had one call to make before we reached Tahlequah. Late that afternoon we rode down a valley until we reached a two-room log cabin. An old man was in the front yard repairing harness. He looked up as we rode up.

"Light and come in," he called. We tied our horses to the fence and entered the yard.

"Your name Jenks?" Callahan asked.

"Sure is," the old man replied.

"Where's your son, John?"

"Down in the bottom field plantin' corn."

"I got a warrant for him—some shooting at a dance."

"He shot in self-defense—got two-three witnesses that'll say so."

"But I've got to serve the warrant."

"Fust time he was in trouble," the old man persisted.

"Can you call him?"

The old man went to the door of the cabin, got a cow horn and blew three blasts on it. "That'll bring him," he said.

We sat on a couple of logs and talked about the weather, chances for a good yield of crops, and what sort of breed our dog was. Within half an hour the boy came in. With him was his mother, a sister about twelve, and another boy, a little younger.

"This is a depity, John, and he's got a warrant for you," the old man said.

"I had to shoot in self-defense," John said, as he unhitched the horses. "Got witnesses that'll say so."

"Can you get your witnesses to Fort Smith?" Callahan asked.

"Not right now. Been so wet everybody's behind with their crops."

"About when could you get them there?"

"As soon as crop's laid by—in August."

"Tell you what I'll do, then," Callahan said. "Bring your witnesses in August and I'll tell the chief deputy about it. Better camp on this side of the river where there's good pasture. Don't get to drinkin' or the old judge'll send you over, sure."

"I'll be there the first week in August," John said.

Nothing was said about bond. It was a sort of unwritten law when dealing with that class of people. The boy wasn't a criminal. The deputies and the judge knew that the boy wouldn't run away. Those hillbilly folks never deserted a family.

"John'll be there along the first part of August," the old man assured us. "It would be hard to have him go now. I'm all crippled up with rheumatiz."

I had turned and was going to get my horse when the old man spoke. "Better feed and water your nags and eat a snack with us," he said.

I looked at Callahan and he nodded. It would be a change from eating sardines and crackers.

"We've got some coffee," Callahan said.

"Sure be glad to get a drink of coffee," the old man said. "Ain't had any for a long time."

I got a pound of Arbuckles coffee out of the saddle bags and we ate supper with them. Fat bacon, corn bread, and some sort of homemade jam. We sopped our bread in the grease that had cooked out of the bacon. It was a crude meal, but filling. Those hillbilly folks ate it 365 days a year. All of them, from the youngest to the oldest drank the coffee. It was a treat to them.

We left their cabin about eight o'clock. The old man directed us.

"There's a trail leading outa this valley and it angles around toward the west till it comes to the Tahlequah trail and from there on it's a plain road."

We rode for a couple of hours. By then the moon had sunk below the trees and we couldn't see. We came to a little stream and tethered our horses.

There was plenty of good grass there for the horses. We went about fifty feet farther up the creek and found a grassy spot which would answer as a bed for ourselves. We spread our saddle blankets and used saddles for pillows.

I was just falling asleep and thought Callahan was asleep when he spoke, "Damfi don't recognize you now. I knew we'd met before."

"Sure—in Honolulu," I replied.

"Naw, before that—in Manila."

"I don't remember meeting you in Manila," I said.

"I do. It came to me while I was laying here. I remember a few of you birds, sixteen or eighteen, was marching along, your guns across your shoulders horizontally, making each man look like a letter T, and taking up the whole street."

"We did that once in a while," I acknowledged.

"But this time you fellows looked like bums the way you were dressed. I was an orderly at the general's headquarters and the old man himself was sitting out on the porch. He watched your squad coming for fifty yards or so. When you got near the flag someone gave an order and you closed up ranks and saluted the flag.

The old general let out a yelp, "Tell the commander of that platoon to come here.

"I remember now. It was you. You had one leg of your trousers torn completely off and there were nasty sores on your leg. You told the gen you had been down east of Zamboango for six months and your lieutenant had got boloed and the non-coms had died off. All the men had ragged clothes and sores on the exposed places."

"I remember that," I said.

"And when the gen told you to go on to your quarters, you fellows did that T formation again and marched away singing a song. What was that song?" I remembered it.

"Raise hell, raise hell. If you want to go with us raise hell.

We don't give a dam for no dam man that don't give a dam for us by-dam."

"That was it," Callahan remembered. "The old gen rose from his seat as if to call you back and give you hell, but sat down again and smiled. He turned to another officer and said, 'From their looks those boys have been six months in hell. And now that they've returned to civilization they can't help but clown. Nothing can get the best of an American soldier.'"

"I remember the incident," I acknowledged.

"I knew I'd seen you before," Callahan repeated.

I was just about asleep again when he spoke. "The man we're going after now is a tough customer. If he sees us first we'll be dead. If we see him first he'll be dead. It's just as simple as that."

The man we wanted wasn't in Tahlequah, so we loafed around the town a few days, trying to get a line on him. We had attended a dance on the outskirts of town one night and were walking back about midnight. The road led past an old deserted log cabin with a wooded hill behind it. The dog was walking just in front of us.

Right in front of the cabin the dog stopped and growled. Crouching, it ran toward the cabin. Callahan put his hand on my shoulder and said "Down."

I dropped to the ground just as a bullet whistled above us. The dog ran on into the house and through it up the hill, but we called it back.

"Wonder who that was?" I asked.

"Why wonder?" Callahan responded. "There's a hundred men here that'd kill a deputy just to be killing a deputy. Let's go over and get a chili before we turn in."

Finally Callahan got wind of where his man was and we left the wagon yard late one night and rode south. Before leaving we tied the dog securely, for we did not care to have it along.

Just before dawn we tethered our horses in a little draw and walked up a hill. For a while we lay there, waiting. With the coming of dawn we crept to the very top of the hill. There was a little cabin just across a valley, about fifty yards distant. We lay there, our guns covering the house, for some time.

The sun was just peeking over a distant hill when the door opened and a man came out the cabin. He carried a rifle in one hand and a bucket of water in the other. He poured water into a pan on a bench near the door.

Just as he had finished something must have warned him. He set the bucket down and raised the rifle to the crotch of his elbow, the muzzle pointing toward where we lay. I don't think he saw us, however.

Callahan fired twice, the shots so close together that they seemed to be one long shot. A look of surprise came over the face of the man, a look of utter surprise. Then his gun fell to the ground, he staggered a little and sat down in the doorway. He sat there a few seconds, then fell over.

I was moving to go across and see where the bullets had hit him, but Callahan put his hand on my arm. "Mebbe more, kid," he cautioned.

We lay there and waited. Little insignificant things made more of an impression on my mind than anything else. An ant crawled along my gun barrel. A bird came down from somewhere and drank its fill from the basin the dead man had filled. A little cottontail rabbit hopped around the corner of the house, sat up, looked around and then went on. A dead human being meant nothing to a rabbit.

After a few minutes Callahan said, "Angle around through the brush, kid. I'll go in front. If you see anyone, shoot. If it's a man shoot for the guts. If a woman, the legs. But shoot first—that's the only way to keep alive in this game."

But the man was alone. Callahan's two shots had taken him in the heart, and they were not an inch apart. Callahan was a good shot, even if he did hijack and bootleg a little.

We found an Indian who drove a wagon and we got the body to Tahlequah. The dog was glad to see us.

A photographer who made tintypes took several pictures of the dead man, as required by law. To collect mileage Callahan had to have that as proof that he had killed the man. It once had been the custom to bring the bodies of outlaws to Fort Smith for identification, but in hauling a body around for several days it became rather smelly. So the ruling about the pictures.

We left Tahlequah early in the afternoon and made a dark camp that night. The outlaw had friends in that part of the country who might want to get revenge. But no one bothered us and we got back to Fort Smith.

When Callahan settled up with the marshal's office the next day he mentioned that I was a good man and should have a deputy's commission. A few days later I was commissioned a Deputy United States Marshal in and for the District of Fort Smith.

In those days a deputy marshal of that district was a poor insurance risk. Some of them lived to scratch grey hairs, but not many.

Callahan was killed a year or so after I left the service, but not by an outlaw. A cook was the innocent cause of his death. As the city marshal of Talihini explained it to me afterward.

"Callahan rode into Talihini late one night, hungry, as usual. He ate some chicken at a restaurant down near the depot. The chicken musta been dead too long, for Callahan got a helluva bellyache and died."

Ptomaine?

40

Deputy US Marshal

I DIDN'T KNOW IT THEN, but a new marshal gets warrants to serve that the old heads can't or won't try to serve. If the new man has good luck and doesn't get killed, he has made good. If he gets killed no one cares much.

I was given two warrants to serve. They were old, but I didn't know the meaning of that. One was for a murderer. The other for the ringleader of a bootlegging gang.

They hung out near Talihini, which was south by west of Fort Smith. I had to buy a horse and a few other things. Just before I left I mailed an order for a shoulder strap holster and a .32 caliber gun to go in it.

The second day out, when I was approaching my destination, I looked for a house deputies had told me I could put up at for the night. But somehow or other I missed it. I rode on and for the next 10 miles I didn't see a house or a human being.

Just after sunset a great mass of clouds came up in the southwest. I knew what they portended—thunder storm, with wind and deluges of rain. And it came.

For an hour my horse slogged along through the brush. I was on a trail, as I could see by flashes of lightning, but it was narrow and the limbs flipped water into my face as I crouched in the saddle.

At one point, during a vivid flash of lightning, I would have sworn I saw a man with a rifle dodge into the brush ahead of me. But when I called out, I could hear no answer.

I was wet through, and although it was springtime and the weather was mild, I was shaking with cold. Right then and there I would have surrendered my commission for a good warm room and something to eat.

I went on, for endless miles. At length, when my horse rounded the side of a hill, I saw a light ahead. When I got closer I could see the light came from a cabin at the side of the trail.

I rode up in front of the place and called. The door opened and in the light I could see a bearded man in the doorway.

"I'm wet and cold and would like to put up for the night," I said.

"Come around to the back," the man said. "There's a shed for the hoss back there."

I rode around and met the man at the back door. He indicated the shed.

"There's oats and hay in the loft," he said. "Make your hoss comfortable and come on in." Then he went back inside.

I fed and rubbed my horse down and went inside, As soon as I got inside the house I did what hillbilly etiquette demands. I took off my revolver, emptied it, and threw it in one corner. I had no cartridges in my rifle, so all I did was to stack it in the corner and throw my belt, having my ammunition in it, in the same corner. Then I turned to the fire.

In company with the bearded man was a young man about my age. He sat in a large chair with a blanket over the lower portion of his body. With a long-handled pan he was frying thick slabs of fat bacon. My, but it smelled good.

"Take a chair and come up to the fire," the old man said. "Damp outside, tonight, eh?"

"Worse than that," I said.

"We'll have something to heat you up in a minute," he said. The bacon fried, he uncovered a pan where three or four slabs of cornbread was cooking, and on the coals farther to the side was a pot of coffee.

Once, while the young man was moving the frying pan and the blanket slipped off a little, I was sure I saw a revolver under the blanket that covered his legs. But I thought nothing of it. Out in the hills it was not exactly safe to take in everyone who came along. Those people had to take precautions.

We talked as we ate. Crops, the rumors that a mining company was going to send men into the Kiamachi Mountains hunting gold and other precious metals. The meal was good, and my clothes were smoking as the water dried out of them. I got out my papers and tobacco and dried a paper so I could roll a smoke and offered them the makings. They refused.

"I never liked store-bought tobacco," the old man said, and he brought down a twist of "long green." They mashed it, stuffed it into pipes and smoked.

I was yawning, for I had been in the saddle since dawn when the old man remarked, "Mebbe you come from Fort Smith?"

"I left there day before yesterday," I said.

"Mebbe you're a deputy marshal?"

"I am," I acknowledged a little proudly.

"Pretty young for a deputy, ain't you?"

"This is my first trip out," I said.

"Mebbe you have some warrants to serve," he continued.

"I have two."

"One of 'em couldn't be for Sam Liming, could it?" he asked.

"You're right," I said. "How did you guess it?"

I saw the young man's hand go to where I knew the revolver was under the blanket. He smiled and said, pointing to the old man, "He's Sam Liming."

I didn't say anything for a moment. But I thought quickly. If I made a move the young man could kill me with the revolver he had under the blanket. Anyway, I didn't have the heart to try anything. Those two had fed me and took me in out of the rain. Aside from that, my guns and ammunition were away over in the corner of the room.

"I'm not serving a warrant on a man that took me in out of the storm," I said. Looking at the younger man, I continued, "Never mind that revolver. If I had one I wouldn't use it against a man that took me in and fed me."

"That's sensible," the old man said. "We've got oodles of kin here in these mountains and you'd never get away. We knew you were coming an hour by sun."

"What sort of a murder did you commit?" I asked the old man.

"See that boy there," he said, indicating the young man. "He could run and jump and do like other boys do till an onery critter shot him through the legs. Ever since..."

"So you got him in revenge, eh?" I asked. "I don't blame you a bit."

"I got him in the guts in a fair gunfight."

"You did right," I said.

I got up and turned my back to the two. They could have shot me easily, but they didn't.

"I'm dead for sleep," I said. "Where do you want me to bunk?"

"Spread your blankets in front the fire," the old man said. "Son and I sleep in the bed."

The bed was a homemade affair with but one supporting post, the other three being the walls.

I spread out my blankets, which the rain had not soaked very much, as they were wrapped in oil cloth; and in 10 seconds I was fast asleep.

When a man was as weary as I was just then he doesn't care whether he ever wakes or not. I didn't.

41

The Second Warrant

THE HEAT OF THE FIREPLACE woke me in the morning. The young man was frying bacon. I got up from my place to allow the old man to boil coffee. We ate in silence. At the end of the meal I asked the road to Taiihini.

"There'll be a man along soon to show you," the old man told me. I smoked in silence. Ten minutes later there was a hail outside and the old man opened the door.

"All honkey dory?" called the man in front.

"Sure," the old man said, and then turned to me. "Gabe, out there'll show you the way," he said.

I saddled my horse, collected my weapons, and joined him.

"I'm going part way to Talihini," the man said by way of introduction.

As we jogged along he became talkative. "Got along with the folks all right, eh?"

"Fine," I said.

"He's my first cousin," my companion explained.

"You knew I was there last night?" I asked.

"Sure. We knew you were coming in last night."

"You knew I had a warrant for him?"

"Lowed you might have."

"I didn't serve it," I said. "I'm not going to serve a warrant on a man that took me in out of the cold."

"Sensible of you. You couldn't've gotten away with it, anyway. Too many kinfolks in these hills. Who else have you got a warrant for?"

"Clem Rogers. Know him?"

"Sure, He ain't no kinfolk, so I don't give a damn. But you ain't got him yet."

"I will, though."

We reached a real good road right where a road from the east came into it. My companion stooped his horse and pointed to the road from the east.

"Rogers lives about three miles up there," he said. He turned his horse back to where he came from.

As he did I thought of something. "How'd you like to join me as my posse-man?" I asked.

"Couldn't," he said. "If I ever got to Fort Smith and they saw me they might remember a few years back and jug me."

"All right. Thanks for bringing me this far."

"No thanks at all, stranger. Wish you luck getting Rogers. If you fail, why there's a real good cemetery over at Talihini."

With that he put spurs to his horse and galloped away.

I studied a few moments and decided to ride into Talihini and investigate a little before going after Rogers. I wanted to find out a few facts about him before tackling him. Anyway, it was almost noon and my breakfast hadn't been much. Talihini, a railroad freight division, had a good restaurant in the station.

I ate at the lunch counter and just behind me was a table occupied by four men. There is where I made my first mistake.

"You know Clem Rogers, living near here?" I asked the waiter.

"They're sitting just behind you," she said, nodding toward the table occupied by the four men.

They gave no indication that they heard me, but left before I had finished my meal. Then I strolled out in the direction of the livery stable. Before I reached there the four men came out of the stable, mounted, and rode rapidly away.

I got my horse and followed. I did not intend to try to serve the warrant that day, but thought I would sneak up under the cover of darkness and spy on the layout while I perfected my plans.

Just before I reached the place where the Rogers road turned off from the main road there was a sharp turn. I was riding along, half asleep, think-ing of nothing much, when I rounded that bend in the road. Before I could even think, those four horsemen came from the trees lining the road and surrounded my horse.

"Well, dam if it ain't our little deputy," one of them exclaimed. This little man did all the talking. The man I spotted as Rogers, a big man, said noth-ing. I tried to bluff.

"You Rogers?" I asked the big man.

"Yes, that's the boss," the little man said.

"I've got a warrant for you, Rogers," I said, but I was quaking in my boots. "You'd better come with for they'll get you anyhow."

The big man smiled. The little man laughed.

"Like hell he will," he said.

I was on the point of arguing some more when one of the others hit me on the back of the head with a gun, I think, and things went black.

It was dark when I came to, lying at one side of the road. For some time I couldn't recollect what had happened, but finally it all came back to me. I had no horse and no guns. My head felt like a trip hammer was working in it.

I got to a little creek and washed some of the blood off my face and hands. I was bloody all over. I couldn't dress the cut on my head, but after I had washed it in cold water it felt better.

I can't explain it now, but a great wave of rage came over me. Those hillbillies had made sport of me, had left me out there with nothing but my clothes. I felt inside my pocket and found my billfold intact, but my warrants were gone.

Without thinking clearly I walked up the Rogers road. As I was fixed I didn't have a Chinaman's chance to get my man, but for want of anything else I would set fire to what buildings they happened to have at the Rogers place. I was sore all over, but rage kept me going. At length I reached a spot from which I could see a light. Then, as my eyes became more accustomed to the dark I could see a big building I took to be a barn and a smaller one, from which the light came, probably the house.

Then a great fatigue came over me and I knew I couldn't do more that night. I climbed a hill from which I could overlook the buildings, found a place between two rocks where leaves had gathered. There I slept.

Daylight woke me. I was cold and my head hurt worse than the night before. I went around to the other side of the rock, and when the sun rose I sat there and got thawed out.

About sunup a man came out of the house with a bucket and was in the barn quite a while. I deduced he had been milking. Then, for quite a while there was no activity that I could see from where I was. I waited for perhaps an hour.

Then the little talkative man came out, went into the barn, and presently rode out on a horse. An hour later, just when I was beginning to get warm and was feeling better, two more men came out, went into the barn and after a time, during which they saddled their horses, they rode away.

None of those three men was Rogers. I knew him, because of his size. If he was alone in the house, I decided, I might as well reconnoiter.

Three horses remained in the barn, Also two saddles. Neither horse was mine. Then I scouted over to the house. There was no one about, outside.

I reached a window of what was a living room. A glance showed me that Rogers was there, sitting at a table. He had a revolver taken apart and was oiling it and replacing the parts, one by one. I noticed there was a rifle hanging over the front door, on a couple of carved cow horns.

No other weapons were in sight. The more I thought of what they had done to me the angrier I became. This led me to try a hundred to one shot that, if it didn't click as I expected, would result in my death. In my frame of mind just then I didn't care. Again, I always had a sneaking notion that I could outwit a coward. I knew Rogers was a coward or he wouldn't have stood for what his men did to me.

I planned to push the front door open and in just one motion grab the rifle. If it happened to be loaded I had a chance. If it was empty—well, as the man had told me the morning before, there was a nice cemetery at Talihini.

I crept up on the front porch and reached the front door. Suddenly I pushed it open, and at the same time reached up and got hold of the rifle.

I got the gun before Rogers knew what was happening. Looking up and without rising from his chair he hurled the dismounted revolver at me. I dodged it and swung the gun around to cover him. In doing so I probably pulled the trigger, for the gun went off and Rogers put his right hand to his shoulder. He got up and I flicked the used shell out and heard another come in place. This time I pulled the trigger purposely. I got him in the right shoulder.

At the sound of the last shot a Negro woman ran into the room and I turned the gun on her.

"Fo' lans sake," she exclaimed.

"Get over there in the corner," I ordered. "Get over there before I put a bullet in your guts."

"Fo' lans sake," she repeated, but did as I ordered. Rogers, with a bullet through both shoulders, was a madman. He called me all the names in the calendar, adding some I never heard.

"The boys'll catch you here and you'll burn, you'll burn, you lousy, sneakin' deputy. Killing's too good for the likes o' you. We'll burn you, starting at your feet."

"Go get some water and see what you can do to his wounds," I ordered the Negro woman. "Don't try any funny business or you get a bullet through you. Hurry."

She made shift to put bandages around his shoulders and all the time he was telling me what his men would do to me when they caught me.

I paid no attention to what Rogers said. When the woman had finished the bandaging I made her tie both arms to Rogers' body with a saddle girth that hung near the door.

"Now go get me something to eat," I said. "Just what you had for breakfast. Don't cook anything."

She brought in some bacon, two biscuits, and two fried eggs that were cold, But I didn't care for that. I ate everything she brought.

"Now," I ordered, "come out to the barn and saddle a coupla horses."

She went out and I left Rogers and foraged in the kitchen. I found a sack of soda crackers, a side of bacon, a sack of Arbuckles coffee, and wrapped them up in a saddle blanket with a frying pan and coffee pot. I wasn't afraid now, for Rogers was helpless and I had a good rifle with a belt of cartridges I had found in the kitchen. I'd have fought off the whole gang.

I punched Rogers and got him to walk out to the barn. He was still giving me hell and he had a vocabulary of expletives that was endless.

The Negro woman was slow in saddling the horses and I thought probably she was trying to kill time until one of the men would return.

"Get going, woman," I said. "If you don't hurry I'll set fire to this barn after I have tied you to one of the posts. Get going."

Finally she had two horses saddled and we got Rogers on one. I got on the other and was about to ride away, when I thought of something.

"Come here, auntie," I said. "Back up against this post."

"You ain't going to burn me, is you?" she asked, her voice quivering.

"No," I said. "This post is fifty feet from the barn. You may get a little hot, but you won't burn."

She backed up to the post. I threw a rope around both the woman and the post and tied it. If she tried she could get loose within ten minutes. Then I drove the third horse out of the barn and threw a match or two up into the haymow. That hay burned quickly.

I left, leading the horse on which Rogers rode. He was still giving me the devil, but I could see that he was growing weak from loss of blood.

I didn't follow the Talihîni road down to the forks. At a point where I knew they could not detect the footprints of the horses leaving the road I left it and struck out across a country unknown to me. I followed a valley for several miles and then crossed a ridge into another valley. I kept on, the smoke from the burning barn being visible for miles.

That night I camped right up next to a little waterfall in a narrow canyon. By camping here I had but one direction to guard—downstream. I cooked some bacon and ate it with crackers. Rogers, a little out of his head, refused food.

Long before sunup I was on the road again, or rather I wasn't on the road at all, but just following a little stream for a while, the crossing over a hill and following the next one and so on.

I think it was the second day when we reached the cabin of an Indian. No one was there but an old Indian woman. I asked her if she could fix up something for Rogers, for he was swelling badly and long since had gone out of his mind. She gave him some stuff, but it didn't act. She also put some sort of salve on my head cut, for it was sore and I thought I detected maggots in the blood I wiped off.

I never could recall all the events of that nightmarish trip. It seems that I led a horse up to a boulder a dozen times to get Rogers onto his horse. He was swelling up until he looked the size of two men. I could reach up and scratch the sore on my head and underneath my nails would be maggots working in the blood. I found out afterward it was a five-day trip.

Early one morning we came out of a patch of woods and struck a nicely graded road. I realized we had crossed the line and had reached Arkansas. A few miles farther and I came to where a man was driving a herd of Holstein cattle into a closed pasture.

"How far is it to a doctor?" I asked.

"There's a doctor down about two miles," he said. "Second house to the right. Come in and have breakfast."

"Thanks, but I can't. Got to get a prisoner to Fort Smith. How far?"

"About ten miles."

The doctor fixed me up, but Rogers was beyond fixing. He had swelled to twice his size and was in a coma. The doctor's wife fixed me up a good breakfast. Then we rode on.

Three streets converge into Garrison avenue at the upper end. I was turning into Garrison from one of them when I happened to notice a man enter a saloon. I recognized him as the talkative man in the Rogers outfit. I took a side street to the marshal's office. I delivered my prisoner and then collapsed.

Two days later I was able to get up and went back to the marshal's office. Half a dozen men were loafing there.

"How about that warrant you had for Sam Liming?" the chief clerk asked. "Didn't you serve it?"

I explained the circumstances and was waxing eloquent on the injustice of arresting Sam Liming for avenging his son's crippling when the whole bunch let out a shout of laughter.

"What a chump," the chief clerk exclaimed. "That boy right now is more active than you are. Old Liming pulls that gag on every new deputy we send out. What we want him for is the wounding of an express messenger during a holdup."

They had a good laugh at my expense.

Later, one of the deputies present said, "Buck Rogers died the night after you got him here. We've noticed a number of his men in town, but we haven't a thing against them. But you'd better be careful or you'll get plugged."

"Is that a joke like the one Sam liming pulled on me?" I asked.

"Not at all," the chief clerk said. "We don't mind if a deputy gets his out in the territory, but we'd hate for it to happen right here in town."

"I'll watch out," I said, but I thought it was just another practical joke.

I laid around in my hotel for a few days, going to a doctor every morning for treatment. My head began to feel all right. There were no more blood or maggots. Along the last of the week I went up to the marshal's office to draw my mileage and another detail.

Uncle Sam is a funny old-fellow. I had brought in one of the leading bootleggers in the southern part of the territory, but I had brought him in by a roundabout way. I had brought him from near Talihini, so my mileage bill counted from Talihini. But the United government said it was so many miles from Talihini to Fort Smith and that was what I was to be paid for, even if I had brought him in by way of Chicago. The government said it was so many miles from Talihini to Fort Smith and it was right, always right.

I tried to argue, but it was of no avail. I was paid according to the code.

Then I mentioned the horses. I had lost a good horse, and could I take one of Rogers' that I had brought in? That, too, was impossible. Those two horses were in a livery stable and would stay there until they were sold at auction.

The clerk, in a moment of good-heartedness, told me I could petition Congress to refund me the value of the horse I lost.

How long would that take? I asked.

Oh, maybe Congress would act on it in ten or twelve years, if they got around to it.

I took what mileage I could get and had to be satisfied with it.

Those two horses had been good to me in the trip over the hills. No matter what sort of a man owns a horse, there was never a horse that was a criminal. Those horses had carried me and a swelled carcass of a man across the hills. I took three or four drinks and decided to go down and see them.

Down on the river bank at Fort Smith was the reservation. It consisted of six or eight houses. The livery stable in question was just across a vacant patch of ground from the reservation.

I could hear them playing pianos and dancing in the houses constituting the reservation. The houses were ablaze with lights. I wasn't interested in such places and merely noticed them.

I visited the horses, saw they were being fed well, and was walking back to Garrison Avenue. A high board fence surrounded the livery stable. I was nearly at the end of that fence, when I would be in the lights of Garrison Avenue, when I heard something click. I didn't know what it was, but I dropped to my knees. As I did so, I heard a bullet plunk into the boards of the fence.

I lay there in the weeds for half an hour, but no second shot came. The pianos and dancing were still going across the vacant patch of ground. If they had heard the shot they didn't notice it or maybe didn't care. After lying there about half an hour, I ran, crouching, into the lights of Garrison Avenue.

I went back to a saloon and took several more drinks. As I was taking my second I looked down along the bar. At the far end I saw that half-breed and his tough white partner. The breed looked at me with murder in his eyes. He nudged his partner, who looked and then both left the saloon.

42

The Owl Hoot Trial

I DIDN'T RELISH THE IDEA of having so many enemies loose who would shoot me in the back or waylay me in the dark. Aside from that, I was fed up on being a deputy marshal.

I went to my hotel room and had been there but a few minutes when there was a knock on the door. I drew my revolver and jerked the door open. It wasn't an enemy standing there, but the hotel clerk.

"Here's a package came for you this afternoon," he said, handing it to me. I thanked him and he left. The package contained the revolver and shoulder holster I had ordered.

Next morning, after selling my big revolver back to the pawnshop where I bought it, I left town.

Three days later I got off a train in Sherman, Texas. It was late at night, but I could see the town around the union station looked much the same as it did when Shorty Hurd and I had collected coins with which to buy dynamite to bomb the new jail.

Across from the station was Pete Fay's saloon. He kept hotel rooms above the saloon and had a crap game going in a room to the rear of the barroom.

I walked over to the saloon and took a drink. Then I wandered into the back room and saw the crap game.

I risked a quarter and won. I let it lay and it doubled. When my quarter had reached the sum of four dollars the gamekeeper told me to draw down and pass the dice, as house rules did not permit further pyramiding.

Twice I ran a quarter up to four dollars. Then I began to lose. I threw several times when my turn came and lost. I suspected the gamekeeper of switching dice on me. Getting hold of the dice again when my turn came, I held them in my hand while I turned away from the table to get a better light by which to examine them. As I did so, the gamekeeper said: "No switching dice here, pardner."

"I'm not switching dice," I explained, "only looking at them."

"Keep 'em in front of you."

"As long as they're my dice I'll look at them any way I want to."

I noticed two men who had been standing behind the game keeper edge around and range themselves on each side of me.

"Throw those dice over here and get out," the gamekeeper shouted.

"I'll throw them, all right," I assured him, as I threw them at his face as hard as I could. They drew blood. One of the men at my side took a swing at me, but I dodged. I sprang from the table and as I did so I pulled my revolver from my shoulder holster and backed toward the door.

As I backed everyone watched me, but no one followed. I was just pushing open the door that led into the saloon when a policeman came in by a side door that led to the street. He saw right away something was wrong.

The gamekeeper was wiping blood from his face. Those dice had surely cut.

"Holdup." he shouted.

The policeman reached for his gun. Mine was already in my hand. I was a good shot and didn't care to kill the policeman. So I fired at his hand as he drew the revolver forward.

I saw blood spurt. His gun fired, but I don't know where the bullet went. I saw him look at his bleeding hand as if it was something apart from his body.

I had been in Sherman before with Shorty Hurd and knew they had a fine jail there. I didn't want to sample its hospitality. I turned and ran through the saloon and out the front door. I smiled as I ran through the saloon, for the bartender ducked behind the bar. He had heard the shooting and saw the gun in my hand.

The instant I was outside I knew I had given myself away. As I pulled out my gun I had pulled out some letters. They could identify me by them. I was afraid to go back after them.

Once outside the saloon I waited for a few minutes under the platform of the railroad station. At the end nearest the saloon it was about three feet from the ground. Wagons could be backed up to it to load baggage.

I watched several men come to the door of the saloon, look out a moment to see if they could locate me and then dodge quickly out of sight. They were in the light and I could have picked them off easily. They knew that.

I saw several go out the back door and run around the building, evidently bound for the main part of the city, several blocks west and south. Telephones were not numerous in those days and it is possible that Fay's had no instrument.

I did not know exactly what my next move would be. I did not want to be caught as I would have been charged with wounding an officer of the law in the commission of a holdup with deadly weapons. All those in the gambling room would swear to that, I knew.

While I was figuring out what I would do I heard the whistle of a train. I had entered the city from the east, coming over from Bonham with a freight crew making what was called a "Sherman turnaround." In other words, they came to Sherman and then turned around and went back to Bonham, after switching in a new train.

When I heard the whistle of that train I tried to orient myself, but couldn't. All directions were the same to me. But boarding that train was better than hiding under the station platform, where the officers would soon find me and take me to their fine jail. And I really thought that train was bound north.

Within a minute or two its wheels clattered over the railroad crossing not a hundred feet distant. I stayed in the shadows until the locomotive had passed, waited until I judged the middle of the train was passing and then caught the side ladder of a car and swung myself between them. I breathed freely again. As we passed what might have been a freight station a block or so farther along I saw the semaphore set for green, That meant the train would not stop there.

I really thought I was on a northbound train. Denison was nine miles north of Sherman and but a few miles from the line of the Indian Territory, now Oklahoma. I could cross the border and be safe.

Presently the train, which had been making good speed, whistled for a station. I thought it would be Denison and prepared to get off before the train stopped, but it rattled right on through. As it did so I read the name on the end of the station building: Van Alstyne. I was headed south instead of north.

Once, when the train stopped at a water tank I dropped off, ran some distance from the tracks and hid in the weeds. The rear brakeman and the front end man walked down the line of cars until they met, then crossed over and walked back, looking for hot boxes or dragging brake rods. As the train pulled out I ran back and caught the handrails again. I did not have time to look for an empty car.

It was good daylight when the train stopped at the crossing of another railroad and I saw tall buildings in the distance. That would be Dallas. I dropped off and hid under a culvert while the train passed. Then I walked toward the city.

I knew my gun would be a dead giveaway if I happened to be arrested, so as soon as I got nearer the city I hid it and my coat and vest near a milepost.

I could locate the things if I ever was lucky enough to get back there. The weather was warm and if I wore a coat I would be spotted as a traveling man, a transient. Without a coat no one would notice me and, if anyone did, he would think I was just a local man.

Across from the T&P and H&TC station in Dallas was a clothing store. I went in there and bought a cap and a thousand-mile shirt. The owner let me put them on in the back room. I gave him my discarded hat and shirt.

As I left the place, I smiled to think that here I was in a thousand-mile shirt again—I, a colonel in the Guatemalan army, a man in whose honor a banquet would be given if and when I returned to that country. Now I was dodging United States and Texas officers.

I went into a saloon next door and got a drink. I ate breakfast at a restaurant next door to the saloon. While eating I looked over a copy of the *Dallas Morning News.*

That paper carried a column story about the holdup of the Sherman saloon and the wounding of a policeman the night before. My description was accurately given, as was my name. The bartender must have grabbed all the money that was in the cash drawer or cash register, for he claimed that I had taken it at the point of my gun.

The story never mentioned the crap game. Perhaps that would have been libel, for gambling was unlawful in Texas at that time. But they surely had things on me, enough crimes to keep me in prison many years. As things were, it was up to me to disappear for the time being. I walked south out of Dallas.

Ten miles or so below the city I came upon a large gang of men surfacing track. I picked out the foreman.

"Need another man?" I asked.

"Go down to the tool car and pick out a shovel," he said.

So I went to work tamping ties for the Houston & Texas Central Railroad. I might have held a position as train dispatcher or trainmaster, but I would have been too conspicuous in such a position. As it was, I was one of about fifty men, all callous-handed. All just snipes, shovel stiffs, working for a pittance in a job where no one ever noticed an individual. I was better concealed there than if I had holed up in a city.

I worked on that job two weeks. Men came and went. We slept in bunk cars, one bunk above another, all along the sides of the cars. We ate in two cars at long tables through the center. The food was plentiful, plain and nourishing. We received $1.25 for a ten-hour day, and fifty cents of that was deducted for board, leaving each man seventy-five cents a day net. On

Sunday, when we did not work, we paid the same fifty cents a day for board. Our wages ran exactly $4 per week.

I knew no one ever noticed a snipe, or section laborer. When trains passed the gang stood so close to the track that no one on a train could recognize an individual man. My thousand-mile shirt, too, was an effectual disguise. No one would ever recognize me as the well-dressed man who shot the Sherman policeman.

Of course, I had no one to blame for the trouble but myself. If I had handed the dice back to the dealer or even pitched them on the table and walked out, I might have left Sherman openly instead of sneaking away as I did.

At the end of two weeks I told the foreman I wanted to quit. He wasn't surprised or sore. Men quit the gang every day and new ones came in. He gave me an "identy"—a slip of paper giving my name, length of service, rate of pay, deduction for board and hospital fees. I could take that paper down to the roadmaster's office in Corsicana and after waiting for about a day, and get a check for my wages.

I didn't collect, for I had a good reason for keeping that piece of paper with me. The H&TC Railroad still owes me for those two weeks' work, but it wasn't the fault of the company. Besides, I had a little more money sewed in the seat of my underwear.

That identification paper would stand me in good stead if I happened to be arrested as a vagrant. By it I could prove I was a working man. So I held onto it.

In pulling out my revolver in the Sherman gambling house I had also pulled out some papers bearing my name. I had read a good description of myself in the *Dallas Morning News*.

But my "identy" from the track-surfacing gang would prove that I wasn't that man at all. I was Pete McCarty, railroad section snipe. And I surely had my calloused hands to show for it. The first day's work brought blisters. The second day they broke. They calloused about the third or fourth day.

Before I started south I walked back to where I had hid my clothes and gun, boxed them and shipped them to Alpine, Texas. Then I journeyed on to Alpine, via the box car route or, as printers call it, I traveled "lower case."

Houston. I dodged through the town and caught a freight train west to San Antonio. By that time I really looked like a section laborer, for I hadn't shaved for three weeks. I don't believe anyone would have recognized me for the well-dressed man who got into trouble in Sherman, yet I cringed every time I saw a policeman.

Finally I landed in Alpine, on the northern border of what is known as the Big Bend country of Texas. The express agent at Alpine looked at me suspiciously when I handed him the receipt for my package.

"Got anything else for identification?" he asked. I brought out the identy.

"You might have found these," he said.

I was getting worried, This man was too inquisitive. But I saw a way out.

"I addressed that shipping tag," I said. "I can duplicate it if you'll lend me a pen."

He silently handed me a pen and shoved over a pad of paper. He watched me write my name and the Alpine address.

"Brother," he said, "there's something fishy as hell about you. You have a snipe's identification card and you write a telegraph hand."

"WTB?" I queried.

WTB was the hailing sign of the Order of Railroad Telegraphers. When working with a new man a member always gave him the WTB to learn if he was a brother member. WTB meant "Wear the Button?" which most union telegraphers did. I was not a member but I had been queried many times.

The man laughed. "Well, I guess you've got your own reasons for being as you are." He handed me the package. "Where are you going now?"

"Down into the Big Bend country."

"It's your funeral, but I'd go a long way somewhere else before I'd go into the Big Bend."

43

Theoretically Dead

THE BIG BEND COUNTRY, a section of Texas about the size of Indiana, had long been a hangout for outlaws from all over the world. The name came from the fact that the Rio Grande River made a big bend down into Mexico. It was a region of boulders and bare mountains. Some of its streams ran with poisonous water. Wild animals and snakes of every description made living precarious. Once down in those wild hills a man could gang up with other outlaws and be reasonably safe. He could live by smuggling. Occasionally officers went into that country after a criminal. A good many of them never returned.

I had about $50 when I landed in Alpine. I bought a horse and an old saddle for $42. I bought food, mostly sardines, cheese and crackers, a slab of bacon, and two packages of Arbuckles coffee with the balance of my money. Then I rode south.

For three days I rode through about as desolate a country as one could imagine. I met no one. Once I saw a horseman on a ridge a mile or so ahead, but he disappeared before I could take a second look.

It was late in the afternoon of the third day when I rode up to a small cabin built against the side of a hill. The hill answered for the back wall of the cabin. I called out, but no one answered. I got off my horse and walked into the place.

A man and woman lay on a pallet on the floor. I could see they were dead, and I could tell by the flies swarming over them that they had been dead for some time.

Gagging, I was about to walk out when a small form crept from a pile of straw or hay in a corner, rubbing its eyes. The kid was about two or three years old, good looking but very dirty.

"Buenos días, muchacho," I greeted.

"Mamma sleep, daddy sleep," the little fellow lisped. "Dick hungwy."

The kid wasn't a Mex at all!

A closer examination convinced me the couple had died of smallpox, induced by dirt and malnutrition. I had met up with the scourge several times before.

I took the kid outside, fed him some crackers soaked in sardine oil and a bite or two of the sardines, and then he fell asleep on my saddle blanket.

I searched the house for food. All I could find was the remains of a rabbit, cooked and partly eaten, and a ten-pound sack of flour, mouldy. I could find no papers of identification on the man. I did not search the woman's body. The bodies were beginning to smell bad so I only made a hurried search of the place.

I hunted around and found an old adz. With it I started to dig a grave. A long-handled frying pan answered for a shovel. I was down about six inches when four horsemen rode up from the south. They were armed to the teeth, and they looked like officers of the law.

I thought I was a goner, for my gun and scabbard were beside the kid, about fifty feet distant. Also, in my saddle bags were papers that might have identified me as the man I was. If those men were lawmen, I was certain to be taken back and sent up to Sherman. If they were outlaws I might have a chance. I never did find out who they were.

"Whatchu doin'?" one of them asked.

"Digging a grave for a man and woman."

"You kill 'em?"

"Naw, smallpox."

The spokesman rode to the door of the cabin, looked in, gagged, and then they rode away toward the south. Those men rode away without another word. They may have thought I was a fool for staying around where a person had died of smallpox. But when I was younger I had a spell of variloid, a mild form of small pox. I was immune thereafter. The kid seemed to be immune, too.

After the men rode away I decided it would be too much work to dig a grave so I set fire to the cabin. Then I rode north with the baby sitting in front of me.

About thirty-six hours later I rode into a small village on the Southern Pacific Railroad. I had got off the trail back to Alpine. I was out of grub and knew that I couldn't keep the child, but I didn't want to leave him in the desert-like country to starve. I had washed him and his few clothes at a creek we had crossed. He was presentable, and a good child.

He enjoyed riding a horse. I tried to find out the name of his parents, but couldn't. He was Dick. His parents were mamma and papa or sometimes daddy.

I rode into the little village about an hour before sunset. No use mentioning the name of that village now, for those people gave the law the merry ha, ha!

The wife of the station agent, the wife of the section foreman, the wife of the storekeeper, the wife of the saloonkeeper, and the wife of the resident Texas Ranger and deputy sheriff took that kid to their hearts. All were childless.

After dark that night I took a bath by stripping and standing under the drip from the railroad water tank. The station agent, because I could read the messages coming over the wires, got chummy with me and lent me his razor. I slept that night in a clean bed. I ate well at the section house and was told that my money was counterfeit and I couldn't spend any in that man's town.

Next morning the saloonkeeper told me the drinks were on the house as long as I wanted to stick around. I was taking my first drink of the morning when the Texas Ranger walked in. We had a drink together, talked a while and then he said, "I want to see you over at my office."

When he said that, I knew I was due to go back to Sherman and stay in that nice new jail if the populace didn't decided to mob me.

I didn't like it, of course, but I couldn't bear to leave a little baby to starve or be eaten by wild animals down in the Big Bead country. If I had left the kid down there, my conscience never would have let me sleep again. Now, of course, I'd sleep a few years in the penitentiary, but I'd sleep with a clear conscience.

I had to make the choice. I made it back there at that cabin. I could kill a man that needed killing, but I couldn't desert a little boy and let him starve.

In his office the ranger showed me a printed circular giving my name and a good description and detailing the crime I had committed, leaving out any mention of the crap game. In a few words, I told the ranger just what had happened. Then I took off my shoulder scabbard and handed it with the gun in it to the officer. I was caught and the kid was the innocent cause of it.

"I could fight it out with you, ranger," I remarked. "But you people have made so much over the kid that I wouldn't want even to try to hurt anyone in this man's town."

The ranger waved me back as I handed him my weapon.

"Keep your gun, kid," he said. "You see, I had to kill a man a week or so ago when I found him robbing the depot," he went on to explain. "He had nothing on him by which he could be identified, and we buried him just across the right-of-way. The section men dug the grave and they know he was good and dead if any question ever comes up. Give me your identification papers and I'll send 'em up to Sherman with the news that I killed you while you were robbing our depot."

I gave him all the papers I had with my real name thereon. He let them lay on the table before him while he filled and lighted his pipe. Then he looked up with a broad smile.

"A man that'd ride his head into the pen to save a white kid from starvation ain't going to be sent up from here. Why, our wives'd poison us."

He stuffed the papers into a big envelope, addressed it to the Sheriff of Sherman, Grayson County, Texas, sealed it and rose.

"I gotta mail this. Come over and have a drink."

So I was theoretically dead. I sold my horse and traveled west to El Paso. Anyway, I had a name. I still had the identy from the H&TC saying my name was Pete McCarty.

44

Owl-Hooting in Mexico

SOUTH OF THE BORDER you may lose your identity if you wish to lose it. You just pick out some name and remember it. Nobody cares.

I had about $40 when I left that little town on the Southern Pacific. I had sold my horse for that amount, and the two days and nights I had spent there cost me nothing. They wouldn't even let me pay for a package of smoking tobacco and a book of cigarette papers.

I left at night and the saloonkeeper insisted I take a quart of whiskey with me. He was tickled pink because those childless families had drawn straws and he and his wife had won the privilege of keeping the baby the first week. They had wired San Antonio for the best in baby beds, baby clothes and baby toys. I left with the satisfaction of knowing my protégé was in good hands.

The station agent fixed me for a ride on a through freight to El Paso. I was a friend of his, he explained, and was a hobo telegrapher hunting a job. That train made passenger time all the way through.

At a station where there was an eating house the conductor woke me and insisted on me accompanying them to a late dinner. I told him I had money to pay for my own eats.

"Hell," he said. "Never mind that. I'm making three cents a mile riding this drag and you're not making a cent riding it. Come on and throw a bunch of victuals into you."

El Paso. The city from which I started my hobo career, if one could call it a career. I didn't tarry there. A private from Fort Bliss to whom I spoke told me my old outfit wasn't at the Fort anymore. In fact, he'd heard that the Signal Corps had been shoved in with the Engineers. So I didn't visit the Fort.

It cost a dime to cross the international bridge and since I wasn't carrying baggage the customs officers didn't give me a second glance. I was just a Yankee tourist going across for a night's drunk.

It was growing dark when I reached the railroad yards. A man with a dirty shirt was walking down a string of cars checking seals and number. He would be the conductor, I knew, but he wasn't the type of conductor you see above the Rio Grande—smooth-shaven, cleanly clad, smart, alert. He had a week's growth of beard on his face.

"What's the chance of going down with you?" I inquired.

"Railroader?"

"Iron Mountain. North Little Rock," I replied shortly.

"Just gapin' or runnin'?"

"Runnin'."

"Trouble with the law?"

"Trouble with the law."

"Waycar's back there about five car lengths. Left hand front bunk's empty."

"Thanks," I said.

"Tahell with the thanks. You don't suppose I'd be runnin' a train down here with two greaser brakeman if I could get a job above the line, do you? I always help a man in trouble."

An hour or so later the train pulled out and I sat and read a newspaper. The conductor went to his desk and checked waybills.

A Mexican brakeman, barefoot, sat in the cupola and watched over the train. The track was rough and the engineer appeared to be trying to see how much speed he could get out of his engine. The caboose hopped around as if the wheels were going over cobblestones. I still had most of the whiskey that had been given me and I took a big drink, gave the conductor the remainder and went to sleep. There were no bedclothes in the bunk, but I could sleep anywhere.

Later in the night I woke to find the train standing still. The air was chilly and there wasn't a sound except the exhaust of the air pump on the engine at the head end of the train. The caboose was empty.

I went to the rear platform and looked around. We were at a little station tagged "Horcacitis," if my memory serves me right. The conductor was sitting on a baggage truck on the station platform. I went over to where he sat.

"Laid out for something?" I inquired.

"Been laid out for two hours. We met a train here carrying follower signals and the second section hasn't showed up yet."

(Follower signals are green flags or lights displayed on the front end of a locomotive to indicate a second section is following. At that time, on the Mexican Central, flags in the daytime and lights at night were carried on the ends of the pilot bar.)

"No agent here?" I asked, hearing a telegraph instrument clicking inside the station.

"Was one, but be went south last week," the conductor explained. "Usually we carry a rear brakeman who can telegraph, but they're shy now and it's been a month since I've caught one."

I told him I could telegraph.

"Hell," he exclaimed. "You gotta job."

He opened the station door with a switch key and we went inside. I cut in a wire that was silent, for the one I could hear was operating on commercial stuff. Once I got the train wire cut in I listened to see if I had the right wire. A dispatcher was sending a train order. I waited until he had completed it and broke in.

"DS, DS, DS," I sent. Then I held the key open.

"What's the call for this station?" I asked.

"Damfino," he replied.

As soon as I closed the key the dispatcher came in, very impatiently.

"DS," he said. "Sign." Meaning I should give the call letters of my station. I didn't know them.

"DS," he clicked again. "Sign."

"This is new man at Horcacitis," I began. "Don't know sign."

"HO," he snaps hack.

I turned to the conductor. "What's your train?"

"Extra South 217."

I began again with the dispatcher. "Extra South 217 held here by follower signals on north bound train. Want orders."

"What train north?"

"What train north?" I asked the conductor.

"Number 21."

"Number 21 carried follower signals," I told the dispatcher. "Second section hasn't showed up."

"Second section was work train that ran only to Allego," the dispatcher told me. "Crew forgot to take in signals. Take a 31."

I got my pencil, found flimsies and carbon sheet, and copied the order.

"Extra South engine 217 will run Horcacitis to Bernalillo regardless of all trains."

The engineer, a youngish man, had walked up from the engine and stood beside the conductor. I shoved the pad of flimsies over for them to sign.

"You sure you got it right, kid?" he asked. "Number 3 should be coming up and meet us this side of Bernalillo. It'd be a sweet smashup if we met on one of those curves."

"I'll repeat it," I said, and did so, and got the dispatcher's OK. The engineer still looked doubtful, so I queried the dispatcher about number 3.

"Number 3 is two hours late," he said, "and may be later."

"Let's get outta here," the conductor said when I told them. He turned to me and said, "You gotta job, kid."

I had a job. All the rest of the way down to Chihuahua I rode the cupola while the Mexican brakeman rode the "swing" or middle portion of the train.

At intervals along the railroad there were boxes attached to telegraph poles which contained instruments and train order blanks. We met trains and we passed trains. If we got stuck, I would get to one of those boxes and ask for orders.

We were tied up often. The railroad was using very small engines that could not pull long trains. So freight trains were so thick along that division that it was difficult to get over it at all. A train would be in a siding about half the time, waiting for some train coming against it. We reached Chihuahua late in the afternoon, a 220-mile trip.

The railroaders ate at a Chinaman's restaurant near the shops. With my conductor, Al Osborne, I went there for supper. We had eaten little coming down, some enchiladas, frijoles and tortillas we got along the road from native women. The American-like food served by the Chinaman tasted good. There we met the other crews who happened to be in—rusty-looking, hard-boiled men who could not get jobs above the Rio Grande because of being blackballed for some reason or other.

There I met the train dispatcher I had first worked with the night before. He was an oldish man, one of the shabby genteel. The clothes he wore were tailor made and in style, but were wrinkled and out at the elbows.

"You're on the Owl Hoot Trail, eh?" he mentioned after we were introduced. "A good many of the boys down here are, but I'm not. But I can hold a job down here while I couldn't hold a job above the Rio Grande shoveling snow after they learned my name. Went to sleep one night and let two freights come together between Logansport and Wabash, Indiana. No one hurt, but the wreck was a mess. They wouldn't let me ride on the Wabash even if I bought a ticket."

"And you have no desire to go back to the United States?" I inquired.

"None whatever. Down here I can do what a please as long as I get trains over the road. Of course, in a few years the Mexicans will be able to run their own railroads. But until they learn the Americans will continue to operate them. By the time these Mexicans learn railroading I'll be dead and forgotten."

Tired out, after eating supper I went to the waycar and slept.

45

Personalities

MY NEXT TRIP WAS SOUTH out of Chihuahua to Jiminez. I caught another conductor, a man named White. He had been blackballed out of the United States when he got into an argument and used his fists on J. H. White, superintendent of the Cotton Belt Railroad at Commerce, Texas. White, unable to secure work in the United States, had come down below the border, where his services were in demand. He did not drink, and once, when I climbed down from the cupola for a drink of water, he was sitting at his desk reading a Bible.

It was the custom then, when we carried traveling natives in the box car portion of the train, to collect as much as we could from them for passage. It was less than passenger fare, and we did quite a business in that line. This money we divided among the American members of the crew when we reached our destination.

White always took his share of the money and usually read us a lecture on the beauties of sobriety. And the lecture usually didn't take. But he never "turned in" (reported) a man for drinking. Someone composed a song about him that ran:

"Every day, when night had come,
We would spend it all for rum.
And it made the old conductor feel so bad."

There were half a dozen verses to the song.

White saved his money and bought American gold in $25 pieces. These he sent up to San Antonio where he had a safe deposit box. Someday, he declared, he would go back home and buy a little patch of ground and raise flowers and preach at some little church whose congregation could not afford a salaried pastor. He was the only trainman on the two divisions who was religious, but the boys all respected him.

They had reason to respect him, too. One day a couple of brakemen got into an argument with him and were going to beat him up. White put the two on the ground with a couple of lefts and rights, and then knelt down by the unconscious men and asked the Lord to forgive him for giving away to anger. But on all the trips I made with him he treated me well, and he was a good conductor. He knew his onions.

The Mexican Central was operated on a sort of first-in, first-out arrangement, so that a man might not catch the same conductor once a month. There were more conductors than telegrapher-brakemen, and the latter were on the first-in, first-out system.

Not all American railroad men were down there because they couldn't live in the United States. Many of them were there just as a sort of lark.

One of these was George Samuels, who ran a freight engine out of Chihuahua. He was a third-year student at Illinois University when he decided to go to Mexico and learn practically what he had learned theoretically. His major was railroad operation and he had practiced on the locomotives loaned to the university by the Big Four and Illinois Central railroads. He had dropped out for a year to see what he could do down in Mexico.

George never drank. Once I asked him to have a drink with me, and he explained his refusal, "Dad keeps all sorts of liquor at home—mostly for guests. I've never taken a drink because I've watched guests take drink after drink and then grow talkative and give away all the business information they had and then some. Dad's a banker and he's learned a lot of things that were supposed to be secret by just listening to a drinker talk."

Samuels never returned to his university studies. Someone up at the financial headquarters of the Mexican Central in New York learned of a man running a locomotive down there who had engineering knowledge. George was called up when a master mechanic quit. From the master mechanic's position, he went on up until he was a big man in the mechanical department of the system. Then one day his father and a few private carloads of bigbugs came down to see the country below the Rio Grande. In the group was a girl with whom George fell in love. Within six months he resigned, went back east and married, and prospered until he died a few years ago.

There was another man there whose name I will not mention—a conductor. Afterward he made the front pages of the newspapers, regularly. No one down there ever knew much about him or his past, but he was prince of a good fellow. He wore glasses and that is why we called him "Four Eyes." I didn't know how far up he would go until I heard him talk—years afterward.

One night I was caught for a number of hours in an Ohio city and drifted into an auditorium to hear the speech of a candidate for Congress. As I sat there and listened to him I recalled a little incident I had long since forgotten:

Late one chilly night our train pulled out of Juarez, bound south. (It gets pretty cold at night on the Mexican plateau.) As we pulled out the conductor—"Four Eyes"—handed me a bunch of train orders as I climbed into the cupola, and then sat at his desk to check waybills. After a while he climbed up beside me.

"We've got four cars of dynamite in those SP cars ahead," he said. "If one of those cars happened to ditch it may mean goodbye to us."

Billy Skinner was pulling the train and he was shoving the engine for all it was worth. There had been quite an argument before we left. Skinner claimed he had had but three hours' sleep and was not in condition to take a train out, but enginemen were scarce and he was finally persuaded to go. I knew he was sore as a boiled owl and was trying to get passenger speed out of an old freight engine. It looked bad.

"Maybe they'll stick to the rails," I said, but the thought of those cars loaded with a deadly explosive made me rather sick. When and if I got killed I wanted to die whole and not have my pieces picked up in a basket.

We had made it over about half the division and were going good when I smelled a hot box. The conductor had gone down into the caboose and was getting a wink of sleep. I dropped down and woke him, telling him about the hot box. A hot wheel box will smoke for a while, then blaze, and then, if the train not stopped and the box cooled, the axle will break, causing the wreck.

We left the caboose and ran over the tops of the cars, climbing down each side ladder, hunting the hot box. We found it under the second carload of dynamite.

We swung our lantern to stop the train, but no one noticed our signals. We were making between forty and fifty miles an hour over rough track. Skinner evidently had fallen asleep, as he said he would before leaving Juarez. We had but four or five cars equipped with air brakes and they were next to the engine. We could not stop the train by pulling the air.

"I'll climb down and uncouple that car," Four Eyes called. "Then you set the brakes on this end of the train, and I'll uncouple the car from the front end and set brakes on it. We'll let Skinner and his end go on."

"But if the car catches fire and you're on it and explodes, you'll be..."

"That's my lookout—I'm running this train," he called as he swung down between the jolting cars.

Those cars were weaving and jolting so that I could hardly hold my feet on the running board. As he came up I began setting brakes on my end of the train. The interval between the sections lengthened and I sat on a brake wheel and watched.

I saw the lantern go down at the front end of the now blazing car, and after what appeared to me to be an hour, but was only a few seconds, it came up again. The lantern swung around and around and I knew Four Eyes was setting brakes on the blazing car. The front end of the train went on. Then the light went down the side ladder of the car and disappeared. That deadly car was now a quarter mile from my rear end of the train. The blazing car was isolated, but I was wondering what had become of Four Eyes. He walked back to me a few minutes later. His lantern had gone out when he dropped from the lower rung of the side ladder of the blazing car.

The quirk of this little incident was that the dynamite never did explode, although it made a great fire—something like an oil fire. Billy Skinner made about fifteen miles before he noticed the taillights of the caboose were not following the train.

I heard Four Eyes, that conductor, make a great speech in that Ohio town and I knew that under his carefully tailored, properly manicured exterior the candidate had something that counted more than anything else he could ever have—nerve, guts, or whatever you might call it.

He was frisked away to catch a train before I could contact him. But I took pride in following his career in Congress although he differed from me politically.

And I have to tell about old "Jumpin' Jasus" Smith and his heroism.

Smith had worked on the Mexican Central since it was constructed. His exclamation when he was excited was "Jumpin' Jasus," and that earned him his nickname. He never drank and his only amusement was to go into the slums of Chihuahua, sit down somewhere and throw coppers to the dirty little children gathered around. Wherever he went in Chihuahua a crowd of children followed, and he never disappointed them. Away from the children, he was a dirty-mouthed old fellow and none of us ever ganged with him.

A crew had quit while in Juarez, and I was deadheading up to bring a train down, acting as extra conductor. I caught a special pulled by Smith—eight coaches and a baggage car. That outfit was some sort of religious gathering that had visited the City of Mexico, for during the early part of the night they had put in the time singing religious songs. I tired of the singing and walked through the baggage coach to the cab of the engine and rode a while on the fireman's seat.

Sometime later, while shoveling in a scoop of coal, the fireman hit his hand on the firebox door, injuring it badly.

I knew this fireman well, a good-natured, smiling young Mexican. So when he injured his hand I told him to go back to the baggage coach and get first aid and I would fire the engine until we would meet a freight and pick up another fireman.

A "norther" was blowing down from Texas, and with it came a fine, misty rain. Firing that engine was no picnic, either. I would shovel in three or four scoops of coal, shut the firebox door, lean out the gangway to get a breath of fresh air and then repeat the operation. Smith had her "in the corner" and was making a good fifty miles an hour. He was humped on his right-hand seat, his hand on the throttle, peering ahead. We had headlights worked with acetylene gas, which threw a faint beam ahead.

I had just shoveled in a quota of coal and leaned out my side of the gangway when I felt a jerk as Smith pushed in the throttle and set the air brakes. He sprang from his seat far enough so he could extend his left foot. That foot hit me in the middle of the back and I toppled out the gangway. I had a split second's view of him as I fell. He was back on his seat jerking at the reverse lever. Then came a crash, a helluva crash. I heard it as I rolled down the sandy fill.

Several cars had been blown from a switch a few miles ahead and were coming down the track. Smith saw them coming in time to bring his train down to a slow speed. He hadn't had time to explain the danger to me, so he had kicked me out.

No one was hurt but Smith. The passengers were barely jolted. The locomotive took the brunt of the impact. One car climbed clear over the engine to the cab, broke a steam pipe—and old Smith was roasted.

He might have jumped, but he didn't. He might have let his passengers bear the brunt of the crash, but that would have violated his own code of ethics. An engineer is supposed to think of his passengers first. Old Smith stuck to his engine. Talk about your Christian martyrs.

46

Murderers

I HAD BEEN WORKING out of Chihuahua several months, and had been advanced until about half my trips were made in the capacity of extra, or relief conductor, when something happened that forever lost me my rights on the Mexican Central Railroad.

This day I was working as brakeman, but I was just as much of a murderer, in the eyes of the Mexican law, as if I had been conductor. Laws were cock-eyed down there in the time of Diaz.

My train was second section of a regular freight train, and we had met a passenger train at a little station where there was no agent. The first section of the train had pulled up past the siding and then backed in out of the way of the passenger train.

There were several cars on the siding, so my train headed into the passing track and, after the passenger train passed, we had to back out.

We were backing out slowly. I was on the rear platform, signaling the engineer. The conductor, Harry Baldwin, was inside asleep, as we had been on the road nearly twenty-four hours.

A native, either very deaf or wishing to commit suicide, got on the track right in front of the caboose and started walking the way we were going. I yelled at him but he paid no attention. The rear end of the caboose struck him and he went under the wheels. I did not have time to signal the engineer and there were no air brakes that far back on the train.

I ran in and woke Baldwin. When I told him what had happened he was awake in a second. At that time, according to Mexican law, it was murder to kill a native in any way—if he shed blood during the killing. This Mexican had been cut to pieces and he had shed all the blood he ever had.

We dropped off the caboose and waited for the engineer to bring his end of the train so that it would clear the switch. We showed him what had happened, which was easy, as pieces of that man were strewn along the track for fifty yards or more.

According to the law, the engine crew was as guilty as the train crew. We pushed the train into the siding at the other end of the switch, cut off the engine and ran to catch the first section of our train. We caught it in less than twenty miles.

At the next siding we backed the engine in the clear, pulled the fire and then hid in the cars of the first section until we reached a point three or four miles from Chihuahua.

There we got off and intended to skirt around the city, where a crew would be notified to watch for us and take us on down, hidden somewhere on the train. According to law, we were murderers.

But I never got below the city.

47

Wives!

WHILE I WAS RAILROADING out of Chihuahua, I carried my shoulder-strap holster and revolver. While I was actually attending to my duties on a train, however, I left it in in the caboose as it made too much of a bulge in my thousand-mile shirt. It was the first thing I grabbed for when I realized we would have to make a quick getaway to escape imprisonment for the crime of murder.

I had explored Chihuahua thoroughly in my days off, hobnobbing with natives of all classes, eating and drinking with them.

One of these places, away out in the west end of the city, had become almost home to me. An old woman operated a cantina there and made excellent chicken enchiladas. Aside from this she had two reasonably presentable daughters, who could sing well. I taught them to sing "Give My Regards to Broadway," although they didn't know what the words meant.

Her place appeared to be a hangout for a bunch of tough-looking men who made frequent trips out and were gone for a month or so on those trips. I suspected these men of being smugglers.

In the course of time, I became well acquainted with the old woman, her daughters and the evil-looking men. I spent money rather freely and those men did the same. It was natural that we should treat each other and become friends. The bandits and the family became well enough acquainted that they called me Francisco or Ponchota.

The old lady told me several times she liked me well enough to want me for a son-in-law, and would let me be one at any time for but $10, which is how you marry down there. If the priest was handy after you have bought the girl from her parents, you go through another ceremony. But the parents had to be fed.

She added further that if I stayed in Chihuahua after marrying one of her daughters, she would board both of us for $5 a semana, which means a week.

So when the train crew had to skirt the city to get below it I quit them and went to that estanca.

The other members of the crew warned me that I was headed to prison for life, but I had my gun and knew I could take care of myself. I did not believe the officials could identify me as one of the crew as long as I was not with them.

I sat and drank late with the bandits. I was on the Owl Hoot Trail myself, I told them, and was ready for anything. After a time, they adjourned to a distant table and held a caucus among themselves, three of them. The girls sat across the table from me and sang songs and brought me drinks and chicken enchiladas.

Their caucus ended. They called me over to their table. Did I have any money?

I had about $400, but admitted having $300.

Was I a good shot?

I offered to shoot the stub of a cigarette out of a man's mouth at fifty feet and not even touch his lips. They did not take me up on this exhibition of my pistol prowess, which shows their prudence and good judgment. I had had too many drinks to shoot at anything and hit it.

Did I care to join in with them?

I might.

Even if it happened to be unlawful?

Laws were made to be broken, I said.

Then they came out with their proposition. I could double my money, they declared, if I would come with them and run a little opium across the line into the United States. They were leaving that night and would be glad enough to have another man along, especially if that man was an American who knew how to use a revolver if and when the occasion required. They had never had a Gringo in the outfit, they said, as many Gringoes were not to be trusted. But they knew they could depend on me, for hadn't they drank and talked with Ponchota until they knew his thoughts and were certain of his courage.

I accepted their proposition on the spot and gave them money with which to buy me a horse and saddle. They knew of a man nearby who had the required transportation for sale. Details settled, they left with my money.

I had been drinking several hours and was feeling good and liberal. While the men were out purchasing my horse I told the old woman I had never met two finer girls than her daughters, and that it was impossible for me to make a choice between them, and if she would take $20 for the two, I would pay her and during my absence I would decide which one to keep for good. If I never got back she would have both the money and the girls. She consented and I paid her the $20.

This transaction changed the complexion of things. Before the bargain the girls wouldn't come nearer me than across the table. But after I had paid the money, they came and sat on the bench beside me and told me how sorry they were I was going to leave, and that they would be waiting impatiently for their tall Americano caballero.

I had twelve or fourteen Mexican silver pesos in my pocket, and I divided the coins among the girls. They exclaimed over the liberality of their new man and begged me to stay over even a day or so and they would surprise me by the fine dresses they would buy with my money.

Then the men came back with my horse and saddle and the old woman sent the girls to bed. We had another drink while the shutters were being put up at the windows.

My new mother-in-law-to-be embraced me when I left and kissed me. She had been eating chili peppers and garlic, but she meant well.

We rode away in a northeasterly direction.

48

Smuggling Opium

IT WAS A LONG way up to the Rio Grande the direction we traveled, hut we took it easy, not having any specified time to get there. At a village a few miles from the Rio Grande, we stopped at a cantina operated by a Chinaman. We slept there and next morning got down to business.

The Chinaman would sell us a certain amount of opium for $100 Mex. If we delivered it to a certain party above the river, he would pay us $100, United States money for it. We could bring the United States money back to the Chinaman who would give us $200 Mex for it. Thus we doubled our money.

But it wasn't as easy as it sounds. United States customs officers, what was left of the Rangers, and a few deputy marshals had a nasty habit of snooping around.

When one of those aforesaid lawmen met a smuggler he usually shot him full of holes and left him to the buzzards. Three members of the gang I was with had been killed recently. That was why I had been recruited.

The opium smuggling was pretty well-organized. We would get our supply from the Chinaman and go up to the Rio Grande. There we would wait for a signal. To let the men across the river know just where we were, we would strip a small bush of its limbs and stick it upside down in the sand at the very edge of the water on the Mexican side.

This sign would not be conspicuous enough to attract the attention of anyone across the river who was not waiting for it. After having placed the sign we would wait, concealed.

Next morning, just across from our sign we would see a similar one. Sometimes this one leaned upstream, sometimes downstream. We went up or down stream as the sign leaned until we found one standing straight up. There, we knew, it would be safe to cross, and we did so.

After we had crossed the river we would see no one for several miles, but occasionally there would be a sign similar to the one at the river, guiding us. Perhaps we would see a horseman on a hill. If he took off his hat and held it on the saddle horn every few minutes, we knew it was our man. If he used binoculars, we knew he was a lawman.

After we had identified each other satisfactorily, we'd meet. He'd take our opium and we get our money. We dealt one at a time. Two of us would stand with our guns ready while he settled with the other two. This was to guard against a possible hijacker, or perhaps men of the smugglers' gang, who might decide to take the opium without the formality of paying for it. In that business you trust no one, not even the man you are dealing with.

Sometimes smugglers returning from a rendezvous were hijacked and murdered, but I was never molested. We always rode back single file, with an interval between each man. And we kept our guns handy.

I had ridden more than twenty loads across the border when I became possessed of a brilliant idea. I would get the stuff across without riding or going across in person. I talked a lot and finally sold my companions on the idea. But in trying it out I was to pay all the expenses of the experiment. Then, when we delivered our next shipment across the river, I had to sell the idea to the man who paid us for the stuff.

My plan was to make small balloons, attach packages of opium to them and when the wind blew from the south let them go at a point where it had been signaled as safe to cross.

I made balloons of silk, of which the Chinaman had plenty. Silk was smuggled across the border, too, but it was bulky and my gang wouldn't handle it. There are specialists in all businesses. Our specialty was opium.

I inflated a balloon with hot air, as I had seen done at county fairs in the states.

The whole population of the village, about one hundred counting the dogs, watched my preparations and speculated on the outcome. Even if the plan was a failure, they commented, here was an Americano who had strange ideas. Everyone in that village, above the age of ten, was connected in some way with the smuggling game. Before I had been there a week I knew every one of them by name, even the babies.

The first balloon load was a success. The wind carried the balloon over the river about a mile before it began to deflate when a cloud covered the sun.

About an hour later the man who paid off rode to the edge of the water and signaled me across and paid me $400 United States money, for what I had that morning paid the same amount in Mexican money. It was easy.

I was patting myself on the back, synthetically, as I forded the river coming back with my $400.

I would send a balloon, maybe two, five or ten, across every day and make a mint of money. In a year or two, I calculated, I would be able to go somewhere and buy me a little railroad of my own, or perhaps a daily newspaper. I was happy—for a while.

On second thought, I realized I could never own anything and live like a gentleman. And what money I had would slip through my fingers or I would give it to some girl as I had done with the other large sum I had—the money I had made in New Orleans. I would give it away if someone didn't bilk me out of it.

My second attempt was a failure. I must have inflated the bag too much, or perhaps the sun was shining too brightly. The balloon, with its $400 worth of opium, rose and kept on rising. We watched it and we knew men across the river was watching it. That's all. We just watched it.

The last I saw of it was when it was a mere speck in the sky far to the north and going higher every second. It may have landed in Canada.

The loss of the $400 worth of opium didn't break me by any means. We had made many trips across the line successfully. But the failure of my plan disgusted me. It shattered the ego in my cosmos, as it were.

I rode back to the village, disconsolate. When my partners started out next morning with loads I refused to go with them. They sympathized with me, and told me it would do me good to rest a few days.

I had explained to them that I didn't mind the loss of the opium but I did regret the failure of my great idea. They saw my point of view. One of them told me of having looked, in his younger days, at a saddle in a show window every time he passed that way. His one ambition was to own that saddle. One night a great storm came up and while it was at its height he broke the window and got the saddle. When he examined it by daylight he found it had only been made for show purposes and was only the fork of a saddle covered with paper colored to look like leather. He, too, knew what disappointment was like.

They rode into the dawn, three dirty, be-whiskered Mexicans, foul-mouthed, drunken, devil-may-care fellows who would cut a throat in a fight, but who would stick to a friend unto death. Ever since the night we had ridden out of Chihuahua together I had been their friend, their "amigo," their crack pistol shot. To them I was a brother, I was Ponchota, the good Gringo.

I loafed around the village. I drank occasionally at the Chinaman's estanca. I threw small coins to the little children in the street, who would bite each coin they picked up to see that I didn't run in any counterfeits on them.

I sat in the shade of what had once been a market shelter and whittled out little windmills for the children. I attended the funeral of a small boy.

Three young men of the village marched with me and played "After the Ball" as a funeral dirge.

A week passed and my partners had not returned. Hijackers of the law had caught them for they would have returned. All three had money on deposit with the Chinaman. I rode to the river several times and set up the usual sign. In the morning there was no answering signal. Something surely was wrong.

I really mourned those partners. With me out of the gang they probably had ridden in a group, which could be ambushed easily. When I was with them I insisted we travel about a one-hundred feet apart, so that if one was ambushed the other three could help him. Somehow or other I blamed myself for letting them go alone.

I waited another week. Then I got all my money from the Chinaman one morning and rode down the river.

49

Salina Cruz

I RODE DOWN THE RIVER, eating at dirty little villages, sleeping where I happened to get sleepy, drinking a little where I found a place drinks were sold. I met a number of rurales, but they never questioned me and I never conversed with them more than to wish them a good evening or good morning, according to the time of day.

Early one morning I rode into Sabinas, quite a little city as cities go in Northern Mexico. I didn't know where to go. I sold my horse and took a train into Eagle Pass.

I sat for a whole afternoon on a pile of ties near the railroad station in Eagle Pass and mapped out routes. No route suited me exactly.

Somewhere, at some time, I had read a little poem, four lines of which stuck in my memory:
"There is something about the tropics
That will get you, sure as rum.
You get away and you swear you'll stay,
But they call—and back you come!"
I realized what was wrong. I was homesick for the tropics again!

I had money and it would be nice to go up to some clean city, get a job and hole up for the winter, eating good food, sleeping in a bed with sheets on it, associating with clean, well-dressed people who bathed and spoke English. I had experienced that sort of life the winter before in Columbus. To decide which way to go I took a coin and tossed it on the ground.

"Heads I go north, tails I go south," I said.

The coin came up heads—but I went south!

Four days later I got off a train in Buena Vista station in the City of Mexico, went across to the Dos Republicas bar, and asked for a drink. The one sole other customer was an American. I asked him to have a drink with me.

224

"I'm running from cold weather," I mentioned as we drank.

"I just came up from the hot country a few days ago," the man said. "I'm going back tonight. Too cold and high for me here."

"Where did you come from?" I asked.

"The Isthmus of Tehuantepec," he replied. "Still got my rights on the Tehuantepec railroad—just got thirty days leave. Wasn't thinking of going back, but I will."

I went down with him, via Vera Cruz. At Rincon Antonio, headquarters at that time, there was nothing doing in the way of employment, so I went on to Salina Cruz, a port on the Pacific Ocean, terminus of the Tehuantepec Railroad. A British firm of contractors, Pearson & Son, Ltd., London, was building the port works there.

In building the port works, great blocks of concrete were molded. These were carried out to the end of the piers in cars and dumped into the water. Hundreds were dumped until the last blocks dumped extended above the water line.

Then steel verticals were sunk on each side, bolted together, and were used as a mold into which to pour liquid concrete. This hardened around the blocks already dumped into the water and made a solid wall in the sea.

There were two of these jetties extending out into the ocean, about half a mile apart. The idea was that the river flowing out between the jetties would wash out a deep channel.

The engineer who planned the port works was good. The river did as he figured it would. Salina Cruz now has a depth of water right up to the wharf which will accommodate any size vessel.

Switch engines carried the cement up a long incline and dumped the contents of loaded cars into a hopper, where the mixtures were fed into a mold. About thirty of these little locomotives were used there, but not all at once. Normally about twenty operated each day.

Because the company was British, an applicant for employment had to fill out a blank before being hired. In it you gave details of your previous employment.

I asked for a job and filled out an application. In it I mentioned my services as master mechanic of the Ocós Railroad. I was told to report for work next morning. I was given a numbered brass check for identification.

As I was entering the shops next morning, the timekeeper at the gate glanced at my check, referred to a paper he held in his hand and said, "You are to report to the master mechanic instead of going into the shops."

The master mechanic was a Yank, as I was. When I introduced myself he said, "You've been master mechanic, I see from your application."

"At Ocós, yes."

"I've heard a great deal about your work from men coming through. Could you handle a gang here?"

"I see no reason why I couldn't," I told him. "Railroading is the same everywhere."

"Then report back at six o'clock tonight," he instructed. "I'm going to put you in as roundhouse night foreman. You'll be responsible for the engines from the time they're delivered to you at quitting time 'til you send them out in the morning. See that the engines are ready to start work each morning at seven o'clock. Think you can do it?"

"Certainly."

"Then report back here at six this evening. The man who has the job now wants to go down to Panama to get in on the canal work when they've started it. He'll show you the ropes for a few nights."

"OK, sir," I said.

"Got eating money?"

"About $2,000 Mex."

"Hell," he exclaimed. "I don't see why you want to go to work with all that money," he laughed. "You hoboes are a queer sort. From what I've heard of your ability, you could hold a good job up in the States. And here you are looking for a little job down here with a coupla thousand dollars in your pocket."

"It's the itchy foot," I explained.

"I know it," he agreed. "Come around at six tonight. The Chinaman over at the hotel will fix you out for quarters."

50

Jamaicans

THAT'S HOW I TOOK CHARGE of about fifty Jamaicans and half a dozen English and American machinists. I was allowed six machinists, but they came and went. One night I would have but one, next night the whole six. Every skilled man below the Rio Grande was heading for the Panama Canal.

The one machinist who stayed with me was an Englishman named Gants. He had been imported under contract and had stayed after his contract expired. He was saving his money with the intention of going out to Australia and starting a sheep ranch and becoming a millionaire. What made him think a good machinist would become a good sheep herder I know not, but that was his ambition.

The Jamaicans had been imported under contract. Most of them were good workers. About one out of fifty was educated, and it was educated ones that gave trouble. The others were happy-go-lucky fellows who seldom took themselves or anything else seriously.

The other Jamaicans were a lovable lot. I became fond of them and they came to me with their personal problems. And they had many of them.

Many of these Jamaicans married Mexicans, after a fashion. In fact, I was in on such a marriage.

It was our custom to work until midnight and then take an hour off for lunch. I usually walked over to the Chinaman's for lunch, as he kept open all night. One night I followed my usual custom and got back to the office with time to spare. I was sitting at my desk, smoking, when one of the Jamaicans came to the door. I looked up.

"I would consult with the mastah about a matter of business, sah," he began. They used the longest words they knew and used them indiscriminately. I caught myself talking that way sometimes.

"What is the business?" I inquired.

227

"It is not good for man to live alone, as is read from the Bible. I would enter matrimony."

"So what?"

"I have excellent wife sorted out. But the father him Indian man and he say I must pay him five dollars for my wife I got sorted out."

"And then what?"

"I am so involved in poverty that I do not have five dollars for the wife I got sorted out."

"And?"

"Maybe the master have kindness of heart to borrow me five dollars."

"This wife you sorted out—she good cook?"

"Super cook, sah."

"You got house?"

"She build house—two-three days. She super with building house."

I knew the kind of house it would be. A cane shack with a couple of stones over which to cook.

"I borrow you five dollars," I said. "You pay back recently?"

"From each week—fifty cents."

I gave him five dollars and for many paydays he would come in and give me fifty cents. I think he repaid the loan fully.

It was the usual Indian wedding. You paid your money and you got your wife, F.O.B. her father's shack. But that sort of marriage was good for life. Those Mexican Indians knew no such thing as divorce.

I saw the bride that cost five dollars few days after the marriage. She was a solid, sturdy women, almost as black as her husband. She was not as young nor as slim as my wives in Chihuahua, but she appeared a great deal cleaner.

The groom must have told his fellow workmen that I was good for a touch. Almost every night in the latter part of the week they would come to ask for a loan of small amount, and I accommodated them. I never kept books, as the sums I lent were too insignificant to bother about. But every Saturday night—Saturday was payday—the Jamaicans would come in, give me a few coins, tell me how we stood, and ask if it agreed with my books. Their figures always agreed with mine, because I kept no books.

They had their superstitions, too. One night while I was walking across the round house I caught my toe on one of the rails of the tracks inside the building. I did not fall, and would have gone on, but several of the Negroes cried out. I stopped and asked what was wrong.

"Mastah, mastah, go back and cross over the rail once again," one of them cried. "You go on and something sure happen to mastah."

I knew it was a foolish superstition, but to please them I retraced my steps and re-crossed the rail without stubbing my toe. I appreciated the fact that they did not want me to get hurt. If they hadn't liked me they would have let me go on without warning, and if the hex got me it would have been all right with them.

51

Boosted Up

IT WAS GOOD LIFE I led in Salina Cruz—too good. I had fallen into a rut again, something I disliked.

The City of Tehuantepec was about twelve miles up from Salina Cruz, and sometimes on Sunday I would walk up there, eat midday dinner at a hotel, and catch the afternoon train down to the port.

Tehuantepec was inhabited by a unique class of people. They were almost lighter skinned, tall, well-formed, and intelligent. They spoke the Zapotec dialect, many words of which resembled ancient Hebrew. I have often wondered if, at some distant time, a colony of Hebrews hadn't crossed the ocean somehow and landed near Tehuantepec, there to start a race of Zatopecs.

I would put in several hours every Sunday when I went up there. Some of those Tehuantepec girls were beautiful and stately—but they wouldn't give an American hobo a second glance.

I had been there several months and Christmas was approaching when one day the master mechanic sent for me before I reported for work.

"I've got a job up on the Southern Pacific," he began. "I'm to take charge January first. I've recommended you for my place. Can you find a man to take the night job?"

I could. Gants could take over and do my job with some help on reports. He wasn't much on education.

"You've got along famously with those men from Jamaica," the master mechanic praised. "Ninety percent of the men on the day shift have made application for night work. And getting along with the men while getting out the work is half the battle of a supervisory foreman."

We went over to the chief engineer's office where I submitted to a severe cross-examination. But those engineers were nice about it. They were gentlemen, those Pearson engineers.

My record in rehabilitating the Ocós Railroad was a point in my favor, although my moral record, as revealed in articles published in the *Mexican Herald*, was not so good.

I explained to the engineers, however, that my life in Ocós had been much the same as in Salina Cruz, and the articles published in the newspaper had been highly colored. I had to be rough, I explained, to clean up things down at Ocós, but I cleaned them up in good shape.

"This may not be a permanent position," the engineer said. "We have a man coming from Suez. Just when he will get there is uncertain, but when he comes you will have to go back to the night roundhouse job. Will that be satisfactory?"

I assured him it would be all right with me.

I had been getting $400 a month Mex, equal to $300, US money, but with my promotion this was increased to $750 Mex.

"I want to educate my two children up in the United States," the master mechanic explained after I had been chosen to take his place. "Up there I'll be foreman at $210 a month, but the children will learn to live with their folks."

My new job was largely white collar. I was boss of the mechanical end of the port works, under the chief engineer and his assistants. As long as everything clicked efficiently in the mechanical department, they seldom said anything other than the usual day's greeting. They were fine men, those Englishmen, even if they did clip their words a little and call a pair of shoes "boots."

But there was one fly in the ointment, one flea on my hide. The climate of Salina Cruz was ideal. Food and living conditions were excellent. A constant breeze off the Gulf of Tehuantepec made sleep-in a pleasure. I never took more than a drink or two a day, usually after leaving my office in the afternoon. My clerks, half a dozen young educated Mexicans, were efficient.

But I wasn't spending any money.' There was no society in Salina Cruz, and if there had been I wouldn't have been interested. Out of my salary I spent about $100 a month. Sometimes for several months I would return my pay check to the paymaster. He would send it up to the general offices of Pearson & Son, Ltd., in the City of Mexico, where it would be held subject to my order.

April came and my feet grew itchy. I began to imagine how things looked when spring came over the land above the Rio Grande.

I thought so much about spring coming over the States that I dreamed about it. I would dream of the wheat waving in the breeze and smell the sweet smell of the prairie after a rain had passed over.

I would wake after a dream of riding in a street car with a lot of clean, well-dressed, intelligent people and look out over the plaza and see the dirty Indians squatting around and swear I would quit that very day. But after I got to my office I would forget it in the routine of running the port works mechanical department. But the itchy foot had me in its grip and it was only a matter of time until I would have to move.

If I happened to think of it when I met the chief engineer I would ask about the man from Suez. I never got a direct answer.

Those British engineers had a club where they resided. Their servants were mostly old English trained men. Of course I couldn't join the club, as I wasn't an engineer or an Englishman.

As soon as they discovered I could use the proper forks at the table and didn't try to eat peas with my knife, they got in the habit of inviting me to their club for lunch once a week. They did not dress for luncheon, but for dinner—always. As I had no dress suit I was never invited to dinner there.

I had made a trade with the master mechanic of the Tehuantepec National Railways that helped me in the engineers' estimation. The shops of the railroad were located at Rincon Antonio. The shops there had less equipment than I had and we made a bargain by which I would do some of the big work for the railroad on a time basis.

There were lulls in the work at Salina Cruz and I did this extra work without interfering with my regular work. For this I got a compliment from the chief engineer. I ran my department as if I owned the whole thing, and kept within my budget.

But the itchy foot was bothering me. One day I put it up to the chief engineer. "When is the man from Suez coming in?"

He smiled. "I am not sure," he replied.

Then I went on, "My feet are itchy. I'd like to go back to the States. I can get you a man within a week who will slip into my routine without a hitch. I will stay here until I am sure you are satisfied and draw no salary."

"Who is this man?" the chief engineer asked.

"The master mechanic of the Tehuantepec up at Rincon Antonio. An Englishman who has been trained both in England and on the railroads of the United States."

"Then he is the man from Suez," the chief engineer said with a smile. "Bring him down and we will try him out."

52

Caroline and...

ON THE ROAD AGAIN! The City of Mexico, where I drew my deposited salary checks from Pearson & Son, Ltd., and deposited them in the Chinese bank.

One of the company officials with whom I conversed for some time after having completed my business with the company, invited me out to his house for dinner that evening. His wife was a native of Baltimore, he said, and liked to entertain Americans.

He had mentioned me to his wife, he went on to say, how I seldom drew a salary check and how I was a colonel in the Guatemalan army. He had talked with her over the telephone while I was engaged with the cashier, and she would like me to come and meet a group of her friends and some visitors that evening.

I was frank with him. "If an Englishman is in the jungles, a thousand miles from civilization," I elaborated, "and has nothing to eat but baked iguana, he will dress for dinner. An American will not. To make a long story short, I have no evening clothes. I never have had."

"But you wouldn't want to disappoint my wife, a Yankee like yourself, would you?" he protested. "It wouldn't be sporting, what?"

The result was that I spent about $150 for a monkey suit—soup and fishes. The tailor was about two hours fitting the suit to my frame. It had been worn before but you couldn't detect that fact.

When I had clothed myself in these glad rags and was in a carriage going out to Colonia, I thought of the other time I had landed in the city from the south with nothing to wear but a tropical suit of clothes, no money, and a red slip of paper with Chinese characters.

The host and hostess were gracious and soon put me at my ease. She introduced me to some twenty-odd men and women whose names I forgot as soon as I turned around.

Going into dinner I was paired with a woman a few years older than I was. She was careless about her dress, but was a good-looking woman at that. My hostess had mentioned she was a writer. I knew she was an English woman from her habit of clipping her words.

I was about to start a conversation about shoes to make sure she was English, for if she really was she would speak of them as boots. But she got the start.

"So you're the notorious El Señor Diablo?" she exclaimed. "I expected to see a big, fierce-looking man. Offhand, without knowing who you were, I would class you as a haberdasher's clerk."

The name of El Señor Diablo surprised me. I had not heard the name in a long time.

I queried: "What is a haberdasher and what does the clerk do? And how did you hear of El Señor Diablo?"

"A haberdasher sells men's gear, ties, shirts and the like. I read all about El Señor Diablo in the *Mexican Herald*. That is why I prevailed on Mrs. Coleman to pair you off with me."

"I did nothing down there but run the railroad and the district," I explained, "and to do that successfully I had to be a little rough."

"And a harem?" she asked, smiling.

"I never had a harem," I declared, "or anything like that. I never associated with native women."

"I came across to Mexico to get material for a lot of stories about Mexico," the woman elaborated. "You're the first real character I've met and you've turned out to be commonplace."

"You knew Mrs. Coleman?"

"I brought a letter from a mutual friend of ours in London."

"Don't write too much about me," I cautioned. "I may come to London some day and check up on you."

"If you ever come to London," she returned, "I'll show you the city."

"I may take you up on that," I said.

"Do so," she invited. "London is full of pitfalls for young men from the wilderness. I am several years your senior. I'm a widow by virtue of a decision of the divorce court, and I know my way around London."

"Have you seen all of Mexico City?" I asked.

"The hanging gardens, Chapultepec, and a few other points of interest."

"You've never been to El Oro, climbed Popocatapetl or things like that?"

"No."

"Perhaps I can take you around?" I suggested.

"Nothing would suit me better."

"I haven't a thing to do," I told her. "If you will give me your name and address I'll..."

"You failed to get my name?"

"Absolutely."

She scribbled her name and address on a piece of paper. I noted she was living in a foreign section of the city.

"How did you come to live away out there, Miss..." I hesitated, while I referred to the piece of paper.

"Oh, call me Caroline," she said. "And I live in that neighborhood to get the real Mexican atmosphere. I have rented half a house. I have an old man and woman, husband and wife, for servants. The woman can speak a little English, and I can speak a little Spanish."

"I'll call for you at ten o'clock tomorrow," I promised as she got up from the table with the other feminine guests.

She was eating breakfast when I called next morning. I ate a second breakfast with her and asked where she wanted to go first.

"Popocatapetl."

"We'll start tomorrow morning, then," I said.

"Today."

"But," I protested, "if we catch the afternoon train down there we can't get up the mountain tonight. Guides will not go up after dark."

"But we could start earlier next morning?"

"Of course. But I'm not sure of the accommodations at the station from which we start our climb."

"We'll not worry about that," she said. "I'll dress for mountain climbing and meet you at San Lazaro station at three o'clock."

"OK," I agreed.

There were no hotel accommodations at the village from which we were to start our climb, but I found a family who agreed to let Caroline sleep in a sort of mud lean-to at one side of their house. She had a blanket and they furnished her another. I slept in the railroad station where the night operator emptied a table that answered for a bed. My coat furnished the pillow.

At daylight I got up and looked out. A cold wind swept down the sides of the mountain. From where I stood I could see nearly to the summit, the peak of which was covered with a haze. I wondered why I ever agreed to climb a mountain when I could have stayed in the comfortable hotel in the city.

An old woman who ran a sort of estanca furnished me a drink, and I told her to prepare something to eat for a señorita. I was seated there when Caroline entered.

"Sleep well?" I inquired.

"I have slept better," she said.

"So have I."

She shivered, much as if she was doing a hoochie-koochie dance.

"Are you that cold?" I asked. "We'll have some coffee in a minute."

"I fear it isn't cold," she said and shivered one more.

"Then what do you attribute your shivering act to?"

"Do we have to go up the mountain today?" she asked.

"No. Nor any other day," I said.

"The nearest bath is probably away back there in the City of Mexico, isn't it?" she asked.

"I think so. These people seldom bathe. It's too cold."

"I'm aware of that—now."

"Meaning what?"

"Lack of bathing facilities breeds little bugs—vermin—that take pleasure in crawling over the body of a human being, it is said."

"Lice?"

"Yes. Have you ever been afflicted with them?"

"Several times."

"What did you do?"

"Stripped. Burned my clothes and bathed and put on clean ones. Even then you'll miss one or two and they'll raise a new family. When they do you go through the whole routine again."

"Ugh."

"Another way is to go down to the hot country. Those little bugs cannot live when one sweats."

All the way up on the train we sat in separate seats. I could see Caroline try to compose herself, and then wriggle vigorously. She was too proud to just relax and scratch.

She did not invite me in when we reached her home. We didn't even make an appointment for another time. But I knew neither of us would ever climb old Popocatapetl.

53

The Serape

I HAD REGISTERED MY mail address with the post office authorities as the office of Pearson & Sons, Inc., and called there almost every day. It was the custom in the City of Mexico to register your address so that the police could check up on you. It answered as a credit reference, too.

As I knew which forks to use at a table, and did not slurp my soup, I received a number of invitations to dinners from the British colony there, members of which were not too high-brow for me. Caroline attended all of these, so we met again.

One morning, while in the Pearson offices I was introduced to a man who was building a cement factory out near Guadaloupe. He was a high-class Mexican and proved to be a good fellow.

He was in search of a man who could take charge of the installation of the plant, which was to be powered by a huge Hamilton Corliss engine. I took the job.

I was out there all day and came in in the afternoon. It became a habit of mine to go to Caroline's for dinner after I had dressed and bathed. She cooked the meals herself and they were far better than I could have gotten in a hotel. After dinner we would explore the city, returning before midnight. Usually we had a light lunch before I went back to my hotel.

We explored the out-of-the-way sections of the city, where tourists seldom penetrate, and I took her to dives that no foreigner would attempt to visit without a police escort. But no one ever bothered us. We went window shopping, and sometimes, when stores were open, we bought souvenirs.

Caroline wrote nearly all day and she put me onto a little of the technique of the short story. I rented an old blind Caligraph typewriter and wrote a story myself, revised it, and sent it to New York.

I was a month installing the cement plant. During that time I usually spent the evening guiding Caroline around the city, or we attended a dinner at the home of some member of the British colony.

I had finished the plant, settled up with the owner, who gave me a bonus and went as usual out to Caroline's place for dinner. I found no dinner and no Caroline.

"Where is the señora?" I asked. The mozo went out and called the owner of the house, who occupied the other half. When she came in I asked her about Caroline.

"I thought you were aware she left this morning for Vera Cruz," the woman said.

I was surprised, as Caroline had never hinted about leaving.

"Did she leave anything for me?" I inquired.

"Yes, señor," the woman said. "She left the bill for the rental of this house for two months. I would have asked you for it sooner, but the señora said you were going to stay after she left and I knew you were employed at Pearson's."

"Anything else?" I asked caustically.

"Some things came for the señora this morning and she asked the messenger to leave the bill here for you to settle."

She handed me a bill from an expensive women's furnishing store. The bill was made out in my name with the prefix "Mrs." Caroline had established a credit there because I was supposed to have been employed by Pearsons. The store had checked my mailing address.

Among the things on the bill was a serape, $125. I remembered then that we had passed the show window many times and each time Caroline had admired the piece. She had it now.

I paid the bills, but remained peeved. She had been good company in our excursions about the city. She had egged me on to writing a story. She had instructed me how to put all the suspense I could into the first paragraph of a story, and several other tricks of the writing trade.

After thinking the matter over I didn't regret the money I had spent on Caroline. But she should have at least said farewell.

Next day I paid all the bills and called at the Pearson office. There was a letter for me and a postcard. The postcard was from Caroline. It had been mailed in Vera Cruz and bore the picture of a great fish head, the Vera Cruz breakfast.

"Forgive me for leaving so suddenly, but I have barely enough money to see me to London. If you ever come to London look me up. You will know me by the serape. CAROLINE."

Ships that pass in the night? Perhaps. And take expensive serapes with them.

The other letter was from a New York magazine. "We are accepting your story "The Ratita" and the check will reach you within a few days. We would like to see more of your work, etc."

It had been our custom, when we had been out for an evening and came home before ten o'clock, to buy a few hot tamales from an aged woman known as Magdaline, who kept a basketfull, hot and delicious, about a block from where Caroline lived. Caroline would make coffee, and that was our late lunch before I went back to my hotel. I liked those tamales better than any I ever tasted. So did Caroline.

The morning after I received the card from Caroline, I picked up a copy of the *Mexican Herald* and read the news. On the front page was a little four-inch story about a woman named Magdaline who had been arrested and charged with failing to bury the body of her granddaughter. Police found flesh cut from the girl's arms and thighs and it was thought, the story went, that this human flesh had been converted into hot tamales.

That story and the fact that Caroline had bilked me good and plenty made me sick at my stomach. I made for the nearest place where I could buy a drink.

It was some sort of fiesta day. I took two or three drinks and then moved on and took one or two at every place I stopped. Along late afternoon I found myself away out in the suburbs. I remember standing at the bar of a cantina addressing those present.

"You people celebrate the Cinco de Mayo (fifth of May) and you celebrate the sixteenth of September," I remember telling them. "But you never celebrate the day American soldiers climbed Chapultepec Hill."

"That's about all I do remember," I told the physician in the hospital the following morning, when he brought police to my room to get details of the fight. I was badly cut and mauled. Passing policemen, assisted by a riot squad, had rescued me, I was told. The Mexicans had resented my speech. Chapultepec Hill was still a sore spot with them.

I assured the police it was but a drunken brawl and no one should be punished for it. I even offered to pay for any damage I had done to the others, but it seemed that I was the only one injured. The cantina owner had lost a jug of pulque and a few bottles of aguardiente, and I sent him the money by the police.

As soon as I was out of the hospital I took a train to Vera Cruz. I had intended going on to New Orleans, but my usual luck held. I never started for any place and got there as I had intended.

54

Back to Guatemala

I WAS IN THE OFFICE of the master mechanic of the Interoceanic Railroad in Vera Cruz, talking shop, when he happened to remark, "They've got four engines down on the Panzos Railroad and only two of them can get over the road at all, and those two can't pull more than five cars. They want a good machinist and want him badly. Care to go down?"

"What's the pay?" I asked.

"The man in here said they'd pay $200 gold."

"I might go. If he comes in again, tell him I'll be at the hotel until tomorrow when the Munson liner leaves for New Orleans."

I was sitting in the barroom of the hotel after dinner when I was paged. I told the boy to send whoever it was over to my table. It was the German from Panzos and another one, about as drunk. Both could speak English after a fashion.

"The master mechanic of the narrow-gage informs me that you are an expert machinist," one of them said, after both had seated themselves and I had ordered drinks.

"He's eminently correct," I bragged. "I've been master mechanic of the Ocós Railroad and got it to running better than any other road in the Central American Republics. I made a record as master mechanic of the port works at Salina Cruz. I can put your road in good repair if you have the money with which to pay me. My specialty is rebuilding and rehabilitating things—and letting someone take the profits from me."

"More and more coffee is coming down for us to transport," the German explained. "Our locomotives are in such disorder that we can't haul it all. The finca owners are talking of building a road of their own down to Livingstone, which would put our road out of business altogether. We want a man who can put our engines and track in good condition."

240

"As I said before," I bragged again, "I'm the man if you want the job done efficiently. All you have to do is furnish the money."

"We were intending to pay a good man $200 a month gold and..."

"Chicken feed." I exclaimed. "If you're only paying that much, you'd better fix your own railroad. I'm going up to the States and get a job at five dollars a day where I can live good and associate with clean people."

They consulted for a few hundred words in German, which I couldn't understand. My knowledge of German was, and is, confined to three words—swei bier haben—and I'm not sure I know how to spell those.

But those three words will always bring out two beers if you say them to a barkeep, even if he is a Brooklyn Irishman. After spitting out gutterals for a few minutes one of them asked, "Would you come if we doubled the salary?"

"I might."

"If we don't get our railroad so we can haul all the coffee down, the finca owners will build another road and our company will be ruined."

All the time I had been intending to go at their original offer, but I wanted to bargain a bit.

"Double your first offer is good with me. Get your contract made out and in the morning we'll go to the British consul and have it OKed."

"I thought you were a citizen of the United States," one of them remarked.

"I am a Canadian," I told them.

At that time, and perhaps even now, United States consuls were not highly regarded by American hoboes. As I mentioned in a previous chapter, the consul at Ocós was a German who could speak little English, and so it was all down the line. Where a consul was a real citizen of the United States, his salary was so small that he had to engage in some business to make ends meet. The American consul at Salina Cruz really attended to business when he happened to be there. But his chief source of income was as salesman for several American implement firms.

The result was that United States consuls paid little attention to the American hobo and the American hobo ignored the consuls.

British consuls were young career men. They were not permitted to engage in local business ventures. Many of them had incomes which made them independent of their salaries. If a British subject got into trouble or got bilked in any fraudulent manner, the British consuls were ready and willing to go to the bat for him, regardless.

That is why, when I wanted a contract authenticated, I turned Canadian, which was the same as being a native of the British Isles. I knew nothing about Canada. Neither did the consuls, so they could not catch me lying if they questioned me about the great dominion.

Two or three days later I took a boat down to Port Livingstone. I was in Guatemala again.

55

Blue Indian

THE PANZOS RAILROAD IS ISOLATED. It is but a link in the route coffee must take on its way from the highlands of Eastern Guatemala to the coast. It operates from the head of navigation on the Panzos River to where the river peters out into a good-sized creek.

From Port Livingstone one takes a boat operated by the railroad up the Dulce River, crosses a lake in which there are lots of alligators, and then enters the Panzos river. We chugged along that route all day and finally reached Panzos.

When you get to Panzos you are nowhere. The town boasts about five hundred inhabitants, who spend most of their time sleeping.

I fell heir to a few old shacks that housed a lathe, a planer and a few other machine tools, and four locomotives more or less decrepit. One of these locomotives had been stripped so much to supply parts for the others than nothing but the boiler was left.

Four Negroes constituted my force—two from Alabama, one from Barbados, and one from Jamaica. My greatest work was to keep them from going to sleep. They were passable mechanics, if one showed them each separate operation. But if I left them for any length of time, I would return to find them asleep. It was useless to discharge them, for no other workmen could be found. White men couldn't be paid enough to live and work at Panzos.

The thermometer varied from 98 degrees at midnight to about 120 in the middle of the day. And the only breeze was made by millions of mosquitoes flying around. I never saw mosquitoes so thick. Natives and the four Negroes working for me used a sort of liquid, made by boiling the bark of a tree, to keep the little pests off their skin.

I tried this stuff. Every morning before leaving the screened car in which I slept I would rub it all over me, after the fashion one rubs on liniment. It did not affect the darker-skinned persons, but it turned my hide a bright blue. And I couldn't wash it off, regardless of how I tried.

After trying several things I discovered that if I washed thoroughly with gasoline the blue would come off. But the gasoline was worse than the blue, so I let it stay on. As my stay lengthened I became bluer and bluer.

One day a party of tourists came through—two men and three women. They had been seeing Guatemala with the aid of some travel agency. These five had left the main party at Guatemala City to cut across to the Peten and visit some of the coffee plantations on the eastern slope. From there they had come down to the end of the Panzos Railroad and they arrived at Panzos via one of the regular trains that happened to carry a passenger coach that day.

Arrangements had been made for a boat to come up to Panzos for them, but it went aground on a sand bar in the lake and it didn't arrive. So they visited around Panzos and eventually reached the shops.

Having no occasion to, I had never shaved. My beard is a reddish color and sticks straight out like in the cartoons of a Bolshevik. This, added to the fact that my exposed skin was a deep blue, somewhat astonished the tourists.

"Have they got blue Indians in this country?" they asked one of my men.

He saw a chance for some fun. "Yas, suh," he said. "We've got 'em of all colors down here."

"What do you call that blue Indian?" one of the women asked, indicating me. I was in the cab of a locomotive, installing an overhauled Penberthy injector.

"He's a Whampodompis. He lives on a little island out in the river, and they eats raw fish and little snakes."

The ladies shivered at the thought of such a diet and one of them reached for a little book and pencil.

"What a story to tell to my classes.'" she exclaimed. Turning to the man she asked, "How do you spell the name of his tribe?"

"I don't, ma'am. I cain't spell anything."

"Is he dangerous?"

"Jes sometimes, ma'am."

They watched me a long time, but I never said a word. After having watched me as long as they wished, they left.

At quitting time the boat had not arrived and I knew there were no accommodations for overnight visitors in Panzos. The German lived in a little house on a hill and had a screened bedroom, but that was the only place in town, aside from my car, that was screened.

There was a sort of railroad station there—a building about 10x12, without windows of any kind. I knew that if persons from the north ever tried to spend the night in such a place they would have enough fever injected into them by mosquitoes that they wouldn't live a month.

I had arranged with the Barbadian's wife to cook for me and occasionally clean up my screened car. He lived in a hut about fifty feet from the car.

I set out to hunt for the tourists and found them down near the river, looking for the boat. I knew it wouldn't come, because when a boat got grounded on a sandbar in the lake there was nothing to do but dig up the sand around it. The digging was done by one man while the others kept alligators away. Judging from the force usually carried on those little launches, I knew there was probably two men on the boat. One would dig while the other shied off alligators. At sunset, they would quit and go to sleep, as one can't see an alligator very well in the dark and they would be afraid to dig.

As I approached the tourists began to get on the offensive. One of the men picked up a large stone. Another picked up a stick. One of the women got behind a tree and looked up as if she was figuring on climbing it.

"I won't hurt you," I said in English. "I've just come to invite you to dinner with me."

"It can talk," one of the women explained, and then, evidently thinking of raw fish and snakes they would be served if they ate with me, she gagged.

"Are you really an Englishman?" one of the men asked.

"I am an American," I said.

"Why the savage getup?" another inquired.

"Because it isn't worthwhile cleaning up or shaving," I explained. "I'm master mechanic here and have been pretty busy."

"But that blue color?" one of the women asked.

They walked up to my car with me after having introduced themselves. The men and one of the women were professors at a college up in the corn belt, and had been intrigued by advertising to try looking over the land south of the Rio Grande. The two older women were wives of the men. The remaining woman, it appeared, was a sister of one of the wives. All were more than forty-five years old and it was their first trip to the tropics.

I had my car partitioned off for at one end I had a little office. I slept in the office that night, while my guests made themselves comfortable in the other portion.

The Barbadian woman, proud to be cooking for white guests, did her best. For dinner we had beans, some sort of fish, baked, tortillas, and coffee. The guests refused my offer of aguadiente. I drank that alone. The only thing I didn't have was plates.

Plates are a luxury in Panzos. In lieu of them I had had several old shovels whose handles were gone, polished, and I ate out of them. My guests did the same. After one gets used to eating out of the blade of a shovel it is about as easy as eating out of a plate. I had four tin cups, however. I used one for my usual mixture of coffee and aguardiente, while the other three were passed around among my guests. The coffee was strong and black, but it tasted good. There was no milk, as I never did see a cow while in Panzos.

Three or four weeks after they had passed through the captain of a freight boat coming up for a load of coffee handed me a letter. It was from one of the professors. Enclosed was a clipping from the college newspaper giving a very interesting account of the night they had spent with the blue Indian.

I discovered that enough engine supplies had been shipped in to equip a number of engines. They had never been unpacked.

In one of those boxes I discovered an electric headlight, a new thing at that time. I put it on one of the locomotives and it worked well. It probably was the first electric headlight ever used in Central America.

One night, after I got that headlight to working, I tried a trial run with the locomotive up the line a few miles. Coming back I turned the light on. It was a cloudy night and the clouds hung low. When the engine struck a high joint the light would flash up onto the clouds and back again. The inhabitants of Panzos noticed it and had never seen anything like it before. When I got back to the town those who could had left for the hills. The few that remained in town were praying, thinking the world was coming to an end and that the flashing light was a warning.

As soon as the first locomotive was ready for efficient work the Jamaican who operated it ran it over a big snake or an iguana and derailed it. I never discovered just what it was, as it was twilight when the accident occurred. The train crew ran back and barricaded themselves in a freight car where they stayed until morning, during which time little animals ate the meat of whatever had derailed the engine and carried away most of the bones.

I had to have a "shoo-fly" track built around the derailment to operate the road.

To prevent such future derailments by running over large snakes or animals I put an extension on the pilot, or cowcatcher as some call it. This extension would scrape off anything more than an inch in diameter or height. If the extension struck anything it would bend and double back and ring a bell in the cab, warning the engineer. Such a device is now used on some street car lines in the United States.

Every month the German paid me twenty gold pieces. Twenty gold pieces of that size are hard to hide and I didn't try. I placed them under my bed. If a native or one of the locals had tried to change a $20 gold piece with the intention of spending it, he would have been arrested anyway. They were paid in Guatemalan paper money or silver.

I told the German I would just as soon work until I was ready to quit and then he could pay me the entire amount, but he countered with the argument that if he paid me every month and I lost the money, he would not be to blame, as he had my receipt for each month's salary.

It was about Labor Day in the United States when I got all the engines working. At my suggestion, gangs had put the track in good order. For the first time in years the coffee was brought down to Panzos as fast as the finca owners could haul it to the tracks.

I had my work completed as per contract and had about $1,500 in gold. So I told the German I was leaving.

"Why do you go?" he asked. "We are satisfied with your work. We are operating the railroad efficiently for the first time in six years, at which time our master mechanic went bathing in a pool that happened to contain an alligator."

"I've completed my contract," I said. "I have no complaint about your treatment of me, but I'd like to go on."

"Where?" he asked.

"I was thinking of going back to the States," I told him.

"And freeze to death? If you'll stay here until it is spring in your country, we'll pay your fare to Vera Cruz besides continuing your wages. The finca owners, who hold stock in the railroad, would like for you to stay."

"Why should I stay? Everything's running smoothly."

"What would you do if you owned the road?"

"I'd string a telephone line along it, and train the enginemen so that you could operate a train anytime you wished without having to hold one at a terminal point until the other arrived. You could arrange meeting points by wire. That's how they do in the United States."

"The very thing," he exclaimed. "I'll order some wire and instruments and you'll stay another month and install the system."

I remembered J. B. Camors & Co., of New Orleans. They had sold me a lot of pick handles I had boxed and palmed off on the Guatemalan revolutionists as rifles. It is but fair to the Camors people to say that they knew nothing of the trick I had pulled in New Orleans. The firm is one of the oldest and most reliable in the United States.

I made out the order for the wire and instruments and went down to Porto Barrios to send the order. It was not necessary to go to the port to send the order. What I wanted was to go aboard a United Fruit boat and get a civilized meal. I also wanted to give the purser my money to be sent to the

Chicago bank. The purser of a United Fruit Company steamer could issue a receipt for money that was as good as gold.

It took me three days to get ready to go. I had to wash the blue off the portions of my body that would show when I was dressed. I washed in gasoline six or eight times the first day, and about that many the second day.

In addition to this, one of the Alabama Negroes used a dull scissors and got most of my beard off. After that I shaved and shaved until my face was sore, but all the whiskers were gone. I was astonished to see my face again after so many months.

I reached Porto Barrios Sunday morning. We hadn't paid much attention to the calendar down at Panzos—in fact we had no calendar—so I was a day too early. I had intended landing there Monday morning, as the steamer was due Tuesday morning. Of course there was nothing to do but wait.

I was in an estanca eating a midday lunch when a squad of soldiers entered. One of them carried a piece of paper. He referred to it and asked, "Is this El Señor Kavanaugh?" I used the "K" all through Central America, although there is no "k" or "w" in Spanish.

"I am Colonel Francisco Kavanaugh," I replied. "I am entitled to your salute. Don't you know how to address your superior officer?"

The leader saluted slovenly.

"What do you wish?" I asked.

"The commander of the port wishes to see you."

I wondered what I had done to require my presence before him, but I thought I could take care of myself.

"My regards to the commander of the port, and tell him I will wait on him as soon as I have finished my lunch." The soldiers hesitated and acted as if they did not intend to leave without me.

I half rose from the table and shouted, "Getta hell outta here."

They left.

56

Back to Changes

I WENT OVER TO THE OFFICE of the port commander an hour or two later. I knew I outranked him and wasn't any too prompt in going to see him. When I entered the office a sentry saluted smartly. I introduced myself to the commander.

"You have saved me from having to send a messenger up to Panzos," he said, after we had exchanged the usual salutations. "I have two letters for you—one from the army commander."

He handed me the letters and left the room while I read them. One was from President Cabrera.

"My Dear Young Friend: I am pleased to learn that you have returned to Guatemala. I have instructed the commanding officer of the army to order you to report to Guatemala City. However, if the order interferes with your private business, disregard it. Things have changed and I would like to see you again. Perhaps you can help me. Yours, etc."

The second letter was from the commanding general, whose name I have forgotten, ordering me to report to him at Guatemala City.

I sent a letter back to the German at Panzos informing him I was going on up to Guatemala City and would be back soon to install his telephone line.

Tuesday came and I went aboard the steamer, the Amselm of the United Fruit Company, and got a receipt for my gold with the exception of enough to do me on the trip up to the capital. Tuesday, after the steamer had pulled out, I boarded the little train going up to El Rancho.

The ex-convict at Gualán had disappeared. In his place was a huge Negro from the swamps of Louisiana. He had a native wife and several small children.

"I got me the best wife in Guatemala," he told me. "When I was section foreman on the Northern I had a little .22 rifle and her father wanted it, so we traded. She runs things here, and all I got to do is just sit here and rest."

I inquired about the ex-convict.

"He done sold out and left. Nobuddy knows where or cares. Men come and go down here and nobuddy cares."

The next morning I went on up to El Rancho. They had changed commanding officers in El Rancho. The one I met there this time was a young fellow who had been with the troops at the battle of Esquipulas. We talked late into the night renewing old memories. In the morning he gave me a burro and I started across the mountains.

Guatemala City had not changed, except that it now boasted a number of telephones. Señorita Sagusta had gone to live in the States. My machine gunners had been detached and were scattered among a number of other outfits. An undercurrent of feeling had begun to swell against my friend, President Cabrera. I sensed the influence of foreign money. I bought a new uniform and loafed a few days.

I visited old Welmyer in the San Marcos building and renewed his acquaintance. Things were going haywire down in Ocós again, he said. A band of marauders from Mexico, he said, had crossed the river twice and robbed the port of all the gold the steamers had paid for two loads of coffee. He was trying to get the government to make good the amount.

The government treasury, as Central American treasuries usually are, was deflated. There was no money in it to pay for all that gold. Paper money had depreciated still farther and it would take a shipload to equal what gold you could carry in your pocket. I spoke to President Cabrera about it. He was expecting a revolution to unseat him any day, and there was no money for anything.

"Where are the soldiers I trained while I was at Ocós?" I asked. "I could have taken those soldiers and cleaned out any force that could have come across the border."

"The company probably was disbanded," the president replied. "They were all your friends, according to reports from there. The man who succeeded you was not a military man."

"I understand," I said.

And I did understand. A politician placed in charge of such a port, far away from central authority, had feathered his nest. That company of soldiers had cost too much.

"Would you go down there and look things over?" the president asked.

"Gladly," I said. "I'll see Welmyer and then go down there for a few weeks."

I saw Welmyer and told him I was going down to Ocós for a visit. But I asked him, "Where is this man Hylton?"

"Now on vacation in Mexico. He may never return."

"Who's in charge ?"

"A man named Allen, from the United States. The city has a Spanish name, and the state has an awkward pronunciation. Have you met him?"

"There are a number of young men in the United States named Allen," I returned. "Did he come from the west?"

"I am not sure. I'll send for the file on him."

The file disclosed the fact that Allen had come from El Reno, Oklahoma, where he learned railroading on the Rock Island.

"If I went down there," I told Welmyer, "I want to run things as I wish for a short while. I outrank the comandante there, and I want to outrank everyone else on the railroad. After I get things settled you can take your dinky railroad and go to hell with it. Is that jake with you?"

"It has to be," he said.

One thing I saw in Guatemala City that pleased me greatly was the linotypes. The men I had taught were running them and they were in perfect shape.

Those former students of mine insisted on shutting up shop the day I called. Then we celebrated. They could do almost as they pleased as they were the only linotypers in the republic. We all congregated at the home of the man who had the largest home and had a great reunion. They were of the uneducated Indian type, but were well-educated. They had books in their homes and the books were read and their children were taught to read good literature. The average Guatemalan Indian regards a book as something to sit on or kindle a fire with.

I started to Ocós. Before going I wrote the German at Panzos and told him I would be delayed, but I would certainly return and install the telephone system.

Down to Esquintla, across the branch to Mazatenango. The weather was fine and I was feeling fine, so I decided to walk across from there and examine the mineral deposits as I went.

I had a sort of idea back in my head that if I could locate gold somewhere down there I would mark the place and return sometime and develop the vein and amass a fortune. I wasn't exactly sure what I wanted a fortune for, but I was always seeking ways to make one. Perhaps if I made it I would give it to some girl again, especially if she was a good singer.

I always wanted to amass a fortune. I never did. Perhaps it is just as well.

I had intended to strike the Ocós Railroad at Pajipite, but my usual luck held. I reached it at Ayutla.

The natives along the route had made the trip a vacation pleasure trip. These simple, dark-skinned men and women were always ready to welcome a stranger and more so if he could, as I did, speak a few words of their language. Occasionally I met a man or woman I had known while I was boss of the district. I was sorry when the trip ended at the railroad tracks in Ayutla.

There had been no trains for several days on the railroad, I was told, but one would come up, of a certainty. A train always came up, eventually. So I waited, loafing around the little town.

One day I crossed the river into Mexico to Suchiata, to where the Pan-American Railroad had been surveyed. At that time the tracks had been laid no farther than Tonala, however.

A survey had been made for a bridge across the river when the tracks would reach Suciate and the Guatemalan Central had reached Ayutla. The bridge was never built. Today, passengers going into Guatemala from Mexico are ferried across the river in the wet season or walk across it in the dry season.

The reason for this gap in what otherwise would be a through rail route from Canada clear to San Salvador is that the railroad on the Mexican side is standard gage, 4 feet 8½ inches, while on the Guatemalan side the gage is 3 feet.

At length the train came up from Ocós. Allen was running the engine. He was glad to see me, the first white man to visit him in three months. I rode down in the cab with him and was grieved to see what had been done to my carefully planned and executed rehabilitation.

Weeds and grass were beginning to cover the rails. The salt solution I had sprinkled to kill vegetation had been gradually washed away by rains. Instead of the six track gangs I had kept at work taking care of the track, there was now but a foreman and four men. I said something about it to Allen.

"This road can go to hell for all I care," he said. "I'm going down to Panama, where I can work with white men. I wouldn't live another three months in Ocós if they made me a present of the railroad."

I was a few days getting in touch with the finca owners. They had been holding back their coffee, but as soon as I told them I would see their coffee loaded on the next steamer and their money delivered to them, they ordered cars to load.

Pena Doros had left Ocós and was living near Tapachula, I was told. Nearly all my young soldiers had left Ocós. My nice clean Springfield rifles were gathering dust in a room in the comandancia. The comandante was a good fellow and gave me living quarters.

He explained that he had quit paying soldiers under pressure from the politicians at the capital, and the soldiers had quit the army. Before I had left Ocós I had placed three machine guns and a lot of ammunition on the rafters of the shop storeroom. They had not been touched. I asked the comandante about them and he had never heard of them. In fact, he had never been out to the shops.

"They are useless against the marauders who come across the river from Mexico," he told me. "They came the last time about two hundred strong. What could I do against such numbers?"

I did not tell him that if he had kept Doros and my little army well-fed and paid he could have stood off a thousand men.

But I didn't explain. Instead I took the guns down from the rafters, cleaned and oiled them. After I got them in working order I mounted them on a flat car and ran it out in the jungle with a switch engine to try them out. They worked perfectly. I could cut my initials on the side of a wall with either of them.

Fever had taken its toll from Ocós. I would meet a woman whose face was familiar and ask about her husband and children.

"They are not here now," she would say. "The fever took them."

Again one would look at me and say, "It is not like when the señor was here. Now there are few boats and work is not plentiful. My husband has gone up near Santa Marie to work for a coffee finca, where the cold freezes the fever out of one's bones. I am going to join him soon."

We had filled the warehouses with coffee when the first steamer came into port. We had hardly finished loading it when the second showed up. We were so busy for two weeks that I had no time for anything else but loading sacks of coffee.

As soon as the first steamer anchored off the port I sent a messenger up to the salt fish outfit to ask them if they could get word to the Mexicans across the river that I was hiring men to load coffee. A dozen or more came down and I put them to work.

Instead of placing the gold I received for coffee in the safe at the comandancia—a safe that could be opened with a good strong hairpin—I had it carried openly across the bayou to the shops where I slept while the gold was there. I let everyone know the gold was over there. I had learned that the raids before had ended at the comandancia, where the gold had been stored.

The last steamer loaded and left about noon one day. I paid off all the men.

We were sitting in the Cantina del Baroa de Oro an hour later, finishing midday lunch, when a native ran in, all out of breath.

"The Mexicans are coming," he cried. "Two or three hundred. Many, many Mexicans."

He ran out and spread the news among the grass huts. Women began packing their belongings. Why they did this I do not know, for the bandits would not molest the poverty-stricken Indians. All they wanted was the gold.

"Now I'll have a chance to try out my bone-crusher movement," I remarked. "Let's go over to the shops."

We had barely reached there when three men on the hand car came down the track as fast as they could push the handles up and down. Seeing me, they stopped.

"We have bad news to report, señor. Six men have taken two rails out of the track not two kilometers from here and threw them into the water. The railroad is blocked and we came quickly to inform you."

"They didn't want us to skip with the gold," I observed to Allen.

"Evidently," Allen said. "I'll help you with your plan. But if it fails the sharks'll have two nice white Americans to gnaw on."

57

The Bone-Crusher Works

SOON THE INHABITANTS OF THE PORT began coming across the bayou bridge, carrying what they could of their valuables. I told them I could not run a train up the road, as the rails were taken out, and most of them walked on. It was only eight kilometers to the water tank, where they could camp for the night. The comandante came along with the last.

"Aren't you going to stay and see the fun?" I asked.

"Are you going to try to fight that horde?" he asked. "It is certain suicide."

"An army doctor told me years ago I had not long to live," I said. I remembered what the old Mexican had told me on my trip from Tapachula to Tonala when I thought I had been bitten by a ratita and I repeated the words, "If I die this year I won't have to die next year."

He turned to Allen and asked, "Are you going to stay?"

"You don't suppose I'd desert a white man to go with a damned coffee-colored rat like you, do you?" he replied.

Allen couldn't phrase a sentence like that in Spanish, so I am not sure how much the comandante understood. He looked at Allen, as if uncertain what to do. Then he asked, "May I have the hand car?"

By this time Allen had forgotten all his small vocabulary of Spanish and he exploded. "No. Getta hell outa here. Vamoose. Damn pronto. Keep going." And he motioned up the track.

The comandante joined the procession plodding along the track. I watched them until they rounded the curve. I walked over to the tank to get a drink of water and found a boy of about twelve sitting there in the shade.

"Why don't you go with your family?" I queried.

"Why should I walk in the hot sun when there is shade here?" he returned.

I did not question him farther. He stretched out on a bench and fell asleep.

255

I knew all those folks would go up and take a sort of vacation, then drift back to Ocós again, regardless of whether the Mexicans won or lost.

If the Mexicans won out and stayed in Ocós a week or so, the natives would fraternize with them. An Indian doesn't hold a grudge against someone who happens to rob a white man of his gold. If the white man can't protect his gold it is just too bad for the white man.

The bandits rested during the heat of the afternoon. They raided the cantinas, too, for I could hear them singing and arguing loudly.

The sun beat down with a vengeance. One hundred twenty degrees was not uncommon for an afternoon in Ocós and this afternoon it appeared even warmer. We rested in the shade and listened to the snores of the boy who didn't like to walk in the heat of the sun.

With the setting of the sun I grew active. It was still very warm. I coupled six coffee cars to the switch engine and gave Allen his instructions.

I had planted one machine gun at the edge of the swamp lining the railroad right-of-way, about twenty yards from the end of the bridge. I had a similar plant directly across on the other side of the right-of-way. At sunset I examined each machine gun to see they were in working order. Then, having nothing else to do, we waited.

Allen had got hold of two chickens and while we waited he fried them over the blacksmith's fire after he had cut them in pieces with his pocket knife. The only thing he could find to use as a frying pan was a shovel. At that, the chicken didn't taste so bad and the boy ate his share, for he had awakened at sunset. We had no bread, but some salt. One gets accustomed to eating impromptu meals after he has wandered around Central America a few years.

The bandits had feasted better than we had. Also they had access to all the aguardiente in the port. It was dusk when they started across the bayou bridge, singing and making funny hooting sounds. I knew many of them were still drunk.

"When I give the word," I instructed Allen, "start the bone-crusher."

I squatted at the left-hand machine gun until I was sure most of the force of bandits were on the bridge, the leading ones not twenty feet from the end nearest the shops. Then I yelled to Allen and he started the engine.

The engine gave the cars a kick, a kick that would have sent them clear across the bridge had there been nothing on the track. I could hear the cries of the men as the cars struck them. I could see a sort of phosphorous light in the foam made by the sharks as they got busy with the bodies of those who had leaped from the bridge into the water or had been knocked in by the impact of the cars.

Before the cars had stopped I let go with the left-hand gun, raking the bridge. I fired as many bursts as I could safely without jamming the machine, and then ran across to the right-hand gun. Here I repeated the operation until I could see no one standing on the bridge. The cars had never gotten across the bridge, having been derailed by the bodies of the men they had crushed.

Within a few minutes after the men had started across the bridge it was all over. Then we coupled onto the cars and pulled them off the bridge, some of the wheels bumping along on the ties. We then went over to round up some stragglers, who surrendered at once. They appeared dazed and frightened.

I needed a light so I kicked the door of the comandante's office in and we herded the prisoners in there.

When I had the lights lit I looked over the prisoners. I recognized one of them and he recognized me. He had been one of my soldiers.

"El Señor Diablo!" he exclaimed.

"Yes," I said. "And now you are a bandit?"

"We did not know you were here, El Señor. Our men who were here to help you load the coffee told us of another norteamericano, but we did not know it was our Señor. Had we known that, neither Pena nor any of us would have come."

"Pena," I exclaimed.

"Pena Doros, whom you made captain when we were soldiers here."

"Was Pena with you tonight?"

I asked the question fearfully. Pena had been my friend. Rather than have killed him I would have given him the gold.

"He was leading us across the bridge and..."

"That is enough. Why did Pena leave here?"

"He was compelled to leave. Señor Hylton drove him away. He quarreled with a relative of Señor Hylton and..."

"I understand," I interrupted.

I looked around at the others. Eight or ten stolid Indians, awaiting their fate. They expected to be shot, but their faces showed no fright. They had the typical poker face. Men must die, was their creed, and what mattered if a man died a little sooner or a little later. It was all the same.

"Where is Pena's family?" I asked.

"He has a place near Tapachula," the man informed me. "It is a good place. The raids we have made before has given us means to improve the place and Pena knew how to use machinery."

"So his family will not suffer now that he has gone?"

"Not at all, señor. When the fever got bad here and many left, some of us stayed on. But things grew more difficult. Where you paid us silver for loading boats Señor Hylton paid us in billettes (paper money) which is worthless, even to buy things from the Chino. So when Pena was put out we left with him. The new comandante did not care to pay his soldiers."

I studied a moment. The man probably was wondering how soon he would be shot or thrown to the sharks.

"Had the señor told us he was here we would have helped him protect his gold," he remarked.

"I know that," I said. "You were all my friends. I am grieved that I killed your leader and my best friend for the dirty gold. To hell with it." The last four words were in English. No one but Allen understood them.

"As the señor wishes," the Indian said.

I studied the matter over a few minutes. The Indians stood around, making no effort to escape. The light of two burners in the hanging lamp shown on their dark faces. It was very hot and sweat stood out like little diamonds, each drop reflecting a point of light. Allen rolled a cigarette and passed the tobacco and papers around. Each man made one.

The last man in the circle shook his head as the makings were passed to him. He held up his hand and showed a bloody stump where three or four fingers were missing. The man next to him made the cigarette and handed it to him, lighting it after the injured man had placed it in his mouth.

I had no coat or vest and my revolver in its shoulder scabbard showed plainly. Allen, having no revolver, had brought a rifle over and it was leaning against the wall behind him. The Indians were unarmed.

"Can you and your companions make your way across the river before daybreak?" I asked. "Some of you bear wounds."

"If you will permit, señor."

"Go, then, when you get home tell Señora Doros I killed her husband, but I will regret it all my life, for he was my friend."

"Gracias, señor," the man replied. Silently they filed out.

"I'll be damned," Allen exclaimed. "Those birds could have massacreed us, and here they go and thank you for letting them go across the river."

"You couldn't hire one of those Indians to injure me," I told him. "They were once my soldiers."

"And what do we do now?" he asked.

I went into the bedroom of the comandancia and raised a portion of the floor. It was where I used to keep my store of aguardiente and I wondered if I would find some there—some that the raiders had missed. I brought forth a garafone, full. I went to the kitchen and got two tin cups. We drank.

"We'll take the gold up as soon as we can get an engine hot," I told Allen after the natives left. "And I'm not coming back here. To hell with this lousy little hole."

"I'm only going to wait till Hylton comes back, or I get my bonus from Welmyer. I was to get a $100 bonus if I stayed here three months."

"If you happen to be here when Hylton comes, bat him one for me," I said.

"I'm going to bat him one for myself," Allen countered. "Let's get over and get an engine hot."

58

Missionaries Again

I SHOOK HANDS WITH Allen after he had brought me up to Pajipite and started out to walk across the mountains to San Felipe. I couldn't sleep much during that walk. My conscience kept me awake.

I couldn't help thinking that I had killed a friend to protect a lot of German gold—gold earned by natives working for about sixty cents a day of that depreciated money—about two cents a day in gold.

Pena Doros was worth all the money Guatemala would ever produce. The fact that he had been killed in the commission of a crime didn't change my opinion of him. He had been my friend. As my friend he was justified in doing whatever he wanted to do.

The weather was pleasant. I would stop at a little Indian village or sometimes just a single hut, eat, drink and try to spend a night sleeping. But I slept little. I would doze a while and wake, shivering all over. If I dreamed during these fitful spells of sleep, I would be behind a machine gun while every friend I could remember would pass by and I would mow them down with a blast of the gun, and watch them squirm where they fell. Then I would get up and walk on and on, in the dark; walk until I fell exhausted.

Late one night, after I had walked for hours, I built a fire between two rocks and slept until the sun was up. I had built a great fire, for it was chilly up in those mountains. Before I left the place I noticed that one of the rocks had melted and some sort of a greenish metal had dripped to the ground. I picked up several pebbles of the stuff, hard and heavy, and was going to have it analyzed when I reached Guatemala City. But I lost them before I got to the city. I've often wondered what sort of stuff I had accidentally discovered.

I reached San Felipe, the mountain terminus of the Occidente Railroad and spent the night with the master mechanic, a Louisiana Frenchman. He had been in Guatemala so long he had forgotten about things in the States.

I asked him about a missionary station near there.

"There is an American mission station about five kilometer leagues above here," he replied, "and occasionally a man comes down for supplies and brings me religious papers."

"Are there two women at the mission, or only one?" I asked.

"A man and his wife."

A kilometer league, a unit of measurement used in some Central American districts, is four kilometers. Five of these leagues would be about twenty kilometers. Reduced to miles, five kilometer leagues would be about 12.5 miles. I decided to walk out and see if the missionaries were the ones I had entertained at Ocós for a time and then sent back over the hills.

They proved to be the eldest girl and her husband. The man soon let me know by his manner that I was of the ungodly type which he might tolerate but never love. Perhaps he was right. Even while I talked to them I was thinking of a man I was going to murder when I reached Guatemala City.

I asked about Frances.

"She is serving an internship now," the woman informed me, "or was when I heard from her last."

"She is of the ungodly type," the man added.

"She struck me as being a mighty fine girl," I contradicted.

"I noticed while we were in Ocós that she attracted you," the sister observed. "She attracts men of the worldly type."

I left the mission that night with a bad taste in my mouth. Those people were too holy.

I walked into a little camp where three men and their wives were making charcoal. I sat with the men for an hour and drank. One of them had been at Ocós while I was there and remembered that I had told my mozos to feed him while he waited a few days until a ship came in to load, when he went to work. He got his wife to make some tortillas and we ate tortillas and frijoles and drank rank aguadiente. They warned me to get to San Felipe and stay there through the day and a night, as a storm was brewing out in the Pacific and would blow in. There were no signs of a storm at the time, but it came. How did they know? I leave the guessing to you.

Those Indians had a sort of religion that dated back centuries before the Christians' Christ and they followed its teachings. No Indian ever went hungry while another had food. They were taught not to fear death, as it came to all.

But to give those missionaries their due, they were not in the business for monetary gain. In a country like Guatemala, with its depreciated currency, about all a missionary could hope for would be a full belly, as food, such as it was, could be had for the gathering. But the missionary had nothing to look forward to except what glory or pride was in his work. He followed a routine that led nowhere.

One missionary who came down to Ocós during some trouble up near his station told me he had not handled a piece of money in a year. Once in a while, he said, a remittance came from some church up in the States, but it was not regular, and he could not depend on it. I gave him five dollars Mex to pay his expenses to Tapachula, where he could telegraph some organization in Chattanooga. He wore a suit of clothes more than five years old.

I think the missionaries worked as much for honor as for monetary gain. But the Indians had such an old and satisfactory religion of their own that I regarded the work of the missionaries as something the country could do well without.

59

Revenge Backfires

GUATEMALA CITY AGAIN. THIS TIME I did not intend to tarry long. I wanted to get back to Panzos. But I had an errand to do in Guatemala City. I was going to kill a man. I did not relish the job, but I was determined to do it.

The report I made to President Cabrera and his confidential advisers about conditions in the Ocós district was anything but cheerful. I advised a change of leaders in the district. I advised that Hylton be driven from the district; that someone be sent to the port who liked the Indians and could organize a company of soldiers like I had done. I already had the guns there. I advised that a young medical officer be stationed there permanently. I advised that the port commander be permitted to pay the soldiers and the medical officer from port collections without interference from officials in Guatemala City.

And finally I advised that a scale of wages be promulgated for labor on the coffee fincas and for the loading labor and the workmen be paid in silver.

"Perhaps it is that the señor wishes to go back to Ocós himself and do all this?" one of the politicians sneered.

"If I wanted to live down there," I returned, "I would not have come back here to report. I could raise a little army of my own down there among those Indians and no one could dislodge me. But I am not going to live in Ocós again. I am going to finish my work on the Panzos Railroad and then go north."

I finished my oral report, saluted the President and walked out. Having finished with the politicians, I went to the San Marcos building, Welmyer smiled as I entered his office. I didn't. Had I smiled I might have disarmed him and succeeded in what I had come for.

"You did good work down there," Welmyer greeted, but I could see he knew something was wrong. "Why didn't you decide to stay down there permanently?"

"I killed one of my best friends to protect your lousy gold, Welmyer," I said. "Now I'm going to kill you and when we meet in hell I'll try to do the same thing over again."

I pulled my gun from its shoulder holster.

Welmyer had been threatened many times before and I should have known he would be prepared. I was across a large table from him. He rose, and as he did so he brought up a long club he must have had handy. Before I could fire my revolver he swung the club. He was a huge, muscular man and had the club landed on me it would have killed me.

I dodged the sweep of the club, fired and missed. I saw the bullet strike the wall just to one side of his head. I attempted to fire again, but my revolver misfired. I hadn't fired the gun for a long time and perhaps one of my cartridges was foul.

As he swung again I picked up a paper weight and threw it at his face. I hit the mark squarely and saw the blood fly. He sprang around the desk, swinging the club. I snatched up and chair and threw it at his legs. He stumbled a little but did not fall. I was now on the other side of the table, across from him. I heard a door open at one side and half turned to see who it was. While my attention was distracted Welmyer got in a direct blow. I went out completely.

I woke in the military hospital. The first thing I heard was the doctor saying, "No concussion. Not badly injured. He'll be all right within a few days."

That evening one of my army friends came in to see me. "We have not yet arrested Señor Welmyer," he said, "and will not until we hear what you have to say."

"It would be well not to arrest him," I cautioned. "The quarrel was a private one."

"But it is a crime for a civilian to attack an army officer."

"I was not in uniform, and I am not sure Welmyer knew I was still an army officer. If you wish to please me you and your brother officers will forget the incident."

"If you wish."

"It would be best," I advised. Then I explained how I had killed a friend while protecting the coffee gold. Friendships are lasting among Guatemalan natives. The officer listened and nodded his head.

"I cannot blame you for being angry. Neither do I blame you for asking us to overlook the incident. Life is long. If one fails one time, there are many other times when he can try again."

My head and shoulders were still sore when I left the hospital. I happened to have a few of the $20 gold pieces I had earned at Panzos with me. I gave one to each of the two doctors who attended me, and one each to the two nurses. The doctors, proud fellows, were not going to accept them, until I told them I would be highly insulted if they did not.

The two dusky nurses accepted their gold pieces and thanked me, and as they left the room they were, woman-like, talking about the new dresses they would purchase with the gold.

I sat in my room that night and cleaned my revolver. If at first you don't succeed, try, try again. I was making sure I would get Welmyer at my next try. Later I went down to the cantina near the Central Railroad shops and had a session with the men of that road. In course of our conversation one of the men remarked, "You know that old boss of yours, Welmyer? I hauled him down to San Jose a few days ago. His face looked like it had been in a collision with a pile driver. He took a boat up to Frisco for treatment."

Welmyer had escaped me for the present. But, as they say in Guatemala, there is always another day coming that hasn't been used yet.

60

Conscience Easy

AFTER THE FIGHT WITH WELMYER and my resultant stay in the hospital, I found I could sleep well. Probably it was because I had done the best I could. At least I flattered myself I had.

News of the fight had gotten out and when I strolled into a hotel barroom to get a drink that evening several Americans and a German or two asked for details. I made light of the incident and let it be known that we had quarreled over a settlement of wages.

I was introduced to a big fat German and we had a drink together. He had lived in the United States several years and could speak good Americanese. Like the German who was resident manager at Ocós and went dead via another man's girl, he was a baseball fan. We talked baseball awhile and I mentioned that I was going down to Panzos.

"My brother and I ship our coffee out over the Panzos Railroad," he told me. "They've got that little road running well now."

"I overhauled the locomotives," I admitted, "and I suggested improvements to be made in the track. I'm going down there now to put in a telephone train dispatching system."

"Good," he said. "You go down with me. I leave day after tomorrow. Five burros and two mozos. Plenty grub and drinks."

"I'll be glad to go down with you," I agreed. "But I'll go half the expense."

"Forget the expense. When you go back to the States send me a new Baseball Guide and you've repaid me sufficiently."

The trip down was ideal and I was treated royally while I was with those German coffee men.

I have mentioned Germans often in this tale of a hobo. In all cases I found them to be persons of intelligence, hospitality, probity. They were of the old Germany, the Germany of culture, music, scientific research, laughter and beer.

The new Germany is different. Instead of culture they deal in intolerance, war, pestilence, hunger, death. I do not understand the modern German. The older ones were real people.

Germany, before the first World War, found the Central American republics a virgin field for its overflowing population. The Germans established the first coffee fincas in Central America. They financed the railroads that brought the coffee down to the coast for shipment to Europe.

Today, one cannot get any information about Central America, even from established travel bureaus. Even as far back as 1901 any German travel bureau would furnish a tourist with information about any Central American republic—railroad time tables, hotels, trails, cities, towns and even villages.

In fact, whether from foresight or because the Germans found the Central American republics an easy region to exploit, the infiltration was great. They cultivated coffee lands and made money—millions. Labor was cheap and coffee brought German gold.

They were not interested much in details. They built railroads and let American hoboes operate them. They bought railroad material that had been junked above the Rio Grande and the American hobo did the rest. He built and operated the railroads for the Germans. They paid the hobo well and, in most cases, the hobo did his work well.

There are miles of little three-foot gage railroad in Central America that the officials of the United States government never heard of. Below the City of Mexico clear to Panama was a blank as far as the United States knew. But it is a lush country, full of possibilities.

The United States government erred in neglecting its neighbors to the south. The Central Americas was looked upon as a country of revolutions, fever, poverty. The Germans found it a country full of commercial possibilities and they cultivated it.

So, when the United States discovered it needed the friendship of the southern republics, it found the Germans before it—the Germans who had built the little railroads, raised and marketed the coffee; developed the country. The United States was a stranger to its next door neighbor. True, the hoboes knew and liked these little countries. But the politicians knew nothing of the hobo—and were too proud to learn!

61

Blue Eyes of Bremerhaven

THE TELEPHONE MATERIAL WAS at Panzos when I reached there. I first strung a grounded circuit—one wire which was grounded for a return circuit and found it did not work for some reason or other. In the United States such circuits worked but there must have been some fissure in the earth that acted as an insulator.

Finally, I strung the second wire, making a metallic circuit, which worked perfectly. I had made an error and after I had strung the metallic circuit I had wire left over. The Panzos Railroad was measured in kilometers. Number 12 wire was quoted in the United States by the hundred pounds. In calculating the number of feet to the mile and then reducing that to kilometers I had made a mistake. So I used the extra wire in connecting a telephone to the German superintendent's house, which he appreciated.

As a train dispatching utility it was success from the start. After a few instructions the men could operate two trains over the road at once, even if they ran in different directions. They could also report accidents and delays. In fact, they liked to talk over the wire so much that they never passed a telephone box without calling in if for no other reason than to say they had gotten that far.

It was along after New Year's when I finished. I told the German I was going as soon as I got the blue washed off my body. I told him as we sat in his house drinking tepid beer; heavy brown German beer. He had received a shipment of beer, but there was no ice. We drank it anyhow. It was a change from aguardiente.

"You are sure there is nothing more you can do here?" he asked.

"Nothing," I replied, "and I want to move."

He opened a couple more bottles of the brown beer before he said anything.

268

"The railroad is making money now. Since we have been furnishing good transportation the finca owners have been sending down a lot of coffee they had stored and are extending their plantations. You might as well stay here and watch the railroad. Why not marry up a girl? I know several who are not bad looking and would make good wives, and you could get one for a few dollars. Yah?"

"You give advice that you do not follow," I observed. "Why have you never bought a wife?"

"Ach so! I would not like the dusky wife. There was a girl in Bremerhaven. She had pretty yellow hair that looked like the sunset when it shines on the river. I can see her yet, just by closing my eyes and thinking. But..."

"She would not come out here?"

"I was poor and there was a wealthy husband for her," he related. "I wished her good-bye and the best of luck and came down here. But it was not for me to forget. The blue of her eyes comes back to me and chokes something inside me when I look into the water of the lake. Ach! Have another beer."

He opened a couple more bottles. There were tears in his eyes.

"And is there a girl waiting up in the States for you?" he asked.

"No one is waiting for me," I replied. "There was a girl—once. We did not marry."

"She would not marry you?"

"She was too far above me in everything. She was a genius. I was a hobo."

"I did not know there were classes in the States."

"There are classes, but not classes manufactured artificially by money alone. Classes up there are determined by brains, training, talent."

"You are a good mechanical man," he said.

"Granted. But still I am a hobo. She was an artist. She would have done wrong to have married a man with itchy feet, a man who could not stay put. Think of what a white woman would do in a place like Panzos."

"Then you go, I suppose," he concluded. "If you ever wish to return to Panzos, come back and do something to the railroad."

The four Negroes, the two from Alabama, the Jamaican and the Barbadian and most of the inhabitants of Panzos were down to see me off in the foggy dawn. I was really sorry when the boat chugged away from the landing.

62

Cankered Brains

PORT LIVINGSTONE. A TRAMP steamer was at the wharf. I located the captain, a Swede.

"How much to go north with you?" I queried.

"Where north?" he countered.

"What the hell do I care?"

"You're an American citizen, I guess?"

"You guessed right."

"Hobo?"

"Right again."

"Got money?"

I pulled out a few gold pieces and jingled them in my hand.

"Where did you get it?" he asked.

"Off the Panzos Railroad. I've just rehabilitated that line. Aside from that, I'm a colonel in the Guatemalan army."

"I met a general of some little army down here a few days ago," the skipper said. "Gave him a quarter with which to get a meal. Colonels are small fry down here."

"How much to take me up?" I insisted.

"I'm busy now," he said. He called a steward—the steward, as the steamer had but one. "Fix an empty cabin for this man," he said.

He turned to me. "I'm busy now. We talk after a while. We must leave before sunset or we stay here all night. We talk about it after a while."

(A Guatemalan law forbids ships to leave or enter port between sunset and sunrise.)

I looked over my cabin and then went back to the pier. On the dock was a pile of cases of Canadian Club whiskey. I hadn't tasted North American whiskey in a long time. A young native was checking the cases by counting them several times.

"How much for a case?" I asked.

"I am not permitted to sell," he replied. "I am to see the shipment reaches an Englishman who lives up near Taca."

"If you were short one case could it be explained?" I asked. I reached into my pocket and brought out a $20 gold piece.

"They go in by burros," he explained, eyeing the gold piece. "One might fall from the back of a burro if the burro was bitten by a snake. And it might fall into the swamp, of course."

"There are swamps?"

"Many, señor."

"If that is true, I'll tell you something. If a case of that whiskey is delivered to Cabin C before the vessel sails the person delivering it will get this coin," I said, showing him the gold.

I returned to my cabin and in a few minutes the young man came in with a case of something wrapped in a grass blanket. The steward followed him in.

"So you brought my luggage?" I asked.

"Si, señor."

"It's all right, steward," I told that individual. "He has brought my luggage."

The steward turned to go away. The young native shoved the bundle under my bunk. I hefted it to see that it was not an empty box. I handed the gold piece to the native. That was more money that he made in a year.

An hour before sunset the steamer backed away from the wharf, swung around and headed across the bay in the direction of the Carib sea. Sunset saw us well out from Livingstone.

A few minutes later one of the mates, in passing, remarked, "Dinner time in a few minutes, mister."

"Will I have to dress for dinner?" I asked, thinking perhaps the captain followed the custom of the British and wore dinner clothes. In that case I would have to eat with the men forward, as I had no soup and fish. But the mate didn't get my meaning.

He replied, "Yes, you come dressed. We do not undress unless we go to bed."

I took two quarts of my Canadian Club down when I went to dinner.

The captain, one of the mates and two engineers were at the table. The captain started to introduce me and then remembered he had not learned my name, so I introduced myself. I placed the whiskey on the table and invited them to drink. They did.

"And now, captain, "I began, as we drank our coffee, "what will my passage cost and where are we going?"

"We will talk about that after dinner."

"But where are we going?" I asked

"We will touch at Belize in the morning and may be there several days. We unload some machinery there and load some cargo. After Belize, Vera Cruz. Then across to Liverpool."

"And I can land at Vera Cruz or Belize?"

"If you wish," the captain replied and went on to explain: "There is a quarantine along this coast, but the authorities below New Orleans pay little attention to it. As this steamer is going into a colder zone we disregard it altogether. The doctor at Belize may look at your tongue. But if it is coated with this excellent whiskey he will pass you."

"Are you going to the United States?" the engineer inquired.

"I think so."

"I read a piece in a newspaper I picked up in Aspinwall the other day where your president, Mr. Roosevelt, lost his bodyguards and they had a hard time finding him again."

"Teddy doesn't need guards," I said. "He's popular with all classes."

"Our king goes about the capital without guards," the engineer said. "If he wants to buy something he goes and gets it, like a common citizen."

"You see," I explained, "an assassin murdered the president before Roosevelt. So now our presidents are provided with guards."

"Why should a man want to kill a king or president?" the mate asked. "I don't understand it."

"I'll confess I don't understand it, either," I said. "I've met but a few men in high circles, but those I have met have treated me right."

"A man who kills a king or president has a cankered mind," the skipper elucidated. "A canker can develop in the brain as it does in the skin of your body. Then your brain festers and one cannot think straight."

Before we turned in that night we ate again at about eleven o'clock. Just a light lunch of cold meats, bread, some chilled beer and coffee. It was a great change from the frijoles and tortillas that had been my food while in Panzos.

63

Yucatan—The Ancient Ruins

WHEN I WAS CALLED next morning we were off Belize, British Honduras. After breakfast I went ashore and passed the doctor and customs men without trouble. I had no baggage to declare and was as healthy as I ever had been.

A man named Joe Lewis from New York operated the hotel. At eleven o'clock every morning Belize eats breakfast. I breakfasted with the other guests of the hotel. They served fish for breakfast. In fact, fish is served at every meal in Belize. Fish was cheap and you were supposed to eat fish if you stayed in Belize. I haven't liked fish since. A few more weeks spent there and I would have begun to sprout fins.

After the meal I walked around back of the hotel, where Lewis had an ice plant. I noticed a derrick there. Afterward I mentioned it to Lewis.

"Two men came through here a year or so ago and said they were drillers," he explained. "I needed an artesian well so that I could make ice without distilling sea water. They started the well and got down about 200 feet when they lost the drill in the well. They never succeeded in fishing it out."

"Mind if I look at it?"

"I'll show you."

The drillers had driven pipe and had the well started when they lost the tool. I suggested Lewis let me make a pointed tool and try to push the lost tool to one side so that drilling could be resumed. I would try it a week, I suggested, and if my plan was successful we would talk about a contract.

I had the tool made and for a week I pounded, working all day and far into the night. I had to quit work after eight o'clock, as the noise of the engine disturbed those who wanted to sleep.

An old English professor named Burton who had been in Belize for a month or so was an interested kibitzer. He wanted scrapings from every foot

273

of the digging if and when I got the tool driven to one side. He contended that at one time Belize had been far inland and a new coastline had been made by an eruption in the ocean.

He was an interesting old coot and could figure geometry in his head better than I could with a pencil. He could name the various geological formations, as well as classify stones and earth.

I gave up trying the well one Saturday afternoon and told Lewis my plan would not work. I charged him nothing for my time and he charged me nothing for my board and room.

Sunday afternoon the old professor and I were sitting on a bench at a jutting point letting the trade winds fan us. Burton was disappointed that I had not succeeded in digging the well. He wanted to prove his contention about that eruption and write the results to some scientific magazine in London.

"Where are you going from here?" he asked.

"Think I'll stick around till Tuesday and then take the steamer to New Orleans."

"I've heard of some ancient ruins up in Yucatan," he said. "I would like to go up and see them. As you are at liberty, I would like to have you come along. I am not certain that I can deal with the natives as you can. I have no knowledge of their speech."

"It's still cold up in the States," I replied. "I'll be glad to go up through Yucatan. Do you know anything about the country?"

"Not a thing."

"How'll we get there?" I inquired.

"A little steamer leaves here every Monday morning for Corozal. From there we'll go inland through Quintana Roo and Yucatan on foot. We'll purchase burros to carry our luggage."

"I have no luggage," I reminded him.

"We will have a tent and supplies which we cannot carry on our backs."

"All right. I'll go. You make arrangements for supplies you think you'll need. I'll share half the expense."

"I have sufficient funds," he said.

"So have I," I told him.

The little steamer landed us at Corozal early next afternoon. As we were leaving the boat the skipper, a New Orleans river man and the engineer both shook hands with us.

"I'm afraid it's goodbye," the skipper said. "I've heard tales of how those Mapa Indians treat the whites when they go into their country. Better back out and come to Belize with us on the return trip, where the only danger you're in is from Joe Lewis' fish meals."

"Any one you know gone inland from here recently?" I queried.

"Haven't heard of anyone—but there's lots of stories going around about men who went in there and were never heard of again."

"I think we'll make it," I said. "I never saw a man I couldn't make friends with."

"If I never come out," the professor declared, "I will have the satisfaction of having tried. And I'm old, and about through anyway."

This seemed to be somewhat prophetic. The old man never did return. But we'll go into that later.

We were in Corozal several days bargaining for burros. There were lots of burros in the vicinity, but no one cared to sell. The owners really weren't interested. Why take money for a burro? If one did he would spend the money and then not have either burro or money. A burro cost nothing to keep. It foraged for its food. But we finally purchased two. Then we started out into the country of the Mapa Indians.

The country was largely jungle, but not an unpleasant jungle. After we left the vicinity of the coast we traveled for miles in open woods, something like the wooded areas of the United States.

We had been warned about the ferocity of the Indians, but they proved friendly. Those Mapa Indians were allergic to Mexicans, although they were part of the Mexican republic. The Mexican government wanted those Indians to pay taxes and the Indians wouldn't pay. Why should they pay taxes to someone they knew not? Thus, when the Mexican government sent in a tax collecting crew the crew never got back to report. As we weren't Mexicans, and made no demand for taxes, the Indians were friendly.

We discovered we could have lived about as well if we had depended on purchasing food in the huts and villages along the route as we did on the canned food we had purchased in Belize. The professor, being British, called canned foods "tinned rations," and like all Britishers he referred to his shoes as "boots."

We traveled about three weeks in order to reach the first set of ruins and we camped near them. I loafed around camp while the professor plodded and prodded in what looked like an old stone building that had come out second best in a skirmish with a tornado.

I wasn't interested. Back home there were lots better ruins than those of Yucatan. Usually someone carted the stones away and built a skyscraper on the site. But they interested the professor. He told me those ruins had been there long before Cortez made his memorable visit to Mexico, which was long before my time.

I discovered an Indian village about three kilometers from the ruins and went over there several times. One or two young men of the village could speak a little Spanish and one who had been in Belize several months could speak a few words of English. They wondered why foreigners would come so far just to see the ruins when they had been there for ages.

The young man who had worked in Belize had an old-fashioned phonograph, with cylindrical records and a few records, but couldn't play them because he had no needle. I whittled out a piece of hard wood with a sharp point on it and it answered very well, although the volume of sound wasn't as large as with a metal needle.

The weather was hot, but there were no flies or mosquitoes. Food for the burros cost us nothing. They grazed and slept.

Then we traveled on inland to another ruins, larger than the first one. This one, the professor declared, had been the site of a considerable city along about the time the Israelites were crossing the Red Sea.

After we had been in this camp for a few days, the professor complained of feeling ill. He became worse and could not get up from his cot. We were near a considerable village and I went over there to get help. By making many motions I let them know I had a sick man on my hands.

A number of the men came over and tried to help. But their efforts were of no avail. After a week of nursing, the old man died.

The professor had given me the address of a person whom I was to notify in case of his death. With the help of the villagers, I buried the old man and we rolled stones on his grave so that wild animals would not molest the body. I packed his papers, money, and letters of credit as well as I could and traveled on.

64

The Crap Game

I TRAVELED LEISURELY. THE MAPA INDIANS proved friendly. One night while on the road I camped near the edge of a stream and was trying to build a fire. Rain had fallen all day and the wood was wet. I was having poor success.

A native walked up from somewhere and watched me for a few moments. He was a giant, the biggest man I ever gazed on. Without saying a word he walked into the stream and bathed. When he came out, dripping wet, he stood and watched my efforts to start my fire. Then he touched me on the shoulder and motioned me to come with him.

I led the burros and followed him. We walked some distance and reached a village of huts. He assisted me in driving my burros into an enclosure and then led me into his hut.

He said something to the two women inside and they prepared some coffee and served me some dried beef, which I ate. While I was eating other villagers came in and squatted around the walls of the hut.

When I had finished my meal a young man rose from his squatting position and came over to where I sat. He spoke Spanish after a fashion.

"Who are you?" he asked.

"A traveler."

"From what country?"

"I am a norte americano."

He explained all this to the assembled company in their language. Then he turned to me.

"We welcome the norteamericano. But not the Mexican. The Mexican try to tax our people, We do not pay taxes. Mexicans shoot. We cut the Mexicans in pieces with our machetes. But you may stay here as long as you wish."

I had a happy thought. I still had the remainder of a case of sardines among my supplies. I had eaten so many of them en route that my taste for sardines was atrophied, so to speak. These were the first sardines I had come across that could be opened by using a little key and rolling the top up by turning the key.

I brought in a case and opened can after can and passed them to the Indians. They tasted the little fish, at first gingerly, but after the first taste they went for them eagerly. Before they retired for the night the villagers were full of sardines and my case was empty. I had eaten a can in self-defense. In case a villager died that night, the sardines could not be blamed if I ate a can myself.

None died, and I left the village with their best wishes and a store of dried beef.

I traveled on and began to notice signs of civilization—the hennequin plantations. Natives wearing overalls made in Newark, hats made in New England. Gangs of convicts wearing blue cotton trousers and a hat—and nothing else.

I followed a good road all one morning and about noon reached the end of a narrow-gage railroad. An American engineer was oiling around his engine. He gave me a package of El Bono Tono cigarettes and told me I could go into Merida with him if it wasn't for my burros. He couldn't carry them in the cab, he declared, and the conductor, a Frenchman, wouldn't carry his mother's picture without a pass. There were no passenger trains on that spur.

It took me three days to sell my burros. I sold them for five dollars each.

Merida. I cleaned up and bought some clothing. I mailed the professor's effects to the London address and reported his death to the Mexican authorities. They listened to my tale and did not comment or ask for further details. An English professor meant nothing to them, and if he had died, why he was dead and that was all.

Then, having finished my business in Merida, I boarded a train for Progreso, the port.

I was in Progreso about an hour. I found a little Mexican steamer was leaving for Vera Cruz and took passage on it. After I had paid my passage and we had pulled away from the docks I discovered they did not serve meals to passengers. I should have brought my own rations. But even at that I could manage on such a short voyage. I got on by going down into the engine room and making friends with the second engineer, who happened to be on duty at the time.

A sort of free masonry exists between men in the mechanical trades. We talked engines, rocker boxes, vertical and horizontal thrust, crown-sheet and tubular boilers and all that.

When the chief engineer came down to take his shift I was introduced to him and we also talked a few minutes. After the second engineer had washed up and was ready to go topside the chief suggested I go up with him and have dinner.

So I ate a good dinner at the table while the other passengers sat around on deck and ate cold food they had brought aboard.

Thus I reached Vera Cruz, where I reported to the British Consul and told him the Panzos Railroad had fulfilled its contract with me. After that I went to a native hotel and got quarters. It was still too cold up in the United States go to there, so I decided to loaf around Vera Cruz a while.

I borrowed an old blind Remington typewriter from the master mechanic of the Interoceanio Railroad and he told me I could keep it if I wished, as he had a new one, a "visible."

On that old machine I wrote two adventure stories and mailed then to New York magazines. As my permanent address I gave the bank in Chicago, to which I had sent my gold from Porto Barrios. If and when the editors communicated with me they would have to do so through the bank. I expected to reach Chicago within a month—but I didn't.

One night I wandered into a gambling house and saw the Mexicans had introduced an innovation into a typical gambling house. They had installed an American crap table. When I saw that table it was like meeting a friend from my own home town. The Mexicans were playing it, too.

Shooting craps is the favorite game of every soldier who has ever served in the United States Army. It can be played anywhere. I have played it on a boat deck, on a cot, on the ground, on a soap box. The only paraphernalia is two dice, which can be and are carried in a pants pocket.

The game of craps is known by a dozen other names. Galloping dominoes, Baltimore billiards, Senegambian golf are some of the names. But it is still shooting craps.

As soon as I saw that crap table and the men playing it I knew I was going to try my skill again. In Sherman, Texas, the game had been the cause of me getting into trouble, but that was my fault.

I carried my money in a belt. I still had four or five gold pieces, perhaps a hundred dollars. And I knew I had more up in the Chicago bank. So I went to the wash room, unbuckled my money belt and took out all but a $20 gold piece, which I left for seed. Then I came back to the table, took my place and waited for my turn to come.

I was lucky from the beginning. Before long I had a pile of chips before me and my other gold pieces in my pocket. I played for two hours, winning often, losing seldom. There were few house rules in those Mexican gambling houses, so I could pyramid as much as I liked.

It was getting late when I quit and cashed in my chips. Most of the other players had quit before I did. When I cashed in the dealer gave me back my original $20 gold piece and a big bunch of Vera Cruz currency.

I walked down the stairs and stopped at the bar for a drink. Feeling good and prosperous I treated the house. I treated again. Then I walked out.

I had to walk seven or eight blocks to my hotel. Two or three blocks from the gambling house I was stopped by an old woman, a beggar.

"If the señor please..."

I put my hand in my pocket to get her a coin, got it and extended my hand to give it to her.

I don't think she was a woman at all. She grabbed my hand and pulled me toward her with a jerk. As I came forward two men grabbed me from behind and stopped my forward motion. Then held me while the old woman went through my pockets. Just as they released my arms one of the men hit me on the head with a club.

I did not fall, but was stunned and came to leaning against a pole. I shook my head and it hurt. I leaned against the pole for a few moments more, until I was sure I could walk without falling. I walked on. From that point to my hotel I never saw a soul. I had been held up and robbed.

I knew it would be useless to report the matter to the police. I could give no description of the holdups. The old woman probably was a man dressed in feminine clothes. They had watched me win at the crap table and robbed me. There was nothing to do but make the best of it.

I still had $20, gold. I either had to get to Chicago or get a job in Mexico. I didn't want a job in Mexico. I knew spring was sifting up over the United States and I wanted to get there. But I did not have the money with which to pay fare.

Cuba was a new republic then, and was celebrating its new freedom by passing all sorts of laws. Many of them were of the freak type. But a newly freed country can't always be right. Neither can any country.

One of Cuba's new laws decreed that every person entering the republic must have at least $50 in United States currency or its equivalent in currency of some other country whose money was good. The vessel landing a person in Cuba without the aforesaid $50 was compelled to take that person on to some other destination.

I had heard of that law and decided to get to New York by paying fare only as far as Cuba. Such schemes had been worked before. But I did not know how often that scheme had been worked.

I paid $15.50 for passage from Vera Cruz to Havana. As I was well-dressed and carried that old blind Remington typewriter, no one thought to ask me how much money I carried. I had about three dollars in my pocket.

At Havana the customs officers came aboard and each passenger landing there was obliged to show the required amount of money. I couldn't show it, for I didn't have it. I showed my Chicago savings bank book, however, but that didn't go with the Cubans. The $50 had to be in real money. So I was shooed back onto the steamer.

The steamer was due to leave late that night, and after the Cuban authorities had refused to let me land I knew I was good for passage to New York. I ate dinner aboard as usual and no one said a thing. I was sitting in my cabin when a mate came in. In his hand he carried a long dress.

"Put this on," he ordered.

"Why?" I asked.

He struck me with his fist and the blow on the jaw dazed me. As I shook my head to recover my wits he repeated the command. "Put on that dress."

I knew I couldn't fight him with my fists, as he was a husky man, weighing 75 or 80 pounds more than I did.

I put on the dress, a long one, with big flowers on it. It trailed the floor, as women's dresses did then. Then he produced a floppy hat with feathers on it. I guess I looked like a tall woman.

He took my arm and propelled me along down the corridor, down the gangplank at the cargo entrance, where men were loading barrels. We passed a freight checker and he didn't look up. A customs man stopped us, however. The mate spoke quickly.

"Some of our men smuggled her aboard," the mate explained. "Got to get her away before we cast off."

"Any more on board?" the customs man asked.

"This is the only one, I think," the mate said. The mate hustled me down a dark street. After walking a block or so he ordered, "Take 'em off."

I slipped the dress off, stood on it, tore the hat off and hit him across the face with it. Then I ran.

He didn't follow me. That scheme of paying passage to Havana and then riding on up to New York or even Mobile had been worked too often. It failed in my case. I had been smuggled ashore in the guise of a woman of the streets.

I was on my own in the new Republic of Cuba with about three dollars in my pocket.

65

In Cuba on My Own

I WAS IN CUBA on my own, but I was not worried. I had long ago learned that if anything is going to happen, no amount of worrying will prevent it. So I've never worried. Worry greys a man's hair, puts wrinkles on his face, and dulls his intellect. As long as other people lived, eat and slept in Cuba, I also would.

When Cuba secured her independence, the railroads of the republic were in poor condition. As a railroad man, the native Cuban, oppressed for centuries under Spanish governors, was a good soldier. He knew how to live on a few grains of corn or a few joints of sugar cane for a meal. He knew how to use a gun. But he didn't know how to operate a railroad.

The new government turned to United States capitalists for assistance. The capitalists could furnish all the money necessary, but none of the skilled brains and experience needed to rehabilitate the railroads or to operate them after they were in working order. Brains and experience are not quoted on stock exchanges. So the capitalists resorted to advertising to get these two necessary elements with which to operate the Cuban railroads.

Advertisements extolling the climate of Cuba were inserted in magazines read by railroad men, Standard rates of pay were offered and a bonus in addition if the men stayed for two years on the job. I have a number of these advertisements in my files now.

The climate of Cuban is ideal. One does not need an overcoat while living there. An occasional hurricane sweeps over the islands, but there have been tornadoes in Kansas, California, and Maine. Every word of every advertisement was true. The only fly in the butter, so to speak, is that you can't cut off a piece of climate and cook it.

At the end of two years, instead of receiving the promised bonus, the men were informed that the railroads were losing money and there would be no bonus. Instead there would be a reduction of twenty-five percent in wages. Take it or leave it.

The men couldn't strike. The new republic had a law which made striking by foreigners an act of sedition, punishable by death.

Because of these conditions American railroad men had been leaving the island for several years—as soon as they could get away. In a few cases, natives took the place of Americans, but few of the natives were trained.

It was easy to get a job. The superintendent at Camaguey listened to a story of where I had worked and sent me down to the dispatcher to see if I knew anything about train orders and operation. After the dispatcher had passed me, I went back to the super's office.

"You're a mechanical man. Why don't you go down and hire to the master mechanic?"

"I've been master mechanic several times myself. I'm not going to work under some master mechanic who probably doesn't know as much as I do." I always was a little egotistical.

There was a little branch of a railroad operating from Camaguey to Nuevitas, a port on the north side of the island. A train—a mixed freight and passenger—made the trip every day if it could.

As I was coming down from the super's office after I had been hired, I ran into a man who had been there from the first.

"Been up there after a job?" he inquired.

"Yes. And I passed, too."

"Any American railroad man can pass nowadays. They could use twenty more men right here now. You're going to start in the Nuevitas branch?"

"How did you guess it?"

"They break in a new man on that run every time. If he stays there a month he's either saving his money to get back to the States and get a job digging ditches, or he's so hardboiled he doesn't give a dam what happens."

"Why?" I queried.

"You'll see," he said. Then he went on, "You'll collect a lot of cash fares on that run. It is our custom to keep enough out of the cash fares to make up for what they pay and what would be standard wages. The government's paying the deficit in operating costs so the practice is winked at."

I had to make one trip over the branch to learn the road. The man who made it with me looked me over and said, "You don't look husky enough for this job."

"Why?" I asked.

"You'll see," he said. "And you'd better get a suit of overalls."

"Why should a conductor wear overalls?"

"You'll see," he repeated.

We left Camaguey. There were plenty passengers and all paid cash fares.

But the track! It was up and down and sideways. Wheels left the rails and sunk into soft sand or mud. The conductor had to lug a heavy re-railing frog from the engine or the passenger coach, whichever was nearest the derailed car, and manipulate it after he got it there.

A native brakeman was carried, but he was no help. When the train stopped, he walked back about fifty yards from the rear end and set a torpedo on the rail, then smoked cigarettes until the engineer whistled him in. As there had never been but one train on the branch since it was built, there was no use flagging against other trains, but this brakeman did.

There were several derailments on the way up. We were due at Nuevitas at 10:30. We reached there at 2:30, four hours late. But there were plenty cash fares. Natives seldom bought a ticket. Why a conductor would accept a little piece of cardboard in return for a ride was a mystery to them. They preferred to pay him cash and be sure of a ride.

Standard wages for that run would have been about $100 a month, with extra pay for overtime after ten hours on the road. I was paid $60 a month with no overtime, although I put in plenty.

I had been on the branch about a month and was sick of it. I decided to stay one more month and then go to the States when something happened that blasted my hopes, as usual.

At Nuevitas we switched out the freight cars and then made a running or "flying" switch to get the engine ahead of the passenger coach. The engine backed into Gamaguey.

To make the running switch I coupled the engine to the passenger car and it pulled it until a speed of about twenty miles an hour was reached. Then I uncoupled the engine and it ran on ahead while the coach coasted. A man stationed at a switch threw it just after the engine had passed, letting the coach onto a siding while the engine was on the main line. Thus we got the engine on the other side of the passenger coach.

It was nearly dark and raining to beat the band when I made the running switch my last day on the branch. I was breaking in a Frenchman who said he was a railroad man and I had stationed him at the switch. I never would trust the native brakeman to throw the switch at the right time.

I had uncoupled the engine and let it run ahead and was on the front platform of the coach, ready to apply the brakes when it was in the clear.

I never learned who did it, but someone on the other end of the coach, probably an inquisitive native, opened the air cock. This action automatically set the brakes. The car stopped within a foot.

The sudden stoppage of the car threw me headlong to the track in front of the coach. I was knocked senseless, but recovered and called and the

Frenchman and several other persons came running. I was carried to a house nearby, so badly injured I could not be moved. I told the Frenchman to take the train on down to Camaguey.

While he was getting the train ready to go out I wrote him a note and sent it to him by a native telling him just how much cash fare to turn in and how much to keep for himself, so that it would average about the same as it always had. The other conductor had told me the same thing—but he didn't put it on paper and sign his name to it.

That Froggie must have wanted that $60 a month job badly. Ignoring the superintendent at Camaguey, who would have paid no attention to it, he sent it up to the government offices in Havana.

Of course that ended my railroading in Cuba. Perhaps I had been dishonest, but I was never too honest with anyone who tried to bilk me on wages. I believe the Cuban railroad was the only company I ever worked for where I had to work for less than standard wages.

Probably I should have blamed myself for my predicament, but I didn't. In fact, I would have beaten the head off the Frenchman when he came to Nuevitas but I hadn't the strength to swat a gouty mosquito. Anyhow, the other men learned what he did to me. He lasted less than a week.

By the time I could get around on my own legs I was broke. The men on the railroad told me they had orders not to carry me, even for pay, and anyone doing so would be charged with protecting a criminal.

I wrote to the Chicago bank asking then to send me some money from my savings account, but about two weeks later I got a letter from it saying I should send my book with the request.

I learned to live on one meal a day. I slept in a shed at the freight house. I would meet the train from Camaguey every day and either the engineer or the conductor would take me to dinner. I lived on that one meal a day.

This was the state of affairs when the Antilles Queen drifted into port, and I mean it actually did drift in, as its engines were not working. When I saw it I was glad, for it brought several Americans to the port. But it came within an ace of getting me hanged by the neck until I was dead, dead, dead!

66

The Antilles Queen

A TUG THAT SERVICED the port brought the Antilles Queen to the pier, where it tied up for repairs. I went aboard and interviewed the first mate, the skipper, and the chief engineer, respectively. The result of the interviews was that I got the job of putting the engines in shape. That meant that I ate and slept aboard, which was quite a change after a siege of beachcombing.

I worked more than two weeks getting the engines running smoothly. I had to take them down and go over them carefully as I put them together. Luckily there were several sets of piston rings, rather rusty, hanging behind a boiler. I re-babbited boxes. I filed down metal boxes and shimmed them to fit. The tubular boilers were full of sediment, but I got them cleaned out.

A steamer operating in tropic waters should be gone over every three or four months and most of them are. But the Antilles Queen hadn't been over-hauled, as far as the machinery was concerned, for more than a year. The electric machinery was a mess. I had to solder or braze a dozen connections on the generators.

One morning I tried the engines and boilers and they clicked off nicely.

Most of this time the chief engineer was drunk and seldom bothered me. When I needed a brazing torch and asked him if he had one, he was uncertain. Finally it was located in the forecastle, where one of the men had hidden it.

The cook was a Jamaican, while other members of the crew ranged from a young New Yorker named Hestand, an apprentice engineer, down to Japanese, Kanakas, and other darker nationals. Few of them cared to speak English. The firemen were instructed to help me and they did, but they were surly. I would have to give an order, they would obey it, and then sit down until I gave them another. They volunteered nothing.

Hestand was a fine young man and helped me a lot. He was disgusted with life on the vessel, but could not desert, or he would have lost the time he already had served. He really knew as much as the chief engineer and never drank.

After I got the engines working, I told the skipper the engines would last until he got to a port where there were machine shop facilities. Those engines needed replacement parts and needed them badly. But I could keep them going a while, I said. He considered going across to Havana for repairs, but happened to get a cargo for New York right there in Nuevitas. He loaded that and we started north.

I hadn't signed on as one of the crew for I had no marine engineer's license. The second and third engineers, disgusted with the boat, had deserted at the last port the steamer had touched at on the mainland.

So the Antilles Queen left the Cuban port with me as second engineer, although I had no right to fill that position. The marine law permitted me to do repair work while the steamer was in port. But the moment it left port I could do nothing. I didn't even have the standing of a deck hand.

Just before we left port I learned that the chief engineer and the skipper were brothers. I should have jumped ship then, for officers who are related means trouble for those under them. Many seamen will not sign aboard a vessel whose executive officers are relatives.

The only thing I cared for was to get to some port of the United States. How, I cared not.

The afternoon we sailed the first engineer was sober enough to take his watch and I went to my cabin and slept. We were heading almost due north.

I had slept about five hours when Hestand came up and woke me. The chief engineer, he told me, had brought a bottle of whiskey down into the engine room with him and had taken many drinks. Just before the lad called me, he said, the chief had fallen off a chair and was in a drunken stupor.

I went down to stand watch. I had the chief carried to his cabin by four firemen off duty.

That was a little after midnight. I thought as we were short of help I would have to stand a twelve-hour shift. That would relieve me about noon the next day.

Noon came and no relief. I sent a Kanaka fireman up after my dinner. I waited an hour or two and then told Hestand to take over while I went up to find the skipper. He was locked in his cabin and didn't answer my knocks. It was the same with the engineer. I suppose they were both drunk.

I cornered the first mate. He ordered me back to the engine room. Rather than have trouble I went without protest. The chief engineer came down to relieve me after I had been on duty more than twenty-four hours.

I squawked good and plenty about my hours.

"What'n'll you kicking about?" be snarled. "We picked you up off the beach and you should be thankful we're letting you eat."

"If I have to stand watch all the time," I explained, trying to avoid trouble. "I may fall asleep when Hestand's not here and something will let go that'll sink us."

"Let the dam thing sink," he said. "We've got her insured to the hilt."

So that was it. An obsolete steamer, a big insurance policy on it. The insurance company probably would pay more than it was worth if it sank. Once on deck I investigated a little. One boat, swinging on the davits, was ready to be launched. The others were tied down and it would take some time to launch them. In the cabins of the officers were new cork life jackets. In my cabin the life jacket was so old it came apart when I punched it with my finger. I knew the answer then. The officers would escape drowning. With the rest of us it was problematic. And I was a poor swimmer.

I knew trouble was in the offing. I was never a man to take the worst of it, but I was too light and too sore from my recent injuries to be any good with my fists.

I had sold my revolver and shoulder scabbard to a native in Nuevitas just after I got hurt. I needed the money. So I had no weapon for protection.

Between times, when I was not actually engaged with the engines, I fashioned a sort of weapon from a half-inch steel rod, about a foot and a half long. One end I bent to form a hook. On the other end I drove a short piece of pipe, half-inch inside and a full inch outside.

When I was on deck I let this weapon hang by the hook from the left hand suspender of my overalls. It was handy there. I could reach over with my right hand and get it, much after the manner in which I reached over and got my gun from my shoulder holster. It was a good weapon. A blow with the big end would crack a skull easily. The hook on the other end prevented anyone from grabbing it and getting it away from me. It was a weapon to be proud of.

The weather was fine until we were off Cape Hatteras. Then came a blow that was a blow.

This blow caused me some uneasiness. I was afraid that if the weather got to knocking us about too much one of the boilers would let go. That boiler was leaking as it was. Where the main pipe joined the steam chest a bushing was damaged and a little spear of hot steam would shoot out occasionally.

I packed white lead in the leak and bound it with electrician's tape. This stopped the leak for a while, but I knew the bushing might let go at any time and fill the engine room with hot steam.

I felt rather squeamish when we went into the blow off Hatteras. There had been no new bushings at Nuevitas and I had no lathe on which to turn one.

By the time the blow hit us I was *persona non grata* with the first mate, the skipper, and the chief engineer. They saw the weapon I had made and knew I was sore enough to use it.

The first mate was at the table one day when I came up for lunch. He made some remark about me not changing clothes before coming to the table.

"These clothes are all I have," I told him, "and if I had others I wouldn't have time to change. With a drunken skipper and a drunken chief I'm on duty almost all the time."

"Don't try to make excuses when one of your superior officers suggests something," he warned.

"My superior?" I exclaimed. "You, my superior? What're you talking about? You illegitimate spawn of a Kanaka wench and a father you never knew. I've had better men than you black my boots. And I want you to get it through your thick skull that I've stood as much as I'm going to stand from you birds. The next twitter I hear out of you I'll turn you into shark bait."

After that, apparently, the first mate never knew I was aboard. I obeyed signals from the bridge but no one ever used the speaking tube. If I happened to meet him at the table he never noticed me. There were no waiters and the cook placed food on the table where the diners could help themselves. After my run-in with him he never asked me to pass anything to him. He would reach for what he wanted, even if it was right in front of me. I followed suit.

Hestand was a good lad and knew what he was doing. I could sleep and he would run things. He would catch a nap and I would manage. When the chief engineer came down to take his turn the change would be made without a word being spoken. I usually backed out of the engine room. I didn't want him to attack me in the rear.

That is how things stood when we ran into the blow off Cape Hatteras.

And it surely was a blow! When Hestand came to call me after a short sleep the steamer seemed to be trying to do summersaults. I relieved the chief. Not a word was spoken. I checked the water gauges. The leak in the steam pipe was spewing again, so I got some black tape and wrapped it.

I warned Hestand if it gave way suddenly to yell to the firemen and get topside as quick as he could, for a broken steam pipe can cook the skin off a man in thirty seconds. I then showed the firemen the leak and told them to save themselves if the thing gave way. I was amused at the way they looked up at the joint every time they shoveled in a scoop of coal. And all the time the old Antilles Queen was trying to do summersaults.

67

Mutiny on the High Seas

WE RAN INTO THE WORST of the blow about eight o'clock in the evening. Down where I was I couldn't see the waves, of course, but I knew they were big ones.

At first we wallowed in the seas, but soon I felt the motion change and knew we were headed into the storm, which was good seamanship. But this caused trouble down in the engine room.

The waves were so large and the steamer so small that when the stern lifted the screw would rise out of the water and the engines would race for a second or two, and then as the stern lowered the screw would catch the water and the engines would jerk to the usual speed. It reminded me of someone putting a stick into the blades of an electric fan.

I realized that a few minutes more of this alternate racing and slowing would doom the engines and perhaps the steamer. It would certainly mean a broken propeller shaft and that would put us at the mercy of the waves, as the steamer couldn't make any headway to admit of steering. That was before the days of wireless.

I rigged up a seat from a couple of boxes right in front of the shut-off valve and took my station there. When the bow went down and the stern came up I would slow the engines to a crawl until I felt the propeller bite the water again, when I would give it a full head of steam.

I sat there nearly all night, shutting the engine off and on. Hestand, about four o'clock in the morning, could stand it no longer and flopped over and went to sleep. I was about down and out. I sent one of the firemen up to get me relief, but he came back and told me the mate had told him to get back to the boiler room and stay there.

About daylight the wind slackened and an hour or so later the chief engineer came down. By that time I had deserted the throttle, as the stern did not lift enough to throw the screw out of the water. The jolting, however, had loosened the leak in the steam pipe and the chief noticed it.

"Why in hell didn't you fix that while we were in port?" he yelled, fright in his voice. "It might give way and cook us."

"Why in hell don't you carry spare parts?" I yelled back. "You drunken rat, if you squawk again I'll put you where you ought to be—with the fishes!"

I was so tired and hungry I didn't care what happened. The ship could sink and I wouldn't care. They could have called the crew and had me imprisoned, but they didn't. Whether the crew would have obeyed orders to take me is problematic. They had depended on me through the night. I was sober—the others were drunk. The crew knew that.

"Why you little bum, you..."

He was coming at me across a space of ten feet. I had been sober and he had been drunk. As a result my brain acted quicker than his did. I drew my rod and let him have it across the head. He fell, striking his head on a bolt. He lay like a dead man.

The fireman were changing shifts and I called to them. "Take this man topside," I said. "He fell and hurt himself."

"To his cabin?" one of them asked.

"I don't care," I said. "Throw him overboard if you like."

I woke Hestand and told him to stand watch while I went to see the captain. He was at the breakfast table. I poured myself a cup of coffee and remarked, "That drunken brother of yours came down to relieve me and fell and knocked himself out."

"You're a liar, you dirty bum," he exclaimed. "You knocked him out with that rod you carry."

"Suppose I did. I've been saving your engines all night while he slept. Tell the cookie to bring me some warm grub or I'll give you some of the same."

"Mutiny." the skipper sputtered. "I'll have you hung when we get to New York. I'll..."

I grasped my rod with my right hand and took the two steps that put me between him and the door. I swung the rod tentatively. "Are you calling the cookie or..."

He sung out for the cook.

As the pilot boat pulled alongside off Sandy Hook I had a word with Hestand.

"How long do you have to stay aboard after we dock?" I inquired.

"As soon as we dock I'm free," he said. "I am supposed to report to the Marine Engineers' office."

"Then make yourself scarce, Hestand," I warned. "It might cook your goose forever if you ganged along with me. I'm in for some trouble."

"I'll report to the Marine Engineers' office and then I'll go on home," he repeated. "My folks live over in Brooklyn—and won't I be glad to get home."

We had just docked and I was wondering just what to do when a nice young man came aboard and I saw the captain nod toward me. The nice young man came over to where I stood. "Your name Kavanaugh?"

"It is."

He showed a badge pinned on his vest. "You are under arrest."

"For what?" I asked.

"Mutiny on the high seas," he replied.

He reached into his coat pocket and brought out a pair of handcuffs.

"I'll go along without those," I said. "I'm glad to get off this old tub."

"Regulations, you know," he said, as he slipped the cuffs around my right wrist and his left. "We're not allowed to take any chances with a man charged with a capital crime."

"What do you mean—capital crime?" I asked.

"Mutiny on the high seas is punishable by hanging," he informed me.

We walked off the boat, rather casually, but our wrists were handcuffed together. I slept in prison that night.

68

The Surprise

IT WAS HOT IN New York that summer. The cell I had occupied was hot. The heat of the tropics had never affected me much but the heat of New York did.

Next morning, after a breakfast of a stale roll and a cup of muddy coffee, I was taken into a hot old building and brought before a United States commissioner. The captain and first mate testified. So did I. They testified that the first engineer was still confined to his bed suffering from the injuries I had inflicted. This was not the truth, as he was up and around the day after I had socked him.

I glanced at a morning newspaper someone had left on a table behind which I sat. I saw I had made the front page for a column story. Mutineers were a scarcity just then, so the reporters had gone the limit on me. I was described as pretty much of a thug, hard-fisted, hard-boiled, a desperate criminal. I had been on the beach in a Cuban port, the story went on to relate, when the captain had taken pity on me and given me passage to New York. I had repaid his kindness by kicking up a mutiny and attacking the chief engineer.

The reporter had gathered his facts from the steamer's officers and had made a good story of it. They had not contacted me. If they had they would have wondered how I did what I was charged with. At that time I weighed 140 pounds.

The hearing proceeded and just as I thought it was about over a tall, elderly, hook-nosed man entered the room, greeted the commissioner and the few lawyers present by their first names and seated himself at the side of the government attorney. The commissioner questioned me before binding me over for trial.

"Are you prepared to give bond if I see fit to name a bond?" he asked.

"I couldn't give a bond for ten cents, your honor," I replied. "I received no pay whatever for overhauling the engines of the Antilles Queen. I know no one in New York and no one knows me."

I knew my friends at the Linotype factory could do nothing for me.

"It would be just as well if I named no bond, then, since you can give none?" the commissioner suggested.

The elderly hook-nosed man rose from his seat before I had a chance to say anything. With the court's permission, may I ask a question?"

"You may," the commissioner said with a smile.

"Doesn't it appear rather strange that one man could successfully stage a mutiny aboard a steamer?"

"It might be so, Carl," the commissioner replied. "Just what are you trying to get at?"

"If you will place this man's bond at some reasonable figure I may make it for him. I came here through curiosity expecting to see a very tough character who bullied a steamer's crew. Instead I find him a young man who looks like a decent workingman."

"So you will make bond for this man?" the commissioner asked.

"If the court will make it reasonable. I make it a practice to carry very little money with me."

"As far as that's concerned, Carl, you're signature on a bond will be sufficient."

"I prefer to make a cash bond."

"Are you not afraid he will run away?"

"I don't think he will. He has none of the outward characteristics of a thug or criminal. I have about a thousand dollars with me and if the court will set the bond..."

Things were coming my way, it appeared, but somehow or other it looked cockeyed to me.

"The court will hold the defendant for trial at the next term of the United States District Court and will place his bond at one thousand dollars," the commissioner said. Turning to the government lawyer he asked, "Will that be satisfactory?"

"Quite satisfactory, as long as my eminent colleague entertains such a high opinion of the prisoner at bar."

The lawyers gathered at the commissioner's desk. I saw my tall hooked-nose friend pass a sheaf of bills across to the man who might have been the clerk, who counted them. He finished the count and nodded. Some papers were signed. The men joked a few minutes. Then hook-nose came over to where I sat.

"Come with me," he ordered. I followed him out.

69

Receipted For

I ACCOMPANIED HOOK-NOSE FROM the building. Just outside I was introduced to a young man who had been waiting. I shall always remember his name—Smith.

Hook-nose said, "You are to go with Mr. Smith. Do as he says."

I couldn't figure it all out and I didn't try to. I was outside of jail and that meant a lot. As long as I was free I could take care of myself. The young man in whose charge I had been placed was somewhat larger than I was, but at a pinch I believed I could outrun him. But he didn't appear to want to be boss. We walked along, side by side, like any other two men might have walked. He made no move to handcuff me.

We had walked a couple of blocks when he stopped. He consulted a piece of paper he carried. "We'll go in here first," he said.

It was a barber shop. After that we went to a swanky clothing store. I was being made presentable for some reason or other. In a Turkish bath I got rid of my overalls and came out clothed like a gentleman.

After it was all over I figured it had cost the young man about two hundred dollars. He had paid cash for everything. I looked like a gentleman, although I made no pretentions of being one. Clad in glad rags and smelling clean, I was still a hobo.

Before placing me in a cell the evening before officers had frisked me thoroughly, but hadn't found my bankbook. That was because it was sewed in the seat of my overalls. I had learned that trick from Shorty Hurd while we were selling soap between El Paso and Youngstown. While I was in the Turkish bath I had transferred it from my overalls to my new coat. If I had to make a getaway I would have that to fall back on. As long as trains were running I could easily get to Chicago.

By the time I was looking like a gentleman it was along about two o'clock.

"I don't know why you are doing all this," I mentioned to the young man, "but is there enough dough left for a lunch?" We were in front of a rather ornate restaurant.

"We'll go down here and get something," he said, at the same time looking longingly into the place before which we stood.

I got what he was thinking. He would have liked to lunch at that nice restaurant, but he was afraid I would embarrass him by acting too uncouth. Perhaps I might even guzzle my soup.

Although a new outfit of clothes had transformed me from a bum to a sort of presentable gentleman, Smith knew a change in clothing could not change a man's manners.

So I said, "I know enough not to try to eat peas with my knife. I know which forks to use for what. I have dined in a presidential palace and got by without a faux pas. If you can stand the expense why not let's go in here. It's been a long time since I put myself outside a good meal."

"I'm not standing the expense," Smith said.

"Come on."

While we were lingering over our coffee I took out my bankbook and showed it to him. It was the money I had received from the Panzos Railroad and sent up by United Fruit steamer just before I went up to Guatemala City and on across to Ocós.

"I'll send you back all this money you're spending on me as soon as I reach Chicago," I assured him as I returned the book to my pocket.

"I'm not spending my own money," he returned. "In fact, I haven't any to spend."

"Who's doing all this, then?"

"I don't know. I'm just a clerk for a lawyer, the one who bailed you out this morning. I'm just following orders. I'm just out of college and haven't money to set myself up in practice."

"Is this lawyer of yours a philanthropist, by any means?" I wanted to know.

"Not by any means. He's a lawyer and you know what that means. He's tops as a criminal lawyer."

"What's next on the program?" I asked.

"We'll have to put in the afternoon somehow," he said.

"Can't we take in a matinee," I suggested. "I haven't seen a good show in years."

On the way to the matinee I bought a copy of an afternoon paper. I was still on the front page with about two inches of type and a 12-point head. I had been bound over for trial, the story went, and had been released on bond. The story went on to say that the Antilles Queen had been libeled for wages due the two engineers who had quit the vessel before I became connected with it.

A little inside story told of an investigation having been asked by the Marine Engineers as to conditions that had prevailed on the Antilles Queen.

Reading these stories, I began to see why I was being treated as I was, or I thought I could see, but I was mistaken. I thought the money spent on me that morning was put up by the Marine Engineers' organization. Later I found it came from a source I never once thought of.

We were seated in a restaurant after the matinee when I inquired, "If I took a sudden notion to leave you what would you do?"

"While I was in university I was known as an all-round athlete," Smith explained. "So it might not be healthy for you to try to get away. Aside from that, you are out under bond. You could be brought back easily."

"I'll not try to get away," I assured him, "as long as things go this way."

"If it weren't for my job, I'd like to get away from you this evening," Smith said.

"Why?" I queried.

"I have a..."

"I understand," I interrupted. "You have a date with a young lady and I'd make a bad third."

"Exactly."

"You've heard of blind dates?"

"The very thing," he said, plainly relieved.

"You can introduce me as a client from Central America whom you are entertaining."

"The very thing. Wait here till I telephone." He returned in a few minutes.

"I fixed it up," he said jubilantly, "but I want to explain something. I have bills to show what I paid for your clothing and other things, and I am to be allowed credit for expenses I incur for meals. But you will have to OK the expense account before I leave you tonight. Will that be all right?"

"Of course. I'll OK anything. Did you get a second young lady?"

"Yes. The aunt of my girl."

"Aunt? Omigosh."

"Wait till you see her. We'll catch a subway out there and bring the girls back with us."

On our way out we made plans. I was to be introduced under my own name and my Guatemalan title of colonel. We took it for granted the girls would not connect a colonel with the mutineer of the Antilles Queen—and they didn't.

The aunt proved to be about the same age as her niece—and prettier. They were nice girls, well-educated, refined, but not a bit snobbish.

"Are you really a colonel?" the aunt asked, as we were eating a lunch after the show.

"I am."

"You look too young to have reached such a high military position."

"I got it by doing favors for the president. I thought up excuses he could make to his wife when he wanted a night out with the boys."

"Your spoofing me."

"I know it."

We left the girls at their home and Smith consulted his watch.

"We will just have time to make it," he said.

"Make what?"

"The end of the trial. I've figured out our expenses to a cent. Will you OK them?"

"With pleasure," I replied. "I've had a pleasant evening."

On the subway I OKed the expense bill. After I had done so, Smith asked, "Will you get angry if I tell you something frankly?"

"Of course not."

"I did not relish my task today—that of escorting you around. I disliked being guard over a nondescript. But now, when we are about to part, I want to tell you I've enjoyed the time with you."

"I've had a pleasant evening, too," I admitted I recalled that the night before I had spent in a hot cell.

"I take it you have had many ups and downs," Smith remarked.

"Lots of them."

"And you do not tire of such a life?"

"I love it."

"It's a strange life, especially to a man who has led a quiet life. My greatest thrill was once when I made a home run while playing on a college baseball team. That would seem tame to you."

"I've seen more exciting things. Where do we go from here?"

"I'm to turn you over to another party and take a receipt for you."

"You mean I go back to jail?"

"If it's a jail it's in a mighty fashionable part of the city."

We left the hack in front of a big apartment house, swanky, elegant. The doorman was dressed finer than any Guatemalan general. The elevator boy might have been a small edition of the Prince of Wales in full uniform.

The elevator stopped at a floor and we got out, walked across a sort of hall and rang a hell at the door where a sign made of highly polished silver-like metal core the name of Mlle. Somebody. The name was foreign—Italian, I think.

A neat maid answered the door. Smith extended a little book and a pencil. "Please sign this receipt," he said.

The maid signed the receipt and Smith turned to leave. "Good bye," he said.

"Good bye," I called.

"Will you please step this way," the maid said, leading the way from the entry into an inner room. An electric fan, noiseless, threw a breath of fresh air across the room. Shaded lights gave a soft tint to the furniture outlines.

"Please be seated," the maid invited. She took my hat and left the room.

I had faced machine guns. I had faced men with murder in their eyes. I had risked death while riding on the top of a string of jolting, swaying box cars. But right then I was more frightened than I ever had been.

The events of the days had puzzled me. Why should anyone want to pick up a hobo, dress him like a gentleman, entertain him, and then bring him into a swanky apartment? I knew it wasn't the Marine Engineers. A marine engineer could not afford an apartment like this one. But, after a few moments indecision, I gave up worrying. I was free, my belly was full and I was feeling pretty good. I could take care of myself.

I started to roll a cigarette—an old army habit I had kept up—but I glanced around the room and put the makings back in my pocket, I was ashamed to smoke in such a swell apartment. So I sat still and waited. Perhaps my heart beat a little faster than usual, but that was all.

I waited, five, ten, fifteen minutes.

70

Reminiscences

AN INNER DOOR OPENED and a woman came in. I looked and couldn't believe my eyes. I couldn't move. Then... "Hortense."

She smiled as she came toward me, and I met her and kissed her. She put her arms around my neck.

"My nice man has come back to me," she said.

Then she buried her face on my shoulder and wept.

"It has been so long," she said at length.

"I read the piece in the paper," she explained as we sat together a few moments later.

"I knew it was you—my hard-boiled man. No one else would have successfully pulled a one-man mutiny on a streamer. So I got a lawyer..."

"Old hook-nose?" I interrupted.

"He's the best criminal lawyer in New York and his wife and daughter are intimate friends of mine," she went on. "So he attended to everything—the bond, the apparel and the entertainment until I would be free after the performance and..."

"After the performance?" I queried.

"Of course. I'm playing second lead in a musical play that closed last night for the summer. I'm making more than my nice man ever made, just with my voice. It is lucky our engagement ended with last night's show. We are going to tour Europe until about the middle of August."

"We?"

"You remember the singer who took me under her wing? She is going with us, to her home in Italy. There will be two others—and you."

"Why should I go to Europe?"

"You said once and several times thereafter that when I wanted to marry you all I would have to do would be to say yes. So I'm saying yes right now."

"But conditions have changed, little girl. Think how out of place I'd be with you and your friends. We'd bore each other to death."

"But you promised."

"I know that. But think how it would be—you, an artist, married to a hobo like me. We'd have nothing in common. I'd have..."

A bell tinkled somewhere and the maid came in. "Telephone—for the gentleman."

I was surprised. "Who could be calling me here?" I asked.

"I wonder?" Hortense said. "The best way to solve the mystery would be to go and answer."

I went to the instrument and gave my name.

"This is McLeod of the Marine Engineers," a voice said. "We're investigating the case of the Antilles Queen and would like to ask you a few questions. Been trying to get hold of you all day."

McLeod's voice over the telephone carried so that Hortense, at my side, could hear him.

"Ask them to come up here," she suggested.

"But you..."

She took the receiver from my hand and spoke to McLeod. "Come up right away, Mr. McLeod," she invited. "Come up and have lunch and a drink with us."

She hung up the receiver and turned to me.

"Two officials of the Marine Engineers will be here in a few minutes." She went to a door leading to an inner room and called the maid. "See if the cook has left anything for lunch, will you, please, Millie?"

"There is plenty, madam," the maid replied.

She was turning when she thought of something. "Have we anything to drink, Millie?

"Nothing, madam."

Hortense went to the telephone and was lifting the receiver when she turned to me. "What would my nice man want to drink?"

"Whiskey," I promptly replied.

"And those men?"

"If I know marine engineers, it would still be whiskey."

She ordered some. Then we went back to the sitting room. "So you won't marry me?" she asked.

"Never."

"Never?"

"I refuse to lose my identity and be known as the husband of—by the way, you have taken a foreign name ?"

"A professional name—yes. But my real name is the same as it was when you discovered me."

"You couldn't change it now, even if you and I were married. By the way, all that money you spent on me—the bond and all that—will be repaid. I have money in..."

"You are forgetting the fact that when you left me here you gave me nearly every cent you had. I've still got most of it and..."

"You earned it all, little girl, by doing as you have done. You helped me and my egotism a million dollars worth by letting me rehabilitate you. Since then I've run the mechanical end of a billion dollar port works and rehabilitated another little railroad."

The doorbell tinkled and Hortense went to answer it. Two men followed her back.

"I'm McLeod, of the Marine Engineers," one of them said, as he shook hands.

"This is Mr. Clayton, our secretary," he continued, introducing the other. Then he turned to Hortense, "I'm sorry to have to blunder into your home like this, mademoiselle, and yet I'm pleased. Twice I've paid two dollars just to hear you sing—and I'm Scotch."

"I'm glad to have you here," Hortense replied. "I would like to meet every individual of my audiences personally." We seated ourselves.

"I've often speculated," Hortense went on, "while I was singing, on what went on in the minds of the persons composing the audience; of their hopes and fears, their likes and dislikes, their loves and hates. I am thrilled to meet those who have heard me sing."

"We had to threaten *habeas corpus* proceedings to get track of our man here," McLeod explained, "but finally that lawyer gave us your address. It would solve a mystery for me, mademoiselle, if you would explain how it comes that this mutineer is here in the home of a great singer."

"This mutineer, as you call him, started me on my career. When he isn't mutineering he rehabilitates railroads and singers. That is why I gave bond for him and am entertaining him tonight."

The maid came in. She spoke softly to Hortense, who nodded.

"I have some excellent whiskey, gentlemen," she said. "Shall I make cocktails or do you drink it straight, like my mutineer?"

"Straight," McLeod said.

"Straight," Clayton echoed.

"That is well, gentlemen," and at her nod the maid brought in a bottle of Scotch and three glasses.

"You do not drink, mademoiselle?" Clayton asked.

"No, but I'm not straight-laced. I like to see men enjoy a few drinks."

"What we came up here to see you about," McLeod began after he had drained his glass, "is to get a statement of just what happened aboard the Antilles Queen and the condition of the boilers and engines before you repaired them, We already have a statement from young Hestand. We're sending him out on a big liner next week. Will you write out such a statement?"

"With pleasure," I replied.

"If the two statements coincide," McLeod went on, "we will bring charges against the officers of the vessel for sailing from a port with an unlicensed engineer and undermanned engine crew."

"You'll stay here until you trial comes up?" Clayton inquired, "if it ever does comes up," he added.

"I'll make him stay," Hortense said.

"You were good to help him out as you did," Clayton remarked.

"I had a personal interest in doing so," she explained. "I wanted to get him out of trouble and bring him up here so that I could ask him to marry me."

"And he will, of course?"

"No," I blurted out. "She's too far above me in every way."

McLeod snorted. "Besides being a mutineer, I think you're a damn fool."

"Would you marry a girl so far above you?" I countered.

"A marine engineer has no business marrying until he retires," he asserted.

"Neither has a hobo," I told him.

After the men left Hortense inquired, "So it's all over between us, my nice man?"

"As far as marrying is concerned—yes. I would lose my identity. I would merely be a noted singer's husband, a nonentity, a man to be despised."

"I could never despise you. Had we not been brought together as we were I might still have been washing dishes for my aunt. In desperation I might have married the first man who asked me—and a lifetime of work and squawling children."

"It is better we do not marry, Hortense. It would be foolish. Give me another drink and I'll go."

"Where?"

"I really don't know, but I'll go."

"I'll give you all the drinks you want, but you will not go."

"I shouldn't stay here over night—although the night's almost gone."

"Isn't it rather late in our lives to fear what Mother Grundy will say? I've a spare room here—my sister artists spend a night with me occasionally—and you might as well occupy it

"I wouldn't want to compromise you."

"If you take a few more drinks you will not be able to find your way out of your room."

I took another drink. I had been on the wagon for more than a month.

"Haven't any other men come into your life, Hortense?" I asked.

"I have had two proposals of marriage. Both were from business men."

"And you refused them?"

"Didn't I tell you years ago that if I ever married I would marry you?"

"I thought you were just talking through your hat."

"I meant what I said," she asserted. "Really and frankly, I don't want to marry, but if I ever do it will be a man like you, one who will go after what he wants and get it, a man who is not afraid to tell the world to go to hell. Have another drink."

"I'm afraid I'll be too drunk to go out on the streets," I said, but I took the drink.

"I know it," she agreed, "but you're not going out on the streets until I go with you."

"How much money did you spend on me?" I asked.

"Not as much as you spent on me."

It was about noon when the lawyer telephoned. I was to appear before the United States Commissioner at two o'clock.

That man Smith had forgotten one thing a man needs—a razor. So a barber came up to the room.

71

Shorty Hurd Again

I WAS LOOKING LIKE a gentleman when we went into the hot building that afternoon for another hearing before the United States Commissioner. I say "we" because Hortense insisted on going with me.

When she appeared in the courtroom she held quite an audience, or reception. The commissioner had heard her sing several times; so had others present. She explained that I had started her on her career; that I was an old friend. It all ended by her going on the stand as a character witness for me, although I never had much character.

Hestand testified, too. Now safely protected by the Marine Engineers, he told all. How the chief engineer had been drunk most of the time and how he had fallen and hit his head against a projecting bolt. No one thought to ask him if I had hit the engineer before he fell. Hestand also testified how I had sat through most of the night with my hand on the throttle and saved the steamer from breaking a propeller shaft or wrecking the engines when the waves threw the screw out of the water.

After about two hours of this sort of testimony the commissioner held that no crime had been committed and discharged me. He ordered the bond money refunded.

Nothing would do Hortense but that McLeod, Clayton, and Hestand should come with us to her apartment for dinner.

Hestand did not drink, but the others, with me helping, drained a bottle. We had quite a jollification. Hortense sang and played the piano. McLeod sang several songs and proved to be quite a singer. Clayton, like myself, had no knowledge of music and kept quiet.

A few days ago I had been an overalled bum. Now I had the appearance of a gentleman. The whiskey made me sentimental. Thinking back over things, I explained to Clayton, I felt like the letter that never came arriving with a postage due stamp on it. Clayton, somewhat dazed by the drinks, gravely asked me to diagram what I meant on a piece of paper.

Next day I accompanied Hortense on a round of shopping. I had marched a whole day with a soldier's pack, but I couldn't stand shopping with a woman. I gave up and went and sat in Central Park until time for her to return to the apartment.

At dinner that evening I remarked, "I think I'll leave tonight. I'd like to get to Chicago."

"I don't think you will," Hortense said. "I will leave within a week and in the meantime we could take in the city. We may never meet again."

"You win," I said.

"Then I'll order a case of whiskey and you can invite your friends up any time."

When Hortense wasn't busy with fittings and shopping we took in the city. One evening down on Third Avenue we passed a small vaudeville house and some hunch caused me to want to go in. We went in and watched a couple of vaudeville acts, not bad, and then a lone man came on and did a monologue. It was my old friend, Shorty Hurd. As a closing piece to his act he sang a parody of "The Banks of the Wabash."

"There's a story going round about the Wabash
And it's ringing in my ears both night and day—
I have lived for all my life along the Wabash,
And I never smelled a breath of new mown hay.
But the faro banks are thick along the Wabash
And the savings banks are raking in the dust.
There's another kind of bank along the Wabash,
Where they make a big report and then they bust."

I started the applause and Shorty got a good hand. I whispered to Hortense, "I traveled with that man just after I was discharged from the army."

"Invite him over to dinner," she whispered back, "or rather, midnight lunch."

"Won't you get tired of having my roughneck friends calling at your apartment?" I asked. "Won't the management kick on them?"

"To quote my nice man, 'To hell with the management.' Go back there and see him."

I managed to get back to the one room that answered for a dressing room for all the vaudeville actors. Shorty was washing makeup from his face. I slapped him on the back.

"Get on a thousand-mile shirt, Shorty," I said, "and we'll go sell the yaps some more soap."

He turned, recognized me, and shook my hands with both his wet ones.

"Get into your street duds, Shorty," I suggested, "and come and have some lunch with us."

"Us?"

"Yes, us. I am here with the Mademoiselle and I mentioned Hortense's professional name.

"What'n'll you trying to tell me?"

"It's the truth. She's back there. She came in with me. We're old friends."

"Wait a minute," he said, and went across and spoke to a man standing in the wings. They came back and I was introduced to the owner of the show. He was astonished to learn that an artist like Hortense would visit a lousy little show like that.

"Could you bring her back here?" he asked. "I'd be thrilled to meet her."

Hortense was willing. I accompanied her back and introduced her.

"If I introduced you to my audience," the manager asked, "would you bow and smile? Those men and women out there never have money enough to pay to see you."

I knew Hortense would accept his invitation, for she gloried in the applause of the crowd. She was introduced on a spot-lighted stage and made a talk of a few minutes and smiled at the ragtag crowd out in the seats. She was rewarded by a burst of applause.

We saw the early sun rise before Shorty left Hortense's apartment. We recounted old times, to the amazement of Hortense. We told about collecting money for dynamite in Sherman, and I told of having to wound a policeman in the same town afterward and of how I was theoretically dead in Texas. It was a great reunion.

Saturday. Hortense was closing the apartment and I was leaving New York. Her boat sailed at midnight. I was leaving for Chicago, which was as good as any other place to leave for.

Fearing I would make the journey "lower case" by beating my way on freights Hortense purchased my ticket personally and saw me on the train. I refused the other money she offered me with the exception of two dollars with which to purchase meals en route.

As I kissed her good bye she handed me a package. "Here is a book you can read between here and Chicago," she said. "It's about a man who was down but never out and came up again—just like you do."

After dinner on the train I went forward to the smoker. On the two end seats, as usual, the conductor was sorting his tickets and making out his run reports. We railroaded a while until the train stopped at some station and he had to go out to see about the loading and unloading.

I tore the wrapper off the package and opened the book. I almost dropped it. Between each page of the first ten was a hundred dollar bill.

With the last hill was a note in Hortense's small, legible handwriting:

"This is your bond money, my nice man. I owe you more, but I know you would not take it if I offered it to you. I feel that someday we may meet again.—HORTENSE."

That hope was never realized. Years after, at a little Central American port, a steamer captain gave me a bundle of old New York newspapers. In one of them I saw the account of a singer who was killed in an automobile accident while vacationing on the Riviera, in Europe. The singer I had rehabilitated was gone.

71

Vladivostok, Here We Come

CHICAGO AGAIN. HOT, DUSTY, CROWDED. Men, women and whole families sleeping in parks to get a breath of fresh air. Excursion boats loaded with passengers. Couples sitting anywhere they could, spooning.

I went to the bank where my money was deposited. I went back to the desk of the man who had tried to sell me copper stock a few years before. He didn't remember me until I told him about the incident.

"Copper didn't soar as you said it would," I reminded him. "Teddy the Terror was elected, too."

"This is just a little letup in business," he explained. "Such cycles are recurrent. Things will come out all right."

"I invested my money otherwise," I went on. "I've just returned from New York, where I inspected my investment. It has more than trebled in value."

"You made a lucky investment," he said as he turned to some papers on his desk, indicating that our conversation was terminated.

I went over to the information window, gave my name and asked if there was mail for me. There was.

"Those letters have been here a long time," the information clerk said. "But we had your instructions to hold your mail indefinitely."

"You did right," I said. "Thank you."

One of the letters—I think it was from *Everybody's Magazine*—contained a letter and a check.

The other letter contained a check and no letter. The letter in the first one asked me to let the editors see more of my work. I deposited both checks for collection.

To protect the thousand dollars Hortense had given me I bought a revolver and a shoulder holster and had a tailor alter my coat a little so the weapon would not be a bulge.

Then began a period of loafing. I loafed around the city, occasionally taking a drink at a fine bar and sometimes taking the same drink at a bar in a joint down on North Clark Street, where barrel booze sold for five cents a drink.

The drinks didn't have the desired effect, so I quit them and for some days drank milkshakes or other soft drinks.

The recent meeting with Hortense had done something to me. I really can't describe the feeling. For the first time in my life I worried about the future. And it seemed I had lost my nerve.

One night on the lake front I let a young man hold me up and take all my change, perhaps two dollars. He had a revolver but I could see he didn't know how to use it. He had to extend his arm to its full length to take aim. I could shoot accurately from any position my hand happened to be. He was ten feet from me and going farther when I suddenly realized I was letting an amateur hold me up.

"You didn't get it all," I called. "I've got a lot of currency."

As he drew near I got my gun from my shoulder holster and as he extended his arm again to hold me up and get the rest of the money I used my revolver as a club and hit him across the hand. His revolver fell to the grass.

"Now punk," I said, "learn how to handle a gun before you try it on an old timer."

I picked up his gun, broke it and found the cylinder contained but one cartridge.

The punk was standing there, his knuckles to his mouth, trying to ease the pain. "I'm sorry," he said.

"No use being sorry," I said. "But when you try to do a thing learn just how to do it."

"I'll return your money," he whimpered. "I think you've broken one of my fingers."

"Keep the money," I ordered, "and get the hell outta here."

He turned and ran, still holding his bleeding knuckles to his mouth. I threw his revolver into the lake.

I got a job erecting a linotype for a printing office on the Monodanack Building, if I have spelt the name right. A job like that is worth $25, but the owner didn't have that much money. I took $15 and told him I would call later for the rest. I never went back.

Chicago was dull. Out-of-works panhandled at every corner and in the middle of some blocks. I was somewhat frightened and worried about conditions in a country that should have been prosperous. Among the Guatemalan Indians no one ever had as much as five dollars in cash in a month, yet no one ever went hungry or had to beg food.

I was about to draw out all my money and go back to Guatemala when I wandered up into the instrument room of the Western Union Building. About the first man I met was the man who had started me on the code used by brokers' offices and which led to the job in Columbus. He looked seedy.

"How's things?" I asked.

"Rotten," he returned.

"You're not doing brokerage work now?"

"Operators are not doing brokerage work anymore," he explained. "They've put in telephones and hired kids to mark up. Those kids get $10 a week."

"Come and have a drink?" I suggested.

"Could you make it a feed, as well?" he asked.

"You bet," I assured him. "Several of them."

After eating we went up to the brokerage office in which he had worked just to see the new cheap method of marking up quotations.

Three very young men with headsets took the quotations and marked them on the board. A telegrapher prided himself on the beauty of his figures. Those boys were careless as befitted $10-a-week boys. Their figure fives looked like a three with a little dash after it, the dash answering for the horizontal line of the five. Other figures were as crude.

"There's nothing doing here in Chicago at all then?" I inquired.

"Not a thing," the operator, named Thornton, replied. "Chicago, and I understand the balance of the country is the same, has gone to seed. A panic almost."

"Bad."

"I've been sitting in at the WU for a little time each day, but I don't make enough to eat regularly on. Just an hour or two a day."

"Nothing in sight, eh?"

"The only thing that's showed up in six months is a man who is here gathering experienced men to go to Siberia and put quad (quadruplex, a system by which four messages can be sent over the same circuit at once) on the lines of the Trans-Siberian Railroad. But he hasn't succeeded in getting any men because a man has to pay fare to Seattle and then live there until the boat leaves."

"Men won't hire, eh?"

"Afraid of the country, too. They tell me it's hell."

"Let's go see that bird," I suggested.

He was a foreigner with a funny name, but he knew his oats and could speak English with just a little accent.

He interrogated Thornton and myself, finding out what we knew about instruments, pole line work, figuring resistance, and all that. Satisfied, he gave us a card to a man in Seattle, telling us to report there as soon as possible and he would come after us, arriving there before the steamer sailed.

I was glad to have a chance to see a new country and so was Thornton, as I had promised to pay his fare to Seattle and see him through. The day we were to leave Chicago he made a suggestion.

"I've heard those birds in Siberian cities are so dumb they think the earth is flat. I've got a scheme to coin a little money outside our wages."

"Spill it."

"I know where we can get a whole bunch of old Confederate money for a dime a package. We might..."

"I get you," I interrupted. "Show me this place. We'll buy a barrel of it."

We were in Seattle more than a week waiting for the boat to sail. There we were joined by four other men. This was all the contractor could find who were willing to go to a country with the reputation of Siberia.

We sailed early one morning but something or other slowed us up or perhaps we followed the coast a distance, for the sun was sinking when Thornton and I leaned against the rail and watched the last of the United States fade away.

"Do you know," Thornton observed, "I have a sort of premonition that I'll never return to my native land?"

"Are you sorry?" I asked.

"I can't say that I am," he replied. "But there is something in watching it fade away that sort of gets me."

"I'm becoming accustomed to leaving things I would like to stay with," I remarked. "That's why I wanted to leave New York and Chicago and every other place. I want something I can never have."

"I'll bet it's a woman."

"You might win the bet."

The wind was blowing freshly and the tops of the combers looked pink where the sun touched them. Something came into my throat and I wiped away a tear.

"Let's go down and have a drink," I said.

"I'm with you," Thornton agreed.

A man with a guitar was sitting in the barroom, picking the instrument and singing "Home, Sweet Home" in a low tone. It touched me a little, me, a man who had never had a home. We took our drink and I walked over to where the singer reclined.

"You're getting the words all wrong, old timer," I said. "You should sing it like this:

"And everywhere I hang my hat

Is home sweet home, to me."

He joined the two of us in another drink.

"Give us a toast," he suggested.

"Vladivostok, here we come," I toasted.

"Vladivostok, here we come," they repeated.

END

72

The Final Chapter

EDITOR'S NOTE... Unfortunately, this is where the manuscript ends. Anyone who might have personal information about what happened next is now gone. What we do have are some old, brown, typewritten pages—apparently from Frank. They were found in family papers left by Frank's daughter, my mother, Mary Frances Cooper.

Frank wrote about the problems he had in getting a passport to Russia in 1906. So that gives us a timeframe for the events in this book. And that trip evidently did happen.

He needed to have an accurate age to get a passport, and the Army was his only source of documentation. The problem was that his enlistment records didn't have his middle initial of "J." As a result, the Army sent the records of a different Frank Kavanaugh who was born in 1880. So Frank used this man's passport information while he was in Russia.

In 1910, he wrote about using this incorrect passport again when he went to El Salvador as a representative for an American machine company. So it seems that Frank's travels continued, but perhaps his adventures calmed down.

The next we read of Frank is when he met his future wife, Mamie Radotinski, who was 18 years his junior. Her parents were Hungarian immigrants, and ran a rooming house in Moberly, Missouri. Their letters describe him as still "hoboing all over," but he kept a room there to occasionally come back to.

Ultimately, Frank and Mamie married and moved to Kansas City with the Radotinski family. There Frank worked as a Linotype repairmen for the *Kansas City Journal* and later on for the *Kansas City Star*.

After a life of adventure and excitement, Frank worked a steady job, raised two children, sold articles and humor shorts, and published a family newsletter during World War II–*The Kavanaugh Kronikle.*

He died peacefully in his sleep.

Grandpa Frank with Larry Cooper, circa 1941

Dear Reader

THANKS SO MUCH FOR reading *The Man Who Wouldn't Die*. Frank packed a lot of unique experiences into just a few years. We didn't want his story to be lost to time.

If you enjoyed this book, please consider posting a review online at your favorite store site. Even a few sentences are greatly appreciated.

This isn't all there is from Frank. Be on the lookout for a book reprinting *The Kavanaugh Kronikle*, Frank's WW II era weekly newsletter that featured current events, family doings, humor shorts, and a zany cast of local characters from both real life and his imagination. It's a fascinating and entertaining window into everyday life for those at home during the War.

I'd love to hear from you. E-mail me at **info@kencooper.com** and check out **www.kencooper.com**.

– Ken

www.ingramcontent.com/pod-product-compliance
Lightning Source LLC
LaVergne TN
LVHW050047090426
835511LV00033B/2112